All Possible Wars? Toward a Consensus View of the Future Security Environment, 2001–2025

Sam J. Tangredi

McNair Paper 63

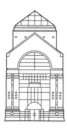
INSTITUTE FOR NATIONAL STRATEGIC STUDIES

NATIONAL DEFENSE UNIVERSITY

WASHINGTON, D.C.

2000

Opinions, conclusions, and recommendations, expressed or implied herein, are those of the author. They do not necessarily reflect the views of the National Defense University, the Department of Defense, or any other U.S. Government agency. This publication is cleared for public release; distribution unlimited.

Portions of this work may be quoted or reprinted without further permission, with credit to the Institute for National Strategic Studies. A courtesy copy of any reviews and tearsheets would be appreciated.

First printing, November 2000

For sale by the U.S. Government Printing Office. To order, contact
Superintendent of Documents, Mail Stop: SSOP, Washington, D.C. 20402–9328
(SSN 1071–7552)

Contents

Foreword.   v

Introduction.   vii

Chapter One
Sifting the Sibylline Ashes   1

Chapter Two
Estimates, Forecasts, and Scenarios   15

Chapter Three
Using the Future—Some Caveats   21

Chapter Four
Assumptions on National Strategy.   31

Chapter Five
Consensus Views   41

Chapter Six
Divergence and Contradictions   93

Chapter Seven
Wild Cards   119

Chapter Eight
Toward a Consensus Scenario   133

Chapter Nine
Conclusions: Effective   141
Defense Reviews

Appendix A
Primary Sources   145

Appendix B
Secondary Sources   161

Endnotes   185

Foreword

This survey is a product of the Quadrennial Defense Review (QDR) 2001 Working Group, a project of the Institute for National Strategic Studies at the National Defense University. Sponsored by the Chairman of the Joint Chiefs of Staff, the working group is an independent, honest-broker effort intended to build intellectual capital for the upcoming QDR. More specifically, it aims to frame issues, develop options, and provide insights for the Chairman, the services, and the next administration in three areas: defense strategy, criteria for sizing conventional forces, and force structure for 2005–2010.

One of the group's initial tasks was to assess the future security environment to the year 2025. This was pursued by surveying the available literature to identify areas of consensus and debate. The goal was to conduct an assessment that would be far more comprehensive than any single research project or group effort could possibly produce.

This survey documents major areas of agreement and disagreement across a range of studies completed since the last QDR in 1997. Because it distills a variety of sources and organizes and compares divergent views, this volume makes a unique contribution to the literature. It also provides a particularly strong set of insights and assumptions on which both strategists and force planners can draw in the next Quadrennial Defense Review.

Michèle A. Flournoy
Project Director

Introduction

There was a legend in ancient Rome about a fabulous set of nine books which contained a predestined history of the Roman people and—in particular—details of all future wars and crises which would beset them.

These oracles, the property of Amalthaea—the sibyl or prophetess of Cumae—were proffered to the Roman government. In a tale of greed, chauvinism, and intrigue worthy of a melodrama, the Romans decided not to pay the sibyl's price for the books and to bargain for a better deal. Upon learning of their decision, an angry and incredulous Amalthaea threw the first three books into a fire where they burnt to ashes. She thereupon asked for the exact same price for the remaining six books.

Again the Romans, wanting a view of the future on the cheap, refused her price and made a lower offer. An angrier Amalthaea burned three more books, and again asked the same price for the last three. Now desperate, the Roman government acceded, and purchased what came to be known as the Sibylline Books.

Because six books were destroyed, there could be no consensus among the Romans on interpreting the three surviving books. Despite sifting through the Sibylline ashes, they were unable to find the threads of meaning that could turn disconnected prophecies into a coherent view of the future. The books hinted that Rome would someday be a great power, dominating and bringing order to the known world. But the fragmented verses seemed to provide no basis for policy. Years later, a frustrated Caesar Augustus destroyed some 2,000 verses as spurious; they warned of things that seemed implausible or could not be understood.[1]

Today, the United States is the dominant world power. We strain to bring what we understand to be order to an apparently chaotic world. Many dream of a future age of freedom, justice, and peace for all humanity.

In the meanwhile, all of us wish to bequeath to our children a nation free from the threats and dangers that beset far-off lands and, potentially, our own: wars, poverty, oppressive ideologies, and ethnic hatreds. We want to know what particular dangers the future will bring. We want to be able to craft policies to protect and defend ourselves against those who would be our enemies, and, where possible, to bring peace to those whom we would aid.

There is no sibyl to offer us a complete set of reliable predictions and thorough explanations of the future threats we will face. There is no predestined chronology or policy which we can follow like a road map. What we do have is a series of learned studies of the meaning of the past and the present, expert assessments on the trends that appear to be developing through current events, thoughtful speculation as to how these trends may change or evolve in the future, and collective worries about what dangers could lie in wait, hidden from view.

This survey sifts through these dispersed piles of Sibylline ashes of our day, in order to develop the nearest to a consensus view of the future issues of war and peace—a view of the future security environment in which the United States will conduct its international relations. The proximate objective is to provide analytical support for the Quadrennial Defense Review of 2001 (QDR 2001), a comprehensive, Congressionally-mandated review of U.S. military strategy, policy, and force structure.

QDR 2001, like its predecessor in 1997, is intended to be a strategy-driven assessment that balances the preparations of the present with the anticipated challenges and opportunities of the future. Obviously, the first step in developing any strategy is the identification of objectives and the environment in which those objectives are to be pursued. In fact, the QDR 1997 report opened with a section that specified the assumptions about the future security environment that were used in guiding the review.

Theoretically, there should be no shortage of futures studies that could be used to form the basis for deriving the future security environment assumptions of QDR 2001. A recent survey identified over 50 academic or professional studies conducted since 1989, the approximate end of the Cold War.[2] As in ancient Rome, the future is a popular topic for serious speculation. However, there are severe problems in attempting to apply the results of these futures studies to effective policymaking. Among the difficulties are the lack of coordination between these studies; the significant differences in their methodologies and the time periods examined; the broad and divergent scope of topics; the presence of underlying and often unidentified biases; and the wide range of contradictory results. Many studies begin with a clean slate, taking scant interest in previous, related work. An unedited compilation of these studies would constitute a modern Sibylline oracle, capable of generating much debate, but not a basis for policy.

To construct a policy requires some sort of baseline consensus from which implications and issues can be examined in an analytical context. This survey attempts to derive such a baseline for the years 2001–2025. The methodology adopted is straightforward, but apparently unique among futures assessments. Thirty-six existing studies concerning the future security environment were selected based on the criteria discussed in chapter one. Conceptually, these studies are representative of views from the range of organizations involved with or interested in national defense issues. All of the studies, with two exceptions, were published between 1996 and 2000. Selecting a publication date of 1996 or later was based on the assumption that such earlier work had been considered by QDR 1997.[3]

The thirty-six studies are then surveyed, analyzed in detail, and compared on a subject-by-subject basis to identify areas of agreement and disagreement.[4] From this comparison, sixteen points of consensus and nine of divergence are identified. The points of consensus do not necessarily represent absolute agreement of sources, but do represent majority agreement.[5] The points of divergence do not necessarily represent a fifty-fifty split, but indicate that there was no clear majority position.[6]

After the consensus and divergence points were developed, they were tested for validity against the conclusions of over three hundred other sources, most of them specialized studies. Most, but not all of these consulted sources are also recent publications. The purpose was to identify dissenting positions on the points of consensus, as well as to validate the fact that the consensus represents a majority view.[7]

Additionally, both the primary and consulted sources were surveyed for the identification of wild cards—unpredictable events that could present a considerable challenge during the 2001–2025 time period.[8] Combined with the dissenting positions, the wild cards indicate changes in the security environment that may require the development of hedging strategies.

The final portion of this essay includes a consensus scenario that describes the anticipated 2001–2025 future security environment in narrative form and a list of possibilities that warrant hedging.

There are conceptual and practical limitations to providing a consensus view of the future which this study identifies, attempting a balanced effort of insight and caution. Chapter one identifies the sources surveyed and details the analytical methodology. The next chapter explores the differences between the three major intellectual approaches to assessing the future, in an effort to illustrate the conceptual difficulties in comparing results among future studies. This is followed in chapter three by a discussion the practical limitations to using any consensus view of the future as a basis for policymaking. These caveats point to the need for serious consideration of dissenting views and wild cards in the development of hedging strategies.

Chapter four is a detailed assessment of the future security environment identified in the QDR 1997 report, using the common subjects. This assessment is an illustrative model of the analysis performed on the other thirty-five primary sources. Additionally, the question of whether the QDR 1997 assumptions remain a valid analytical baseline is discussed.

Sixteen points of consensus are outlined in chapter five, as well as dissenting views on each of the points. Chapter six details the nine points of divergence and their relationship to the consensus views. Then, in chapter seven, the wild cards most frequently identified in the literature surveyed are described.

Chapter eight presents the 2001–2025 consensus scenario narrative, as well as the wild cards that appear most appropriate for consideration in constructing hedging strategies. This discussion is concluded in chapter nine.

The conclusions found in this survey are but a starting point for the public debate on American defense policy for the 2001–2025 period. Critics will undoubtedly contest the points of consensus. The points of divergence are, effectively, intellectual debates already in progress. Nearly everyone has a different future they would prefer to see. Professional futurists often suggest that scenarios should describe the optimism of goals, rather than the pessimism of threats. But for the purposes of strategic planning, and particularly for comprehensive defense reviews involving a multitude of organizations and people—many with conflicting agendas—a baseline view of the future is critical in ensuring that competing choices of action are addressing the same challenges, instead of being built on completely different sets of assumptions.

Unlike the Sibylline Books, this survey does not claim to predict or illustrate all possible wars that America might face between now and the year 2025. Rather, it attempts, through analysis of representative and reputable sources, to incorporate the most likely characteristics of the future security environment into a single scenario, while heightening our awareness of dissenting viewpoints and plausible wild cards. The objective is to avoid the mistakes made by great powers in the past by moderating both the natural urge for economy in defense and impatience with futures that do not conform with the desired outcomes of our strategic vision of the future security environment.

Chapter One

Sifting the Sibylline Ashes

If I always appear prepared, it is because before entering on an undertaking, I have meditated for long and have foreseen what may occur.

—Napoleon[9]

Attempts to gaze into the crystal ball of the future are rife with paradox. On the one hand, most people *believe* that the future—particularly in the details of probable events—is essentially unknowable. On the other hand, humans inherently *want* to know their future, and, more importantly, the essence of all planning—particularly long-range or strategic planning—*requires* an assessment, or at least, a supposition of the situations or environment that will be faced. No plan—except the most general or serendipitous—can exist without some definite assumptions about the future.[10]

To the defense planner, an expectation of the future is an absolute requirement in preventing, preparing for, deterring against, and, if necessary, fighting wars.

At the operational and tactical levels of war, an ability to anticipate the future actions of the enemy has always been considered a defining skill of history's greatest military commanders. In fact, it is a skill that most clearly delineates the successful from the unsuccessful military leader. While personal leadership and courage may be the two elements that bring victory in the tactical situation of the battlefield, even the bravest of great captains have faced ultimate defeat because an unanticipated element derailed the overall plan.

This can also be true of otherwise successful strategists, including the great Napoleon himself—who did not foresee the effects of delay and Russian winter on his 1812 campaign.

On the level of grand strategy—where there is the interplay of the competing efforts of nation-states in defending their security and achieving their vital interests—a detailed assessment of the overall international security environment is clearly the fundamental requirement in the development of a national defense policy.

For the policy to remain effective, the common understanding of the security environment should be continually assessed, and changes in the security environment must be anticipated.

As the United States enters the 21st century, it is certainly prudent for the nation to review its overall defense policy to ensure that its strategy, plans, and military force structure are valid for an ever-changing security environment. In addition to the normal planning processes within the Department of Defense, the Department of State, the National Security Council, and other organizations entrusted with national defense, there has been in recent years a series of Congressionally-mandated defense reviews. Along with increasing Congressional participation in defense policy, the intent of these reviews has been to obtain a formal assessment of American security in order to foster longer-range planning and decisionmaking by the Department of Defense, which has frequently been accused of focusing on the urgent, rather than the important.

The first of these reviews, the Department of Defense Quadrennial Defense Review, was conducted in 1997.[11] Following QDR 1997, an alternative, independent assessment, also mandated by Congress, was charged with critiquing the results of QDR 1997. This National Defense Panel (NDP) provided several alternative defense concepts and force structure recommendations based on a somewhat different view of the future. Currently, an additional Congressionally-sponsored study group, The U.S. Commission on National Security/21st Century (previously known as the National Security Study) is completing a series of reports that includes a specialized look at the future security environment.[12] And a second Quadrennial Defense Review, to begin January 2001, has been included as a requirement in the latest Congressional defense authorization bills. Original legislation indicated a Congressional intent to make QDR a recurring four-year evaluation of American security efforts.

A natural first step in this evaluation process is to determine what is the future, or more properly, the range of alternative futures that we are planning for. What challenges and opportunities will the future security environment present to the United States? What developments should we anticipate? Exactly what sort of threats do we expect to face?

What possible wars should we plan for, prepare our forces for, and, hopefully, deter through our policies, programs, and actions?

From Clear Threat to Cloudy Lens

The need for a continuing assessment of the security environment seems common sense when a security threat is evident. During the Cold War, the NATO alliance and most other nations of the noncommunist world saw the potential expansion of the Soviet empire as a clear and present danger against which well-defined security plans were an absolute necessity. Constant assessment of the trends and shifts in international security were required if the plans were to be valid and deterrence maintained. Entire organizations were created—staffs of intelligence collectors, analysts, and planners, supported by academic assessments of demography, industrial capacity, economic factors, and social trends—to give decisionmakers a clear picture of the international environment. The fact that such clarity was difficult, and that assessments were sometimes invalid, is much less an indictment of these efforts than a validation of the limits of human perception.

Yet, there is an underlying irony that this intensive assessment effort occurred during an historical period in which the international security environment changed relatively little. It was largely a bipolar world in which security issues revolved around or were primarily affected by the rivalry between the two superpowers. Thus, it was relatively easy to forecast the strategic importance of any particular event, even when its occurrence could not be anticipated.

In contrast, the post-Cold War world—a world heady with the collapse of communism and in which the United States remained the sole superpower—proved a much more difficult environment to analyze, particularly after the apparent stabilizing effects of victory in Operation *Desert Storm* and in the absence of a clear security threat.[13] Many thought that the reduction in East-West tensions created a new world order, made possible a "peace dividend," and made extensive security assessments practically moot.[14] As a practical matter, the United States did reorient and reduce its defense structure by approximately one-third. From this perspective, re-assessment of the future security environment appeared difficult and important, but not necessarily urgent.[15] The reduction in defense structure included a corresponding reduction in assessment organizations and policymaking staff.

Arguably, the United States now faces a post-post-Cold War world in which threats are more direct, more dispersed, and, to some degree, more evident.[16] It is a world in which a liberated Russia did not develop a solid foreign policy partnership with the United States. It is a world in which China did not allow the inevitable growth of democratic sentiment, but crushed it ruthlessly at Tienanmen Square and elsewhere. It is a world in which globalization and economic interdependence did not prevent a series of ethnic wars along an Adriatic coast that was rapidly becoming the summer vacation zone of choice for Western Europeans. It is a world in which a thirty-year series of arms control treaties and proposals did not prevent other nations—even states presumably nonaligned during the Cold War—from seeking to build nuclear arsenals.[17] It is a world in which the crushing coalition victory over the Iraqi forces that had invaded neighboring Kuwait did not deter, for all time, the aggressive encroachment of other authoritarian regimes on their neighbors.

In other words, it is a world that did not cease to be dangerous, frequently chaotic, and ruled by power, rather than by law. Recognition of this post-post-Cold War world was a significant motivator behind the current series of Congressionally-mandated defense reviews. The common perception was that defense processes originating in the Cold War or the immediate post-Cold War era might not be appropriate to the apparent and anticipated changes to the future security environment. A fresh look was needed. And, in fact, all of the reviews—with their wide range of current and potential future impacts on U.S. defense policy and structure—sought to define, to a varying degree, the future security environment that American decisionmakers would face.

Consensus and Divergence

Each of the reviews used different methods. QDR 1997 relied primarily on intelligence estimates and forecasts, some of which were later publicly released by the National Intelligence Council (NIC) as *Global Trends 2010*.[18] Supplementing the intelligence community work was a series of commission studies by outside research institutes, along with a series of projects by the Institute for National Strategic Studies at National Defense University.

The corresponding NDP report attempted to construct a series of alternative future scenarios that could provide insight into the range of defense policies that might be considered in the face of an uncertain future. However, this effort was conducted primarily off-line from the rest of study, and the panel's final recommendations appear to have had only limited impact.

In the case of both QDR 1997 and the NDP, much of the logic leading to their respective future assessments is largely implicit or was developed from other sources. Describing the future security environment was but the prerequisite to their overall objectives. In contrast, the U.S. Commission on National Security/21st Century, established in July 1998, attempted to make its views of these threat estimates particularly explicit as a separate phase of the study. Released September 15, 1999, this phase one assessment, entitled *New World Coming*, is (as of July 2000) the latest U.S. Government-sponsored futures work in publication. Given the complexity and attractiveness of this field of study, it will obviously not be the last word on future security threats.

The issue of consensus and divergence in studies of the future security environment studies is an intriguing one, since almost every government agency, Federal research institute, nongovernmental organization, and academic center involved with national security policy issues has—at one time or another—pursued its own assessment of the future security environment. An unpublished study addendum of the U.S. Commission on National Security/21st Century cites 20 studies published since the end of the Cold War which the commission surveyed as pertinent to its efforts.[19] As previously discussed, these studies were chosen from approximately 50 identified futures efforts. Sixteen studies from the mid-1970s also were identified. Whatever the exact number of ongoing futures studies, it is obvious that political decisionmakers, business leaders, and academic observers consider such assessments worthy of considerable time, effort, and expense. Yet, there have been few attempts to categorize and compare the findings of this myriad of future security environment studies.[20] Practically all of the ongoing efforts, particularly those that focus on future scenario development, essentially begin with a clean slate.

The Fallacy of the Clean Slate

While the clean slate approach is intended to avoid intellectual bias and group-think generated by the study of previous futures efforts, it also leads to disconnects between what could be mutually supportive endeavors, as well as to the lack of a corporate knowledge of the cognitive and political factors that influence future analyses.

A dramatic example of the failure of linear trend analysis—the projected future of the manned space program in the late 1970s—is frequently used to explain why the incorporation of previous future forecasts may be detrimental to fresh assessments. Forecasts based on the continuing and incremental successes of the manned space program in the 1960s and 1970s tended to project a robust future for the program—with permanent moon colonies established by 1990, and missions to Mars underway by 2000. Many of the public forecasts were based on internal assessments by the National Aeronautics and Space Administration of the evolution of space technology. Obviously, these events failed to come about—primarily due to political and public disinterest in funding the high cost of manned space exploration, factors not anticipated by otherwise technologically accurate forecasts. It is presumed that clean slate thinking can avoid such traps. Instead of analyzing previous assessments and accepting them as starting points for further refinement, it is argued, such previous efforts should be largely ignored lest they contaminate the intellectual freedom and greater accuracy of current creative thought.

However, it can also be argued that a comprehensive assessment of the future of manned space flight can *only* be developed if such previous misassessments, and the spirit of optimism that generated them, are analyzed and understood. This is an argument for inclusion of context as well as content. Likewise, there is much to learn from previous accurate forecasts. Processes that produce accurate results are appropriate starting points for replication and should not be discarded without careful examination. If the wheel needs to be reinvented at every turn, who will have the energy to reinvent the whole car?

Purpose and Methods

With that in mind, the purpose of this survey is to provide, *not* an independent forecast, but a comparative analysis of current studies of the future security environment in order to support upcoming reviews of American defense posture. It does so by providing background information of futures study methodology, and then surveying both governmental and private studies. In short, the survey technique consisted of first developing an analytical summary of each primary source, and then preparing a series of matrices comparing the conclusions of each study concerning specified common issues. The common issues were initially organized under the categories of anticipated threats, nature of probable conflicts, and drivers.[21] The goal was to identify both consensus and disagreements among the selected studies concerning the following three questions that define the future security environment from the perspective of the United States:

- What are the most likely security threats that the United States will face?
- If conflicts occur, what are the likely nature or forms of these conflicts?
- What are the drivers—such as ideology, economic competition, or advances in technology—that might cause such threats and propel conflicts to occur?

The apparent consensus and disagreements are then more fully developed and discussed on an issue-by-issue basis as findings. The findings are categorized as consensus, divergence, contradictions, and—in the case of forecasts that are confined to a single source, or rare events that are discussed as mere possibilities, but not probabilities—as wild cards and outliers.

In sum, the survey employed a four-step technique:

- Summarize the source.
- Identify topics addressed in each source by the following categories: anticipated threat, nature of probable conflict, drivers, or common themes.
- Compare the sources by building matrices displaying sources, topics, and conclusions, which either supported a view, did not support a view, or did not discuss a view.
- Develop findings, which could be in the form of a consensus view, a dissenting or diverging view, or an outlier/wild card.

The Second Round

After consensus points, divergence points, and outliers were initially identified, these findings were subjected to a second round of analysis. Over 300 other sources were examined and compared to the findings in an effort to ascertain:

- whether the consensus points represent a majority view across the literature
- whether other points of dissent could be identified
- whether the divergence debates were common to the literature
- whether additional wildcards could be identified.

The 300-plus secondary sources were identified from bibliographic searches through various media, including libraries, electronic databases, and the Internet.[22] Searches were primarily restricted to sources published after 1996, except for issues that appeared to require earlier background information. For example, the issue of economic competition led to the identification of concerns between the United States and Japan that peaked in the early 1990s. Material from those years was used for background information.

Criteria for Primary Sources

The underlying objective of the selection process for the primary sources was to collect material that generally represents viewpoints from the range of different types of organizations (and, by extension, individuals) which influence defense planning in the United States. A working assumption was that a representative view could be identified for each of the following types of organizations: Congress (in the form of Congressionally-mandated reviews); the White House; intelligence community; Office of the Secretary of Defense (OSD); Joint Chiefs of Staff (JCS) and unified commanders-in-chiefs (CINCs); war colleges; individual services (Army, Navy, Marine Corps, and Air Force); Federally-funded research institutes; independent research institutes; nongovernmental organizations; independent or ad hoc citizen commissions; private consultants; political opposition; and a range of independent scholars whose work influences the defense debate.

After prospective sources were identified for these organizational categories, standardized criteria were used to determine whether the source constituted an assessment of the future security environment suitable for detailed analysis. In accordance with the criteria, a primary source should:

- focus on the overall future security environment, not just particular drivers (such as population growth or availability of resources) of future trends
- examine multiple subjects affecting the future security environment
- be representative of the collective views of an organization influential in national defense policymaking
- be produced by a source with a solid professional or scholarly reputation
- have been published since 1996

■ be unclassified (if a U.S. Government product) or provide analysis of the future security environment in unclassified sections.[23]

Based on these criteria, at least one source per category was selected; in certain cases, multiple sources were deemed necessary to provide for the representative view.[24] As will be discussed, representative views of the future are not necessarily the official view of the organization concerned.

Once the representative sources were selected, they were summarized and their conclusions categorized in the method outlined above.

Representative Views

Selection of representative sources was meant to be both inclusive and simplifying. At least one view from each type of participant in the defense debate was included. But the sources needed to be kept to a manageable number.

In most cases, the organizations identified do not have official views. As a practical matter, it can be said that the official view of the future security environment for the overall U.S. Government is contained in the President's current *National Security Strategy*. But this strategy is a political document as well as an expression of policy; it represents the public view at the national command authority level, but is not necessarily inclusive of views at other governmental levels. Other sources may have some degree of official standing in the respective agencies. For example, the National Intelligence Council's *Global Trends 2010*, which is developed in consultation with members of all of the U.S. intelligence community (as well as other sources) could be construed as the official unclassified view of the overall intelligence community concerning the future security environment to 2010.

Although developed by defense organizations, other sources are designed as reports or reflections, but are not intended for acceptance as an official view for the respective organization. An example is the Joint Strategy Review (JSR), a report prepared annually by the Joint Staff in consultation with the staffs of the Armed Services, and presented to the Joint Chiefs to assist them in strategy and policy formulation. The JSR is intended as a strategic study, not an official JCS view. Its thematic focus varies year-to-year based on direction from the Chairman. In 1998, the JSR focused exclusively on alternative futures.

Among the services, the Air Force 2025 project appears to be the most extensive alternative future scenario-development effort, but does not represent an official Air Force view of the future. The three selections from Army sources represent the perspectives of three different, though related organizations within the service itself. None is official.

The Navy sponsored significant reexaminations of the future security environment in conjunction with the development of its post-Cold War... *From the Sea* strategic vision in the early and mid-1990s, but since that time has not directly sponsored futures work. To derive a representative view, two sources were surveyed: an alternative futures analysis conducted by the uniformed officers of the Navy Strategic Studies Group (SSG) in 1995 for a previous Chief of Naval Operations, and a personal view of the future security environment written by the Secretary of the Navy. Again, neither can be construed as an official Navy view.

In contrast, the genesis of the Marine Corps sources allows them to be construed as the official view of the Marine Corps during the tenure of General Charles C. Krulak as Commandant. This reflects a deliberate choice on the part of the leadership to develop a consensus view for their Marine Corps.

Within OSD, the Defense Planning Guidance, a classified document issued to direct the Title 10 activities of the individual branches of the armed forces and defense agencies, contains an unclassified section detailing "The Projected Security Environment." This section is the closest to an official view of the future by the civilian authorities of the Department of Defense, and the 1999 version was selected for survey. A subordinate organization, the Office of Net Assessment within OSD, which reports to the Under Secretary of Defense for Policy has long been known for its iconoclastic, outside-the-box studies and analysis of current and future military threats. Its unclassified 1999 Summer Study reports were selected for survey as representative of distinctly unofficial OSD views.[25]

A source that can be construed as contending with the views of the individual services and representative of the perspectives of the unified commands is the "Futures Program" of U.S. Joint Forces Command (formerly U.S. Atlantic Command). The "Futures Program," geared to the development of joint experimentation and identification of future weapons requirements, has not produced a documentary final report. However, a series of unclassified briefings were surveyed as being potentially representative of general CINC concerns toward the future security environment.

Several studies conducted by the National Defense University Institute for National Strategic Studies were selected as representative of the futures assessments being conducted at military war colleges, and that presumably impact thinking within the Pentagon.

Outside Sources

The process of selecting analyses from outside the U.S. Government was intended to capture the richness of the contending voices of the defense debate in the United States. But while there are many contending assessments, there are not many studies that fit the criteria described above. Many outside sources consist of single-issue forecasts, or examine the future security environment only indirectly. Thus, the wider range of debate is captured largely in the secondary sources. However, fourteen nongovernmental sources were selected as representative of differing organizational or individual perspectives.

Two studies conducted by research institutes that are primarily federally-funded were selected: RAND's *Sources of Conflict in the 21st Century: Regional Futures and U.S. Strategy* was produced for the U.S. Air Force, and the *Vision 21* project was conducted for the U.S. Marine Corps by the Center for Naval Analyses.

Included in the primary sources are two studies published by independent research institutes, the Center for Strategic and Budgetary Assessments (formerly known as the Defense Budget Project) and the Institute for Foreign Policy Analysis (or IFPA, associated with the Fletcher School of Law and Diplomacy at Tufts University).[26] Nongovernmental organizations (NGOs) are represented by three studies sponsored by an environmental NGO, a humanitarian assistance NGO, and a project cosponsored by two public policy NGOs. Studies are also included that represent an independent, self-appointed commission, a private consultant on strategic futures, and a political candidate running in opposition to the current administration.

Four studies that are the published work of individuals represent different types of experiences as participants in the defense debate were selected. Paul Bracken and Donald Snow are both teaching academicians; however, Bracken has served on official defense advisory groups, such as the Chief of Naval Operations Executive Panel, and has consulted for the Department of Defense and intelligence agencies. Ashton Carter and William Perry are both associated with academic institutions but have frequently served as defense decisionmakers. After a distinguished career in defense-related industry and government service, William Perry was Secretary of Defense from 1994 to 1997. A retired career military officer, Ralph Peters is a prolific and widely-respected contrarian on defense issues.

Although an enormous number of outside sources could have been selected, these four met the criteria and appeared representative of varying, but influential, perspectives, ranging from teaching academic, to academic consultant, to former defense official, to retired officer. As discussed, other unofficial and civilian perspectives were captured within the collection of over 300 secondary sources. Secondary sources were not subjected to the same rigorous subject-by-subject analysis and comparison as the primary. Instead, they were assessed for their support or opposition to the consensus points or their views on the divergence debates. Readers interested in details on primary and secondary sources surveyed may consult the appendices.

Outliers and Wild Cards

While the relationship between consensus and divergence may be evident, the impact of outliers and wild cards on defense planning is not. The term "outlier" is used to define those findings that appear plausible but are idiosyncratic to a particular study; they lie outside the norm or consensus. Outliers are neither contradicted nor confirmed by other studies, but usually evaluate a topic specific only to its parent assessment. For example, one outlier concerns the development of a standing UN military force. This topic is addressed by assessments directly focussed on the future of the United Nations Organization, but is addressed separately by the broader future security environment studies.

Wild cards are "unforeseen events that could cause a major discontinuity or fundamental change" in an environment.[27] By their occurrence, wildcards literally sweep away the effects of many of the anticipated events and supplant them as the overriding driver and primary planning concern. An example of a wild card would be a cascading economic crisis that impoverishes much of the world. Under such circumstances, the security equation might change overnight, with a shift in focus from deterring major theater war (MTW) to preventing mass migrations, internal conflicts, and the rise of a neo-fascist ideological threat to democracy.

By definition, wild cards are not events that are normally planned for. They can be conceived but not predicted. At best, they are occurrences that could (and should) be hedged against. Their role in scenario building, and futures assessment in general, is precautionary as well as instructive—they encourage intellectual humility.

On the other hand, as elements of future defense planning, they are cards that must be played wisely. Incorporating the conceivable premise that earth could be invaded by space aliens into a significant assessment of national security, tends not to add credibility to the assessment.

Outliers and wild cards are included in this study to reinforce the fact that prudent defense planning must include hedging factors. For the purposes of analysis, there will be no distinction made between outliers and wild cards.

Sum of All Fears

Once the findings—including wild cards—are identified and discussed, this study attempts to incorporate them into a consensus scenario that describes a baseline view of the anticipated future security environment. The objective is to provide a most likely view of future threats against which defense plans and force structure can be evaluated and developed. One of the most frequent criticisms of contemporary American defense planning is that we tend to plan for the last war instead of the next. Part of this problem, of course, is that no one can predict absolutely what the next war will be. The best we can do is combine the lessons from previous wars with an assessment of what kinds of wars might occur.

From that overall assessment, combined with creative thought and a wide range of evaluative tools, a range of defense strategy options—along with corresponding force structure alternatives—could be developed that would best prepare the United States to deter or defeat likely threats, while hedging against the less likely. That is, in fact, the objective of previous defense reviews, as well as the desired objective of QDR 2001. As expressed in the *National Defense Authorization Act for Fiscal Year 2000*:

> The conferees intend that the Quadrennial Defense Review described in this provision should include an effort to determine a defense strategy designed to protect the full range of U.S. national security interests and to identify forces sufficient to do so at as low a risk as possible.[28]

Included in the QDR report would be "the threats to U.S. national interests examined for the purposes of this review."[29] The obvious first step in determining a full range of threats to United States national security interests would be to assess—as methodically as possible—the plausible future environment in which they will arise.

Yet, even as we attempt this task, it is of vital importance to keep in mind two significant hazards. First, it is difficult to compare futures assessments that are based on different methodologies. Second, adherence to a consensus view may be very dangerous in a world of rapid change. These concerns are discussed in the following chapters.

Chapter Two

Estimates, Forecasts, and Scenarios

People have an innate ability to build scenarios, and to foresee the future.

—Peter Schwartz[30]

Three distinct methodologies are used to assess the future security environment, namely, estimates, forecasts, and scenarios.

Estimates

Estimates utilize an assessment of current conditions to identify possible future events. This method is most closely associated with official intelligence estimates provided by intelligence agencies and services, the most significant of which are the National Intelligence Estimates (NIEs) summarizing assessments common to the overall intelligence community.

Such intelligence estimates generally combine current information on a variety of elements—such as industrial production, technology trends, and military orders-of-battle—in a manner that is comprehensive enough to identify probable near-term policies and events. Due to Cold War controversies, as well as natural conservatism and bureaucratic pressures for continuous accuracy, most official intelligence estimates focus almost exclusively on capabilities of potential opponents and shy away from discussion of likely intentions.[31] But whether including intentions or not, the priority remains accuracy, which requires a relatively short time horizon. Department of Defense net assessments generally fall under the category of estimates.

Forecasts

Forecasts represent longer-range assessments, primarily relying on trends-based analysis. Most credible forecasts are issue-specific, generally under the assumption that an issue-area expert is best qualified for making an assessment concerning the continuity or modification of current trends. When issue-oriented forecasts are combined in an attempt at comprehensiveness, variations of the Delphi Method—in which experts are polled as to their views—appear most often used.[32]

Although most future assessments produced today can best be considered forecasts, the term is frequently disparaged by futurologists of the burgeoning "futures industry" who favor the use of scenarios. As one source admits, "the success of forecasting is decidedly mixed, especially so in industries that are experiencing discontinuous change. . . . Forecasting...has a long history of unreliability when it was wrongly used to predict the unpredictable."[33] However, the same compendium advises: "We would suggest that organizations need to employ both technologies [forecasts and scenarios], because forecasting does shed light on how predictable trends may combine to produce significant changes in the business environment."[34]

Forecasts, along with the futurologists themselves, are subject to considerable criticism from policy analysts. As the late Harry G. Summers, a prolific author and retired U.S. Army colonel, argues:

> Although futurologists like Alvin and Heidi Toffler make their livings in claiming to predict coming events, their 1993 effort, *War and Anti-War: Survival At the Dawn of the 21st Century*, like other such works, is at best an exercise in scientific wild-ass guessing. Unless taken to heart and acted upon, most such attempts are harmless, and may even offer some minor insights. But the future is and will remain uncertain.[35]

Ironically, forecasts can be implicit, and as such, appear in almost every analytical work on future policy. This includes the very work in which Colonel Summers dismisses the Toffler forecasts, which is subtitled "A Military Policy for America's Future."[36]

Since forecasts are not necessarily explicitly labeled as such, and appear at least implicitly in every strategic assessment, a first step in evaluating the validity of any policy recommendation is to determine the assumptions about the future, i.e., the forecast, on which the recommendations are based. This is a preliminary step that is not always followed in debates on defense policy.

Scenarios

Scenarios can be thought of as a range of forecasts, but both their construct and intent are more complex. In defense analysis, scenarios can be traced back at least to Herman Kahn's *Thinking About the Unthinkable* approach to analyzing potential nuclear wars that might occur if deterrence failed.[37] The current popularity of scenarios in business planning is largely the result of Pierre Wack's strategic business planning for Royal Dutch/Shell. Wack is often credited as the sole forecaster of the rise of OPEC and the oil crisis of the 1970s; however, scenario builders are quick to point out that their objective is not to forecast a particular future at all, but to help "to make strategic decisions that will be sound for all possible futures."[38] In the words of Wack's collaborator, Peter Schwartz, who had a significant role popularizing scenarios work in the United States, the breakthrough in scenario development came about when Wack changed from "developing simple tales of possible futures" to building descriptions of "full ramifications" designed to "change our managers' view of reality."[39] Thus, modern scenarios tend to be richly developed depictions of alternate worlds based on plausible changes in current trends. "The end result, however, is not an accurate picture of tomorrow, but better decisions about the future."[40] This is the significant difference between scenarios and forecasting; presumably, forecasts *are* attempts at an accurate, ostensibly predictive picture of the future.

The technique of scenario building has become professionally formularized. Usually done with groups of diverse subject matter experts, the initial step is determined by the drivers that will propel future change. Drivers are the underlying factors in current trends, such as population growth or decline, technological development and diffusion, or human factors like the will to power. Changes in drivers result in changes in trends, which, in turn, result in changes in the human environment. A scenario is a depiction of the future based on the selected directions of a series of drivers. Because of the multiple directions possible for multiple drivers, the number of scenarios required to depict all plausible future outcomes can be rather large. The heuristic effect of considering the difference in implications of the multiple plausible future outcomes provides for a strategic conversation that allows decisionmakers to consider implications that may not be evident in the reality of today.[41] The differing implications of multiple scenarios thus provide for a wide range of policy options to analyze. Like theories, and unlike forecasts, scenarios are neither right nor wrong, merely plausible or implausible. Despite the quotation opening this chapter, the innate ability developed through scenarios is not to foresee the future, but a range of possible futures.

Scenario work is used increasingly by defense planners because the development of a range of alternatives corresponds well with the traditional military planning process of anticipating all possible moves of enemy forces. The would-be Napoleons of history rarely considered only one possible move or one possible response.

Of the military services, the Air Force has placed the greatest resources toward formal futures scenario development, with a significant effort culminating in late 1996.[42] *Project 2025*, a study conducted by Air University for the Air Force Chief of Staff, developed eight alternative world futures and conducted an analysis of the defense policy implications of the four assessed as "providing the most stressful planning challenges."[43] Other service efforts have generally focused on two or three alternative worlds, or on specific technological trends.

Methodology

Comparing the strengths and weaknesses of the three primary methodologies for futures assessment reveals implications for policy recommendations. The strengths and weaknesses of the many competing defense policy recommendations are themselves influenced by whether their expectations are derived from near-term estimates, longer-range forecasts, or insights from scenario building. Theoretically, the time frame for which the policy recommendation is intended would dictate the method or mix of methods utilized. However, rarely are the methods used clearly and distinctly identified.

Summary of Strengths and Weaknesses

Methods	Estimates	Forecasts	Scenarios
Strengths	Greater definition Quantitative orientation Application to immediate decisions Appeal to practical decisionmakers	Longer time frame Diverse viewpoints Simplified planning Expert creativity encouraged Holistic approach not required	Longer time frame Heuristic orientation Inclusive of varied options Contrarian thinking evoked Appropriate for developing hedge strategies
Weaknesses	Short time frame Reliance on linear trends Discussion of intent often avoided	Accuracy based on continuity of trends Tendency toward extreme assessments	Translation required for application to immediate decisionmaking Unappealing to practical thinkers

As summarized in the table above, estimates have the strength of a greater degree of definition that appears directly applicable to practical, relatively near-term decisionmaking. But the reliance on accuracy in an environment with multiple variables mandates the examination of a relatively short time frame of events. Political and technological trends often do not proceed in a linear manner, and therefore defy prediction over a long period.[44] Defense policy recommendations based on estimates may assuage immediate concerns but may not capture the range of possible long-term concerns against which a prudent planner might hedge.[45]

In contrast, forecasts capture a longer time frame, but their ultimate accuracy is subject to events that cannot be predicted with certainty. Many forecasts make up for this vulnerability by examining a very specific topic or small slice of possible futures. Presumably, the narrower the topic, the more specific—and therefore the more accurate—the forecast.

Unlike scenario building, forecasting need not take a holistic approach toward the future. For example, forecasts are routinely made on the future profitability of a particular corporation or industry. Indeed, most of the decisions made on Wall Street or in commodity futures trading are based on forecasts with much the same characteristics as the most outlandish writings of futurists.[46] And like the plethora of conflicting financial advice, there is considerable contradiction between forecasts.

The validity of forecasts is assumed to correspond to the expertise of the forecasters themselves. To get the best forecast, the common approach is to find the most experienced or credentialed expert. Indeed, forecasting encourages the creativity of subject matter experts, requiring them to go beyond the safer realm of estimates. The element of creativity promotes the comparison of diverse viewpoints, and many forecasts are compiled by committee in order to ensure all possibilities are considered and analyzed. This simplifies planning and makes the forecast a more acceptable tool for decisionmakers used to relying on the collective wisdom of their staffs.

However, the existence of contradictory forecasts creates an insidious tendency toward extreme forecasting. Outrageous statements are often made in order to attract attention to otherwise responsible forecasts, as often by media reports as by the forecasters themselves. There is an even greater tendency to claim an unjustified degree of certainty.

Scenarios have a heuristic orientation, and thus do not need to demonstrate an accuracy for prediction. The intent is to be inclusive of all possibilities, even contrarian thinking. In order to discourage the perception that scenarios should be predictive, Pierre Wack referred to scenarios as "the gentle art of reperceiving."[47] "Reperceiving" consists of questioning assumptions about the world.[48] Peter Schwartz advises the use of "remarkable people," unconventional thinkers "found in unconventional locations and roles" to ensure the development of inclusive scenarios.[49]

Freedom from the need for direct prediction promotes a longer-range look at alternative futures and allows for the development of hedge strategies toward unlikely, but possible events. However, the heuristic approach requires a methodology for translating insight into practical policies. This translation process often requires more intellectual effort than the process of scenario-building itself. Likewise, it does not necessarily lend itself to immediate, problem solving decisions.

The need for translation makes scenarios less attractive to practical decisionmakers, who are likely to view scenario efforts in the same light as Summers views forecasting by the Tofflers: harmless, and even offering some minor insights. But the process of scenario building lends itself to conferences, workshops, off-sites, and other methods of modern management, thereby ensuring its popularity as an appropriate public demonstration of thinking about the future. Though based primarily on estimates and forecasts, both the National Defense Panel report of December 1997 and the U.S. Commission on National Security/21st Century's *New World Coming* include brief chapters identifying four potential future scenarios.[50]

The inevitable question as to which is the best methodology has a simple answer: it depends on the desired balance between certainty and insight. If time and resources permit, an examination including estimates, forecasts, *and* scenarios would prove the most comprehensive of crystal balls. The sources selected for this study represent exactly that sort of mix.

Chapter Three

Using the Future— Some Caveats

To the extent we foresee the future and effectively address it, then the future will not develop as we anticipated it.

—Richard Danzig [51]

No plan survives contact with the enemy.

—Helmuth von Moltke [52]

While accepting that an assessment of the future security environment—no matter the methodology used—is the essential starting point for all strategic planning, planners must be cautioned against both inappropriate use and the belief in a high degree of certainty.

Perhaps the most telling historical example of these dangers is the development of the British "Ten-Year Rule," and its subsequent unquestioned implementation in the years between the First and Second World Wars. Between 1919 and 1932, the British Cabinet officially advised the service ministries that "major war was not to be anticipated or prepared for at least ten years."[53] This estimate may have, in fact, held a degree of validity based on a survey of the world in 1919, following the defeat and exhaustion of the German-led Triple Alliance at the hands of a worldwide coalition that included even Japan. But its intent as a budgeting tool, intended to reduce the drain of defense expenditures on the British economy, discouraged systematic reassessment. There is no evidence that any such official reassessment or update in light of world events was ever seriously considered.

What was ostensibly a working hypothesis became a barrier against planning for "remote contingencies or ones which were '*beyond the financial capacity of the country to provide against'* (italics in original)."[54] A direct result was the defeat of British expeditionary forces on the European continent in 1940, and, even more dramatic, the complete collapse of the British Empire's Far East defenses in the initial Japanese onslaught—an event that independent estimates began to warn against in the 1920s. "The general consensus of opinion is that while there was much to be said for some broad guideline in the years immediately after 1918, it was a mistake to confirm the Rule in 1928, and put it on a moving basis so that the assumption of ten years' peace was pushed into the indefinite future."[55] The problem of the convenient official assessment was that "ten years is an extremely long time in terms of international relations, but a comparatively short time for a largely disarmed and pacific democracy to rearm for a major war against more than one potential enemy."[56]

But the potential for the retention of originally accurate forecasts in a changing future is not the sole potential pothole in the path of futures assessments. In addition to the unwarranted belief in certainty, there are at least four other factors that justify caveats: the inclusion of normative assessments, institutional bias, emotional reaction of individuals, and the effect of taking action.

Unwarranted Belief

The information age holds the potential for compounding the problems generated by an unwarranted belief in a high degree of certainty. Repeated in multiple media, popular forecasts tend to become common knowledge, and are treated as if proven fact or certain outcome. Such forecasts range from the inevitability of global warming to the irreversibility of the expansion of democratic governance throughout the world. The result is a form of group-think that narrows the popular view of plausible futures. When expectations are later contradicted by events, the results are often shock, surprise, recrimination, and disillusionment. In planning for warfare, the results can be disastrous.

There is a definite linkage between the repetition of an assessment and its popular acceptance as certain. This holds a certain similarity to mass propaganda in totalitarian societies, referred to as "the big lie" technique. It is often argued that the proliferation of modern media is causing the breakdown of governmental control of information in autocratic nations, and there is ample evidence that such has occurred.[57] However, we cannot discount the historical use of the media by totalitarian regimes to buttress their legitimacy. Under such manipulation, even a plausible assessment of the future can be transformed into unquestioned theology.

An excellent example can be found in the history of Marxism-Leninism. It can be argued that both Karl Marx's world of the 1840s and the post-First World War Europe of Lenin's Bolshevik coup genuinely appeared to be ripe for revolutions by industrialized workers. However, the forecast of workers' revolts was transformed into an ideology of fomenting revolution, and then to a theology of the inevitability of communism. Despite its continuing efforts to foment world revolutions, the Soviet Union was unable to replicate the conditions prescribed in Marxist theory, nor force the rest of the industrialized world to do so. Moreover, the theology of inevitability discouraged efforts to reform communism to match the reality of the world economy. By the time Mikhail Gorbachev attempted to introduce reforms, his de facto repudiation of the theology of inevitability caused the complete collapse of the intellectual underpinnings of Marxism-Leninism. Even if the reforms were successful in prolonging the life of the Soviet Union, the forecast of a communist future was shattered forever.

Open societies, awash with information, would seem immune from the unwarranted certainty of forecasts. However, the very plethora of information, with many sources repeating the same assessment, serves to make forecasts appear universal and more certain than a detailed study of their sources would indicate. Political elites may be even more susceptible than tabloid readers, due to their behavior of "constant media grazing."[58] Through repetition, a forecast can become the intellectual version of an urban legend, providing a fascinating myth of dubious plausibility.

Normative Assessments

A significant factor in the transformation of assessment into ideology is the influence of normative desires. Futures assessments, even those based on linear trends in the development of technology, inherently carry the biases of the assessors. Such is inevitable in every social science; humans are unable to stay neutral about human behavior. At its best, realistic forecasting (a description which itself is value-laden) strives to be value explicit rather than value free or value neutral.[59]

The inclusion of normative desires in futures assessments is almost routine. Largely, it extends from "the utopian tradition in ancient and modern literature."[60] The unfortunate aspect is that normative forecasting is often presented as scholarly futures assessment, and a frequent topic of normative forecasting is security planning. The agenda is not always as wonderfully evident as that of a recent article—ostensibly a futures forecast—by United Nations Peace University chancellor and former Assistant Secretary General Robert Muller, entitled "The Absolute Urgent Need for Proper Earth Government."[61] Because various arms of the UN promote futures research, and many normative forecasts are published through organizations such as the World Future Society, it is often difficult to separate rigorous, dispassionate assessments of probable futures from optimistic views of the futures that we might prefer.[62] In the realm of policymaking, the rigorous and the optimistic often compete for attention and acceptance without always being distinguished.

Defense planning does not necessarily remain free from normative assessments. By its very nature, the national security strategy of the United States has as its objective the national security of the United States, and the use of futures assessment is colored by that objective. The very insurance policy nature of defense planning puts a premium on the identification of worst case scenarios. This need not mean that legitimate futures assessments are bent so as to discard plausibility. But it does mean that the existence of such an objective, in itself, colors the likely interpretation of what is plausible.

Institutional Bias

Institutions and organizations, like individuals, have inherent biases. Such biases do not have to be products of deliberate distortion, but may evolve from seeing the world from a particular, often unique, viewpoint. Within the Department of Defense, the individual military services have unique cultures that have evolved from historical experience and the mediums in which they operate. These "masks of war" are filters through which past, present, and future are viewed.[63]

Likewise, the various other departments of the Federal government that are involved in international relations have distinctive viewpoints shaped by interaction with their immediate constituencies. There is nothing particularly sinister in the fact that the Department of Agriculture puts a higher premium on facilitating overseas grain sales than on signaling U.S. displeasure toward another nation's espionage. It is natural that the Department of Commerce is primarily focused on the benefits of foreign sales of U.S. high technology, while the Department of Defense is more concerned with the potential use of such technologies in strengthening the military capabilities of potential opponents. As our primary organization for international negotiation, it is likely that the Department of State would characterize the international environment as having a degree of cooperative behavior between nations, while the Defense Department would look to the potential for conflict.

Similarly, it is natural that nongovernmental organizations (NGOs) would have perspectives different from governmental agencies and, most likely, different from each other. Their viewpoints are partly directed by the particular issue they were formed to address. Researchers have wildly varying perspectives, based on personal beliefs and institutional affiliations.

Assessing possible futures is not necessarily a "where you sit is where you stand" exercise, as much as it is a "your view is your viewpoint" situation in which personal experience and ideology provide the telescope through which the future horizon is examined. A telescope can bring distant images into clear focus, but at the cost of narrowing the panorama to pupil-width.[64] This can be compounded by normative desires of what the future *should* be like and fanned by the rhetoric of scenario building in which participants are advised to *create* their future.

Emotional Reactions

The fact that we are human has two effects on interpretations of the future. On one side it can give us greater understanding. On the reverse, it clouds our judgment.

In a recent address, Brian Sullivan, a scholar who has been involved in Department of Defense futures work, argued that, while specific future events cannot be predicted, the "history of the future" *can* be predicted because it is based on human nature, a subject of which we have some understanding.[65] In Sullivan's construct, previous historical events provide the range of probable futures. While current trends and technologies may create the setting, the primary driver is human emotions, such as desires for greatness, gain, or revenge. Thus, for example, given the corrupting nature of absolute power and the particular circumstances of his regime, we should expect that Iraqi dictator Saddam Hussein will act in ways similar to Adolf Hitler in attempting to create his desired world order. His moves, therefore, are predictable.

The problem with this approach is not necessarily the methodology, but the fact that there is no common acceptance of what constitutes human nature, and that popular views on its nature tend to change. There is an immutable division between those who view human nature as basically saintly and those who view it as basically sinful. And, as previously observed, there is a division of interpretation based on experience. President George Bush and Prime Minister Margaret Thatcher had no problem describing Saddam Hussein as a Hitler; both had witnessed the consequences of Hitler's actions. Their viewpoints were colored by their previous views. Others, particularly those born some generations after the Second World War, may have felt uncomfortable with what they considered inflammatory rhetoric.

Yet, in theory, an understanding of human nature should be a useful tool, and probably deserves more attention than it has received thus far in studies of the future.[66]

On the reverse side, emotional reactions to plausible futures is a factor in determining the range of alternative futures acceptable to study. Witness reactions to both Herman Kahn's initial "thinking the unthinkable" and initial nuclear war fighting assessments of the Reagan administration. Both cases evoked condemnation for the very fact they contemplated so horrible a future, a future whose very contemplation was deemed to increase its likelihood of coming about.[67] Based on factual data alone, the potential for a Cold War nuclear exchange was a very plausible forecast. But, like contemporary understanding of the enormity of the Holocaust, it was a plausible occurrence that many deemed too grotesque to recognize.

While genocide and nuclear war may be extreme cases, there is an evident human inclination to recoil from dire forecasts, no matter their merit. For example, even the most ardent of environmental NGOs fundamentally believes—as an organization—that the human race can and *will* prevent environmental catastrophe from coming about, if only it would listen to reason. War itself is such an emotional topic that it is difficult to separate our desire to prevent it from our understanding of its causes. Our preference for a more peaceful future and our emotional reaction to presentations that portray it as unlikely have at least an indirect, if unrecognized, effect on our defense planning.

Effects of Action

Perhaps the most significant difficulty in developing futures assessments and translating them into policies and actions is the fact that all actions taken have the inherent effect of changing the future. The observations made by Secretary of the Navy Danzig and German General von Moltke at the beginning of the chapter apply here; execution of a plan changes the conditions that inspired it. The dynamics of this change increase through the unfolding of competing actions, such as the plans of a wartime enemy, or his counter-thrusts. In a sense, the future is never what we think it will be, only what our actions—with a whole host of potential unintended consequences—create.

Arguably, the transformation of the immediate post-Cold War world is an example of the consequences—in this case, negative—of this prediction/action (or inaction) cycle. In the immediate aftermath of the dissolution of the Soviet Union, the conventional (and overwhelming) wisdom was that the development of free markets and democratization of Russia and the entire world was inevitable. Market economists argued that it was a natural process.[68] Assumptions were made concerning the expected development of international cooperation. Analysts who suggested that Russia could remain a military threat to the West were dismissed. The result was considerable pressure to take a restrained approach in helping to develop the Russian economic system and cementing mechanisms for bilateral foreign policy cooperation, because it was perceived that the *inevitable* result made such actions unnecessary.[69]

Unfortunately, the miracle of a stable Russian market economy now seems further off than in 1992, as economic oligarchs dominate. Russian support for American-led action for the liberation of Kuwait in 1991 was not matched in the case of NATO actions in Kosovo in 1999. Along with the previous enlargement of NATO membership, the actions in Kosovo were harshly criticized by the Russian government. At the same time, political liberalism did not continue to spread at its anticipated exponential rate. While American inaction was certainly not the *cause* of such events, it is obvious that the anticipation of an inevitably benign future shaped the actions and inaction that occurred. The result was that the future did not occur as we expected.

This does not mean that we should not continue to assess and therefore anticipate the future. Rather, it suggests that the translation of futures assessment into policy is similar to the practice of deterrence. It is impossible to certify when deterrence is effective, only when it is not. If a war does not occur, how can anyone tell whether it was deterred or what means deterred it?

In the theory of strategic nuclear deterrence, a whole series of future actions and reactions were assumed to be prevented by the threat of punishment or denial. In their abstract theorizing of action and reaction, many analysts argued that it was in the interest of the United States to remain vulnerable to Soviet attack. An attempt to develop invulnerable defenses, it was argued, could cause a "use `em or lose `em" attack, or, in a more cynical assessment, encourage an invulnerable United States to attack the Soviet Union. Since a nuclear war between the superpowers did not occur, the policy was, by default, correct.

Unfortunately, the translation of deterrence theory into the prevention of conventional warfare has proven elusive.[70] The fact that the United States had the most powerful military in the world and a nuclear arsenal failed to deter Saddam Hussein from his fateful actions. Yet, does the invasion of Kuwait invalidate the theory of deterrence? How many other potential invasions—such as on the Korean peninsula—have been successfully deterred?

The assessment of future security environments and corresponding actions to prevent threats from developing suffers the same analytical difficulties as the theory of deterrence. In a very real sense, the question of how much is enough in terms of spending on defense resources can never be answered. No one can ever be certain of what did not occur. The very act of preparation may deter the anticipated consequence. Or it may create unintended consequences.

Sum of All Caveats

The importance of recognizing the limitations of futures analysis and the historical caveats concerning its use lie in the realization that the acceptance of any assessment entails risk. As a starting point for defense planning the assessment of the future security environment is essential, but it cannot guarantee the success of any policy based on its premises. But because defense policymaking in a democracy is inherently a political process, the rhetoric of its debate is couched in certainties. As an example, the current argument over the development of a new generation of air superiority fighter is ultimately premised on assessments of the future. Proponents see American advantages in the air superiority mission as dwindling as current systems age and become more vulnerable. Opponents argue that current trends indicate that potential opponents are more likely to invest in ballistic and missile systems and not the manned aircraft that air superiority fighters are optimized to defeat.

In a very real sense, both positions are correct. The issue is where to invest finite resources when there are a multitude of threats to defend against. Which potential threats can be risked with some assurance that there will be time to recover from the wrong investment decision? At the same time, it must be realized that the investment decision itself—whether right or wrong for that time—changes the future by encouraging counteractions by a potential opponent. That is why the issue of *asymmetric warfare*, the current focus of much defense analysis and debate, is such a difficult concept to operationalize and plan for.[71] In essence, *all* decisions provoke asymmetric responses in the security environment. And that is also why worst case planning is so appealing; it is an attempt to neutralize the greatest potential risks.

Thus, the most critical aspect to assess is not necessarily what the future security environment will be, as much as what will happen if it suddenly changes. This strengthens the argument that the alternative scenario method—when properly utilized—may have the most to offer defense planning, precisely because, by its very construct, it postulates uncertainty. And this also brings us back to addressing the trap made evident in our opening example of the British Ten-Year Rule. In a dynamic security environment, an assessment of the future is only as valuable as its facility for being updated.

Chapter Four

Assumptions on National Strategy

I f the value of an assessment of the future security environment is based on its facility for being updated, the obvious starting point for a new consensus assessment is a validation or refutation of the current wisdom as incorporated into the standing defense policy and military strategy.

The current U.S. military strategy of "shape, respond, and prepare now" was codified primarily through the mechanism of the Quadrennial Defense Review (QDR) that concluded in May 1997. Although QDR 1997 was popularly perceived as a resource analysis leading to optimal force structure for a downsizing, resource-constrained Department of Defense, considerable effort was made to develop a strategic approach to the current and anticipated security environment—albeit, an approach considered, in the words of Secretary of Defense William S. Cohen, "fiscally responsible" and based on the premise that "barring a major crisis, national defense spending is likely to remain relatively constant in the future."[72]

The report of QDR 1997 contains a three-page section describing the review's planning assumptions concerning the present and future global security environment. The assumptions were derived primarily from intelligence estimates, including the original limited use publication of the National Intelligence Council study that would be later released as *Global Trends 2010*.[73] Of note is that the 1997 version of the National Security Strategy, also released in May, appears to be based on an earlier set of estimates than *Global Trends 2010*, and does not incorporate the same language as the QDR. In contrast, the 1998 version—released in October 1998—references the "priority military challenges identified in the 1997 Quadrennial Defense Review," and adopts significant segments of the exact language of the QDR report.

The Environment to 2015

As summarized in the tables below, QDR 1997 attempted to balance a view of the current environment with limited forecasts to the year 2015. The tables utilize the first two categories described in chapter one: *threats* and *nature of probable conflicts (and anticipated military mission areas)*. As noted, because the QDR report's future security environment discussion is derived from other sources, it makes no effort to directly identify *drivers* (third category)—with one significant exception: the role and posture of the United States. The QDR report assumes that the actions of the world's sole superpower remain the most significant driver of international security relations. This is an inherently logical assumption, since, as the saying goes, when the elephant rolls over, the other creatures lying next to her have to move. The QDR report makes this driver clear in the form of a concluding caveat:

> Finally, it is important to note that this projection of the security environment rests on two fundamental assumptions: that the United States will remain politically and militarily engaged in the world over the next 15 to 20 years, and that it will maintain military superiority over current and potential rivals. If the United states were to withdraw from its international commitments, relinquish its diplomatic leadership, or relinquish its military superiority, the world would become an even more dangerous place, and the threats to the United States, our allies, friends, and interests would be even more severe.[74]

Regional Dangers

As defined by QDR 1997, the world that the United States faces to the year 2015 is one that presents little or no prospect for war on a global scale, but retains a high propensity for regional crises. Many of these crises will not involve conflict between nations but, instead, constitute conflicts within nations, or situations in which the governmental authority of a particular state has broken down. The latter case, that of failed states, may result from—or correspondingly cause—civil wars, military coups, refugee migrations, or other humanitarian disasters. The events are seen as destabilizing to other nations in the particular region, or to the global international system as a whole. Reflecting overall Clinton administration policy, there is a presumption that, in most cases, such crises ultimately constitute a threat to U.S. national security and will require some degree of American involvement or intervention. From this view, the primary objective of U.S. military power is to provide for

Summary of Threats (QDR 1997)

Threats	The Global Security Environment
Competing Ideology	None identified. "Our core values of representative democracy and market economics are embraced in many parts of the world…"
Rival Coalition	None identified. "Former adversaries, like Russian and other former members of the Warsaw Pact, now cooperate with us across a range of security issues."
Military Near-Peer Competitor	Absent until 2015. Possible beyond 2015. "The security environment between now and 2015 will also likely be marked by the absence of a "global peer competitor…" "In the period beyond 2015, there is the possibility that a regional great power or global peer competitor may emerge. Russia and China are seen by some as having the potential…"
Global Conflict	No. "The threat of global war has receded…" Threat to U.S homeland present via new, "unconventional" means. "While we are dramatically safer than during the Cold War, the U.S. homeland is not free from external threats."
Regional Conflict— Europe	Very limited possibility. "…failing states may create as we saw in…the former Yugoslavia." "Russia's agreements with NATO will assist in integrating it into a larger European security architecture."
Regional Conflict— Mideast/SWA	The "foremost" threat. "Both Iraq and Iran continue to pose threats to their neighbors and to the free flow of oil to the region." "In the Middle East, the potential for conflict will remain until there is a just and lasting peace in the region and security for Israel."
Regional Conflict— Western Hemisphere	Not discussed. However, "illegal drug trade and international organized crime… [as well as] uncontrolled flows of migrants will sporadically destabilize regions of the world and threaten American interests and citizens."
Regional Conflict— East Asia	Significant threat. "North Korea continues to pose a highly unpredictable threat due to the continued forward positioning of its offensive military capabilities…" "China's efforts to modernize its forces and improve its power-projection capabilities will not go unnoticed, likely spurring concerns from others in the region." [There is no mention of Taiwan Straits issue.]
Regional Conflict— South Asia	Not discussed. Regional Conflict—Africa Instability from local conflict. "Failed or failing states may create instability, internal conflict, and humanitarian crises… as we saw in Somalia…"
Terrorism/ Nonstate Threats	Increasing threat. "Other unconventional means of attack, such as terrorism, are no longer just threats to our diplomats, military forces and Americans overseas, but will threaten Americans at home for years to come."

Summary of Probable Conflict/Missions (QDR 1997)

Nature of Conflict	The Global Security Environment
Global War	No. "The threat of global war has receded..." MTW Probable. "Between now and 2015, it is reasonable to assume that more than one aspiring regional power will have both the desire and means to challenge U.S. interests militarily."
SSC Vital Interest	Probable. "Failed or failing states may create instability, internal conflict, and humanitarian crises, in some cases within regions where the United States has vital or important interests."
Space/Space-Based Assets	Potential inclusion in MTW. "Areas in which the United States has a significant advantage over potential opponents and increasing capabilities (e.g., space-based assets...) could also involve inherent vulnerabilities that could be exploited by potential opponents (e.g., attacking our reliance on commercial communications)..."
Information/ Technology	Potential element of MTW, homeland threat, and terrorism. "Information warfare (attacks on our infrastructure through computer-based information networks) is a growing threat."
WMD Employment	Actual employment not discussed; proliferation will affect interactions. "Of particular concern is the spread of nuclear, biological, and chemical (NBC) weapons and their means of delivery..."
Terrorism vs. U.S. Homeland	High potential. "... other unconventional means of attack, such as terrorism, are no longer just threats to our diplomats ... Information warfare (attacks on our infrastructure through computer-based information networks) is a growing threat."
Terrorism vs. Allies and Overseas Forces	Increasing. "Increasingly capable and violent terrorists will continue to threaten the lives of American citizens and try to undermine U.S. policies and alliances."
Chaos: "Three Block War"	Does not use this terminology.
SSC—Important Interests: Peace Enforcement	Enforcement Assumed. As result of failed states and transnational threats.
SSC—Other Interests Peacekeeping	Assumed. As result of failed states and transnational threats.
SSC Humanitarian Ops	Expected. "Failed or failing states may create instability, internal conflict, and humanitarian crises, in some cases within regions where the United States has vital or important interests."
Other Support for Civil Authority	Not directly discussed. Implied under threats to homeland. "The illegal drug trade and international organized crime will continue to ignore our borders, attack our society, and threaten our personal liberty and well-being."

international stability so that the political evolutions begun by collapse of the Soviet Union and end of the Cold War—the growth of democracy, free markets, and economic integration—can continue to create a more peaceful world.

The use of military force in such crises is expected to be limited in intensity and objectives, but may still involve the use of considerable force and resources, in some cases requiring show of force operations, limited strikes, and interventions, as well as such policing and civil assistance actions as "noncombatant evacuation operations, no-fly zone enforcement, peace enforcement, maritime sanctions enforcement, counterterrorism operations, peacekeeping, humanitarian assistance, and disaster relief."[75] These operations are incorporated together into the term "small-scale contingencies" (SSCs). In earlier times, many of these SSC operations might be considered gunboat diplomacy or empire/estate management.[76] However, QDR 1997, in consonance with the National Security Strategy, emphasizes coalition building and interagency operation, rather than expecting the U.S. military to provide a sole-source response. Small-scale contingency operations will also put a premium on the ability of the U.S. military to work effectively with other U.S. Government agencies, nongovernmental organizations, private voluntary organizations, and a variety of coalition partners."[77] International approval of U.S. actions as a coalition leader is assumed. From this it can be inferred that the QDR 1997 security environment is one in which there are commonly accepted international norms. Regional crises, although frequent, are effectively considered aberrations in an international system that naturally seeks stability.

As previously pointed out, although the actions of the United States are not causes or drivers of these individual regional crises, U.S. actions become *the* significant driver in restoring the regions to stability. This creates an analytical quandary in that the actions of the United States are forever changing the forecasts for regions in which crises may occur. The quandary is subtly acknowledged in the opening statement by Secretary of Defense William S. Cohen to the QDR report in which he admits that "we cannot expect to comprehend fully or predict the challenges that might emerge from the world beyond the time lines covered in normal defense planning and budget."[78] Since the normal defense planning and budget is done on a biennial basis with budget forecasts no longer than five years, this statement would seem to contradict the future security environment assessment effort found in the QDR, which extends to 2015.

However, it is more likely that the statement by Secretary Cohen is meant to imply a difference between generalized challenges, such as failing states and regional crises, than the occurrence of any specific conflict.

Hedging on Two MTWs

There are, however, two specific regional dangers identified by the QDR 1997 report that entail force greater than that expected to be applied to a SSC. Both are potential threats that pre-date the post-post-Cold War world: the threat of North Korean attack on South Korea, and threats to the stability of the Arabian Gulf region from either Iran or Iraq. In both cases, the United States has considerable military force stationed in the region and a network of alliances and friendships to provide for regional support of American actions. Both are recognized by QDR 1997 as "significant" and "foremost" threats, respectively, and provide the logic for a two-MTW policy. And neither threat has since been resolved.

Unlike the QDR 1997 assessment, many of the other assessments have discounted the potential of major theater war in those particular regions, contributing to a view that the two-MTW approach is strategically and fiscally obsolete. In commenting on the work of the QDR, the National Defense Panel gave scant attention to the two near-simultaneous MTW potential. An invasion by North Korea, in particular, is seen as an issue of the past. "We envision a reconciled, if not a unified, Korean peninsula," states the NDP, focusing their concern on Japanese and Chinese reaction to inevitable Korean unification.[79] In effect, the QDR global security environment (along with the parent analysis, *Global Trends 2010*) appears the sole holdout to the growing view that a peaceful reconciliation of North and South Korea would occur in the very near future.

Since 1997, North Korean development of intermediate range ballistic missiles has renewed concerns of potential conflict, although this has not necessarily been reflected in the general trend of futures assessments. The RAND *Sources of Conflict in the 21st Century* points out that, even after such multiple crises as the fatal 1976 DMZ tree-cutting incident, the 1983 Rangoon bombing that killed 17 high-ranking South Korean officials, and the 1993–94 North Korean nuclear development scare, no direct military clashes occurred between North and South Korea.[80] Presumably this would indicate the improbability of cross-border invasion during future incidents. However, the staying power of the North Korean regime is itself a caveat to placing any certitude on futures analysis.[81] By all conceivable trends, such as economic decline, marginal agricultural production, and limited access to world resources, North Korea should have already failed.[82] With this in mind, numerous sources assume an impending reduction in the 36,000 U.S. military personnel currently stationed in the Korean peninsula.[83] The NDP recognized that "the risks in Korea remain high," but its report argues that the "challenge in the theater is unique" and not necessarily a strategic justification for the two-MTW construct.[84]

Likewise, the NDP report argues that "our current forces . . . with the support of allies, should be capable of dealing with Iraq, which still poses a serious threat to the region and appears intent on acquiring an offensive WMD capability."[85] But having also mentioned Iran as a potential MTW threat in the Southwest Asia region, the NDP report makes no assessment of U.S. capabilities to deal with Iranian capabilities, which are considerably different from and more robust than Iraqi capabilities.

The issue of whether two near-simultaneous MTWs are likely remains a focus of U.S. defense planning. The key point to be made here is that, as an official Department of Defense review, QDR 1997 was required to take a cautious approach on the future resolution of crises. From this perspective, the future security environment of the QDR is more comprehensive in its timeframe (to 2010) than the competing NDP version.

Critiquing QDR 1997

It is the QDR's effort at comprehensiveness that strengthens its position as a natural starting point for comparative analysis. But does it actually encompass a long-range view of American security interests?

As discussed, QDR 1997 used intelligence *estimates* as its methodological approach. But whether estimates can remain valid for 13 years is questionable. It is also unclear whether alternative-futures work had much influence on its assessment. In contrast, the NDP engaged in alternative scenario development, although, like QDR 1997, it is difficult to discern the impact of the recommendations of the final report.

There is also no discussion of the effects of wild cards on defense strategy in the QDR 1997 report. While that is not a significant criticism in itself—many of the wild cards discussed by futurists would be considered outlandish in a formal governmental assessment—it does suggest that QDR 1997 had no mechanism for incorporating hedging strategies other than two MTWs in developing its study. This is illustrated by the fact that there is no discussion of the use of intensive military force beyond the canonical MTWs of Korea and Southwest Asia. Although the estimate of the lack of a near-peer competitor seems valid, the possibility of a regional competitor more robust than Iraq or North Korea does not seem to have been considered. If security policy is meant as survival insurance, the lack of plans for hedging against a more powerful opponent would be a flaw. Neither Iraq nor North Korea posed a direct threat to the survival of the United States in 1997, nor do they today. But there could be other regional competitors that do, and a conflict involving them could easily require military forces beyond those designed for the canonical cases.[86]

The QDR 1997 report admits the potential for a near-peer competitor beyond the 2010 time frame but sidesteps a discussion of whether the two-MTW force would require modification if unexpected development of a near peer occurred. Obviously, this concern is a prime motivator for the NDP call for "transformation," although at the expense of a two-MTW capability. Again, this points to the issue of incorporating hedging strategies against the unexpected.

Another area that would merit greater concern would be the combat employment of WMD. Although the QDR report expresses concern on WMD proliferation, it sidesteps the discussion of whether the future battlefield will be one of extensive WMD use. The characteristic would be of considerable concern in developing an appropriate future force structure.

Although the QDR 1997 global security environment emphasizes nonstate threats to "Americans at home," the extent of this threat is not clearly defined. If, in fact, the intensity of such threats is anticipated to be high, it would seem logical that significant changes in U.S. force structure might be needed. Such changes are not suggested in the overall report.

Recommendations

In assessing the future security environment, the QDR 1997 appears to do an excellent job in avoiding constraints imposed by fiscal concerns. Conceptual support for the potential for two overlapping MTWs is but one example. However, there are several improvements that could be incorporated into future reviews.

First, the exclusive use of the estimate methodology should give way to *a more inclusive blending of estimates, forecasts, and scenarios.* The use of estimates only limits the long-term effectiveness of the review. If it is expected that a QDR will be conducted every four years, then it would appear that there is no harm in relying on short-term, yet more sharply defined estimates. However, this would not provide any means of incorporating the reviews into a more comprehensive, long-term plan. The image is of climbing a ladder of which only the next few rungs can be seen. The destination still appears unclear. In terms of the procurement of new defense systems, a process that can extend out to almost twenty years, the short-term view provides little input on the anticipated environment in which the system will be used. This adds to the impression that the Defense Department remains chained to preparing for the last war. Likewise, the life span of major weapons systems may be thirty years or more. Is a short-term estimate the best assessment on which to base the procurement of thirty-plus year systems?

Secondly, a *mechanism for incorporating hedging strategies* would appear critical if the future security environment is to allow for unexpected events. As part of this mechanism, *discussion of the effects of wild cards* would also improve comprehensiveness.

Finally, a *greater degree of integration* is needed in incorporating the implications of the anticipated future security environment with overall defense decisionmaking. This can only be done if upcoming defense reviews avoid isolating the assessment of the future security environment as a preliminary discussion, confined to a small introductory portion of the report. Instead, recommendations should be tied directly to the anticipated future. If the anticipated future is one of WMD use on the battlefield, procuring nonprotected systems would seem hard to justify. Likewise, WMD defenses would seem to be a greater priority.

Of course, as the Yiddish proverb says, if we don't know where we are going, any road will get us there. The first step is to ascertain where the likely roads to the future go.

Chapter Five

Consensus Views

U sing the comparative analysis generated by the survey of studies, it is possible to put together a series of 16 propositions that reflect a consensus among sources. These propositions reflect a common assessment of the future security environment and mark the boundaries of the most likely future events. All of the propositions concern the time period 2001–2025, and can be divided into three broad categories: consensus concerning potential *threats*, consensus concerning *military technology*, and consensus concerning *opposing strategies*.

Consensus Views

Threats:
- No rival ideology to compete with democracy
- No rival military coalition
- No global conventional military peer competitor
- Economic competitors (but no resulting war)
- Regional military challengers (but disagreement on who—China, Russia, rogue states)
- More failing states
- More nonstate threats to security

Military Technology:
- Diffusion of advanced military technology
- Commercial availability of significant operational intelligence
- Retention of U.S. lead in an expanding RMA
- Technological surprise unlikely (but by the United States or ally, if any)

Opposing Strategies:
- Continuing U.S. control of the seas and air
- Antiaccess/area-denial strategies by regional powers
- WMD likely in large-scale combat with U.S. forces
- Increasing vulnerability of American homeland to asymmetric attack
- Increasing importance of information warfare

Such a derived consensus does not represent absolute agreement by the majority of sources, nor does it represent complete agreement with the proposition by any one particular source. Rather, it is indicative of a collective wisdom that can provide an appropriate baseline assessment for future choices in American defense policy.

As discussed above, there are inherent limitations in utilizing collective views of the future. The derived consensus is not meant to be a prediction. It is meant to be a starting point from which choices on appropriate future strategies, policies, and force structure can be developed. Stating consensus views as single sentence propositions, as in the table above, provides a solid core for follow-on detailed discussions, including the identification of dissenting views.

Almost every consensus point has a corresponding dissenting or contrary view. In the process of translating the implications of future assessment into policy recommendations, the contrary views certainly deserve consideration, both as caveats to precipitous policy recommendations and as indicators of potential events against which a prudent strategy may attempt to hedge.

The following discussions are structured to identify both the details of the consensus view as well as the arguments of prominent dissenters.[87]

Threats

No Rival Ideology

During significant periods in history, ideology has been a driver of conflict. Ideology played obvious, if not dominant roles in the American Revolution, the French revolutionary wars, and totalitarian-led conflicts in Europe.[88]

The propellant of the Cold War was the ideological struggle between democracy and communism as embodied in the United States and Soviet Union, ending in dramatic victory for the West.[89] Ideology as an element of history did not end, though the rivalry between democratic capitalism and communism did, at least for the foreseeable future.[90] Vestiges of Soviet-style communism are largely confined to North Korea and Cuba.[91] China still claims to be a Marxist-Leninist state, but its philosophical focus appears to be on state power based on nationality and ethnicity rather than ideology.[92] Even the current Russian Communist Party refuses to admit a direct link to the former Communist Party of the Soviet Union (CPSU).[93] Both the current U.S. National Security Strategy and National Military Strategy maintain that "our core values of representative democracy and market economics are embraced in many parts of the world, creating new opportunities to promote peace prosperity and enhanced cooperation among nations."[94]

Consensus View

In this regard, the majority of future security environment studies, both governmental and private, cannot identify other ideologies with global appeal and, thus, cannot foresee a competing ideology before at least 2025.[95] The expansion of democratic values appears a byproduct of globalization.[96] That does not mean there will not be authoritarian nations that claim to be democracies, when in fact their political structure falls far short.[97] However—with the exception of one significant dissenter discussed below—the consensus remains that the future will be one of an evolutionary increase in democratic states.[98]

The consensus view does, however, include room for the potential for public discouragement and disillusionment in democracy and market capitalism.[99] The *National Security Strategy for a New Century* (October 1998 version) expresses concerns that a slowing pace of economic growth could cause resentment of Western-led globalization and a disillusionment with democratic ideals. The report suggests that "if citizens tire of waiting for democracy and free markets to deliver a better life for them, there is real risk that they will lose confidence in democracy and free markets."[100] However, the overall report—which is directed at maintaining Congressional support for the Clinton Administration's foreign policy—is overwhelmingly positive on the expansion of democratic values, given continued American encouragement.[101]

Contrary View

Although not professing to be a direct forecast of the future security environment, Samuel P. Huntington's *The Clash of Civilizations and the Remaking of World Order*, like his earlier *Foreign Affairs* article on the topic, advances the thesis that there are cultural challenges to Western-style democracy.[102] Huntington's view is that cultural identity plays a significant role in global politics and that there are natural frictions between the ethnic civilizations of our "multipolar, multicivilizational world." In particular, the Islamic culture could pose the greatest challenge to Americanized democratic liberalism.

Islam, with its traditional linkage between religious and political authority, appears to be the sole rival philosophy that can claim to be international and not primarily ethnically-based. In contrast, the other cultures identified by Huntington—Sinic, Hindu, Japanese, Orthodox, Latin American, etc.—appear primarily ethnic in origin and do not necessarily reject democracy as a governing principal.

However, this claim for the internationalization of Islam has its limits; Islamic culture primarily dominates those regions of historical Arab or Turkish conquest. Likewise, the dominant face of Islam in international politics is that of the Arab states, whose stature is largely based on their oil reserves, an asset that will eventually be depleted. Also, the lack of a separation of authority between religious leaders and government—which is the primary philosophical challenge to Western-style democracy—is a feature of the Arab world and Iran, but not necessarily a reality in secularized Islamic nations, such as Turkey, Pakistan, or Indonesia (although religious leaders are still influential).[103]

Thus, the challenge of Islam seems to lie in the potential for its radicalization by the so-called Islamic fundamentalists, or by the rejection of Western culture that Huntington characterizes as the "Islamic Resurgence." This resurgence, epitomized in the slogan "Islam is the solution," accepts modernity and development in an Islamic context and, thus, is an alternative to more radical rejection called for by the fundamentalists.[104] Huntington points that "in its political manifestation, Islamic Resurgence bears some resemblance to Marxism, with scriptural texts, a vision of the perfect society, commitment to fundamental change, rejection of the powers that be and the nation state..."[105] However, he finds the Protestant Reformation a more useful analogy. And indeed, the Protestant Reformation sowed the seeds of a philosophical change in the theory of governance in Europe. The question is whether the Islamic Resurgence is radicalized to the point of seeking a confrontation with the nonIslamic world. Huntington cites authorities who view the OPEC oil price hike in the 1970s as being the spear-tip of such a confrontation.[106]

Directly contradicting Huntington's implication on the potential rivalry from Islam is the argument advanced in *New World Coming: Supporting Research and Analysis* that Islamic culture's adaptability to modernity is the very factor that ensures that such a confrontation will not come about; "Islamic neo-orthodoxy is neither militant nor expressly political in nature ... and no Muslim countries beyond Iran, Afghanistan, and Sudan, are likely to develop theocratic governments over the next quarter-century."[107] Other Mideast regional specialists tend to agree with this view and conclude that "like their secular counterparts, on most issues many

[Islamic-oriented political actors] would operate on the basis of national interests and demonstrate a flexibility that reflects acceptance of the realities of a globally interdependent world."[108] Even some of the sources that do acknowledge the potentially destabilizing effect of Islamic fundamentalism argue that fundamentalism is now waning.[109]

No Rival Coalition

In terms of cost-benefit analysis, it is hard to conceive of an overriding motive that could encourage a rival coalition of technologically-advanced states, most of which are democratic, to challenge the United States militarily. The foremost preventatives are shared values and the integration of the world economy. It is a long-standing belief that democracies do not go to war with other democracies, and—depending on how one defines democracy—the evidence appears to support such a belief, although there are detractors.[110] Those who view globalization as creating constraints on the independent actions of national governments also find scant evidence for the development of rival military coalitions.[111] Thomas Friedman, a reporter for *The New York Times* who has done the most to popularize the current globalization trend, has semi-facetiously put forward his "golden arches theory of conflict"—that no war has ever been fought between nations that have McDonald's hamburger franchises.[112] Whether that will remain true in a world in which McDonald franchises are ubiquitous—with restaurants from Moscow to Beijing—is questionable. Yet, the point is that it remains difficult to perceive the development of anti-U.S. military coalitions in light of current trends.

On the other hand, nondemocratic states threatened by the expansion of democratic values might prove more likely candidates for an anti-U.S., or more likely, anti-Western coalition. But the common perception is that the expanding information age is causing nondemocratic states to shrink in number.[113] Thus, there would be fewer candidates to form such a coalition. Another factor is the natural tendency of autocratic states—driven by nationalistic ideologies—to be reluctant to ally themselves to other equally powerful states.[114] There might be the natural fear that a powerful ally could reap a much greater benefit from an anti-Western coalition, thus precluding one's own rise to greater power.[115]

However, Brian Sullivan points to the fact that conflict alliances can be built by nations who hold traditional or ideological enmities between each other. "Consider how racist Nazi Germany allied with Japan in World War II, or how the atheistic, Communist Soviet Union allied with democratic, capitalist Britain and the United States in that same conflict."[116]

Sullivan warns that "future alliances and wars could easily present the same peculiar combinations," although he does not forecast the formation of any particular alliance.[117] A question to be asked is whether these alliances would ever form before, rather than *during* an existing conflict. Yet, Stephen M. Walt, in the same edited volume that contains Sullivan's argument, gives nuanced meaning to the theory of democratic peace: "Indeed democracies may well fight other democracies on occasion, but it seems axiomatic that democracies tend to ally with other democracies far easier than with authoritarian states."[118]

Consensus View

It is accepted that economic and political globalization makes it unlikely that a rival coalition could form to challenge the United States militarily. Various nations may express their displeasure at U.S. foreign policies or the overall specter of American "cultural imperialism," but most would have much to lose and little to gain in an anti-U.S. alliance.[119]

Based on this consensus, Donald Snow goes farther in postulating that the future "First Tier" of nations—centered around the so-called Group of Seven (G-7) economic powers of the United States, Germany, Japan, France, the United Kingdom, Italy, and Canada—is evolving toward a common post-industrial society and culture based on "shared commitment to political democracy and market economy and their equally shared commitment to enlarging the sway of those values."[120] Snow maintains that "the absence of substantial political or economic disagreement among First Tier states makes it virtually impossible to conceptualize military conflict among them."[121] Although other critics may speculate, there have been no serious forecasts that the European Union's interest in developing a unified military force independent from NATO will lead to a potential military confrontation with the United States.[122]

Supporters of the view that a rival coalition is unlikely point to the fact that the desire of lesser-developed nations to join the "First Tier" mitigates the tendency to fuel anti-Western hostility. Russia has been an honorary member of G-7 since 1997. It is likely that China also seeks a closer association with G-7; indeed, in 1999 it was proposed for membership in the World Trade Organization (WTO).[123] The closer both nations are economically tied to the West, the consensus view argues, the less likely that an anti-United States coalition will be formed.[124] Based on current trends, both Russia and China will seek to continue increasing their world trade during the next twenty-five years.[125]

Contrary View

Strategic Paradigm A of Jacquelyn K. Davis and Michael J. Sweeney's effort postulates a "loose" rival coalition driven by "an increasingly more assertive China aligned with a much weaker, authoritarian Russia."[126] Since this appears as a nonlinear trend from the present security environment, Davis and Sweeney explain that in their construct: "Chinese opposition to the United States is not the result of current trends in Sino-U.S. relations . . . [but] developed following a series of poor policy choices by both Beijing and Washington that have moved them into a more antagonistic posture than either state had intended."[127] The primary postulated event is U.S. action to deter a PRC naval blockade of Taiwan in the 2010 timeframe.[128]

The Paradigm A scenario also postulates that the current U.S. alliance framework has gradually eroded in the wake of Korean unification, development of the European Military Union (EMU), and nuclear proliferation. They argue that "while to some extent a worst-case scenario, the potential for both Japan and Europe to turn inward and leave the United States alone to face a major challenge from China and other states is plausible and, as a parameter for future planning, must be considered."[129]

Paradigm A is a scenario rather than a forecast, and the authors conclude that "this paradigm is perhaps the least likely to develop by 2025." However, there have been actions that indicate a desire on the part of the Russian leadership for a symbolic rapprochement with China as a way of countering "global domination by the United States," and particularly U.S. criticism of Russian military actions in the separatist republic of Chechnya.[130] Additionally, Russia sought in late 1999 to recharge its diplomatic relations with the so-called rogue states.[131]

Likewise, there have been suggestions that China would seek to put together alliances that "can defuse hegemonism by the U.S."[132] However, most other Asian states view China as their primary potential threat and the United States as a balancing power, so their willingness to join such an alliance is very low.[133]

In the absence of a competing ideology, the possibility of a China-Russia-led coalition would be the worst-case politico-military scenario for the security of the United States. Thus, it would appear that a critical foreign policy goal of U.S. national security would be the peacetime prevention of a China-Russia military alliance.[134]

No Global Peer Competitor

The issue of the rise of a military peer competitor to the United States suffers from a definitional problem. What exactly is a peer competitor? The QDR 1997 report used the analogy of the Soviet Union in the Cold War, stating that "the security environment between now and 2015 will also be marked with the absence of a 'global peer competitor' able to challenge the United States militarily around the world as the Soviet Union did during the Cold War."[135] However, QDR 1997 held out the possibility of the emergence of a "regional great power or global peer competitor," with Russia and China "seen by some as having the potential to be such competitors, though their respective futures are quite uncertain."[136]

The National Defense Panel of 1997 used the term "hostile peer competitor" in order to describe a future threat against which the United States "should take appropriate policy decisions at that time, including mobilization preparation . . ."[137] The NDP also identifies an ongoing "geopolitical revolution that prompted the collapse of the Soviet Union and that will see the emergence of China as a major regional and global actor."[138]

The debate on whether China will develop into a military peer competitor in the 2001–2025 time frame is extensive, but inconclusive.[139] A significant portion of the confusion is on the lack of a standard definition of the term.

To develop a standard definition, one must ask the question: what can the Armed Forces of the United States do that those of other nations cannot? The succinct answer is that the United States is capable of projecting its military power on a global basis in a sustained fashion. It is capable of inserting its forces into any region of the world and sustaining them through its unparalleled logistics capabilities, including airlift, sealift, an extensive series of alliances, and expeditionary forces.[140]

Few nations can project power on a global basis. Potential candidates include the United Kingdom and France, both of which are U.S. allies. In the 1980s, Britain demonstrated long range power projection capabilities in the Falklands War. France routinely projects and sustains forces in francophone Africa. The Soviet Union was able to project long-range military power, but even then did not quite equal American capabilities; the consensus assessment is that Russia could not do so today.[141] While China continues to increase the reach of its military capabilities, its capability for transporting forces beyond its immediate neighbors is limited.[142] Other nations, particularly those with well-developed economies, have potential for some degree of global military reach. Japan, for example, is building modest power projection capabilities into its Maritime Self-Defense Force.[143]

The National Defense Panel recognized the uniqueness of U.S. power projection capabilities and described it as the "cornerstone of America's continued military preeminence"[144] and as a "central element of U.S. defense strategy."[145] The NDP also acknowledged that the Nation can currently "project combat power rapidly and virtually unimpeded."[146] That statement can be made of no other nation.[147]

Consensus View

If the term peer competitor is defined in terms of equivalency to the Soviet or by the capacity to sustain global power projection, the consensus view is that a peer competitor cannot develop before 2025.[148] It is not simply a question of pursuing the development of power projection capabilities. Rather, 25 years appears too short a time to duplicate American logistics and alliance networks, which result from an effort sustained over half a century. In essence, the United States never fully retreated from its postwar occupation of Germany and Japan and attempted to maintain the good will of its wartime allies—with the exception of the Soviet Union and its occupied satellites, which ironically provided the threat to facilitate this task.

To duplicate U.S. reach requires much more than developing the technology for long-range strike, such as with ballistic missiles or long-range bombers. Russia still retains a considerable slice of these capabilities, and can threaten the United States with a strategic nuclear strike from both land and sea.[149] China has developed its own ballistic missile submarine that could be positioned to strike the United States, and the United Kingdom and France have the capabilities for strategic nuclear strike, as well.[150] But as devastating as such a strike could be, it does not constitute sustained power projection. There is no nation that could transport a significant body of forces to the American homeland and attempt an invasion.[151] This contrasts with the American ability to invade anywhere.[152] Unless the United States made a deliberate decision to forego its power projection capabilities, there appears a very small possibility, if any, that this conventional asymmetry can be overturned by 2025. Thus, there is no potential for a power projection peer competitor.[153]

Contrary View

Since the end of the Cold War, the Office of Net Assessment has maintained an ongoing study of China's changing military strategy and future military capabilities. This China focus has dovetailed with the corresponding Office of Net Assessment study of the issue of a RMA. While there is no agreement that China could develop into a global peer competitor by 2025, the results of a series of Summer Studies suggest that Chinese power projection capabilities could greatly increase through a sustained effort to harness a RMA.[154] The most recent study postulates a plausible future in which China is able to project sustained military power throughout the Asian continent, or, at the very least, prevent the projection of U.S. military power anywhere in Asia.[155] This would be a China capable of being a *regional* peer competitor, rather than a global peer.[156] However, this regional potential could be expanded by an informal Asian condominium between China and India.[157]

Additionally, a Russia-China led alliance could pose the possibility of simultaneous conflicts in multiple regions, which would severely tax the ability of American forces to respond. This would be the closest equivalent to a global peer competitor, but it would still lack the power projection capabilities of the current American defense structure.[158]

Economic Competitors

Propelled by the perception of increasing trade competition between the United States and Japan, the 1990s saw a series of publications suggesting the potential for military conflicts based on economic rivalry. In Japan, several prominent figures indicated dissatisfaction with America's 'bullying' of Japan on economic and security matters.[159] In the United States, publication of *The Coming War With Japan* renewed interest in the once-popular view that war was caused by economic competition and that a war between the two strongest economic powers—separated by vastly difference cultures—was almost inevitable.[160] There was a near immediate effort by the official foreign policy establishments of both nations to smother such sentiments.[161]

Although the particular controversy was even more effectively suppressed—for at least the time being—by the Asian economic downturn of the late 1990s, the view of a linkage between economic conflict and war has remained a lingering byproduct. A staple of Marxist theology and post-First World War assessments, the popular appeal of this linkage was echoed in the oft-stated view that the Gulf War was "all about oil." The potential for China to become an economic power, along with the evolving European Union, have also been cited as precursors to politico-military confrontation with the United States.[162]

Consensus View

Despite popular concerns, the intellectual consensus remains that economic competition need not lead to military confrontation, and that it is very unlikely to do so in the 2001–2025 period. The particulars of U.S.-Japanese economic conflict are largely seen as "reconcilable differences" that will not affect security arrangements.[163] The prevailing view of the phenomenon of globalization is that such greater economic interconnection decreases, rather than increases, the potential for military conflict.[164] However, concerns have been frequently expressed that unequal rates of globalization may create a world of have and have-not states that will lead to regional instabilities. The benefits of a more integrated global economy may not be felt in societies that are unable to absorb or apply rapidly emerging new technologies. As forecast by the U.S. Commission on National Security/21st Century commission: "New technologies will divide the world as well as draw it together."[165] Likewise, globalization holds the potential for increasing competition for resources as potential shortages develop in previously accessible energy sources or such essential natural resources as water.[166]

Nevertheless, the prevailing view remains that, in the long term, the growth of free markets and new technologies solve more problems than they cause.[167]

Contrary View

One diverging view, however, is that of Stratfor.com, the global forecasting and consulting firm located in Austin, Texas. Heavily influenced by Friedman and Lebard, Stratfor.com admits a contrarian belief in the conflictual nature of globalization and global prosperity:

> The predominant belief is that prosperity tends to stabilize the international system. We disagree. Paradoxically, increased prosperity and integration tends to increase political instability. Prosperity leads to greater economic integration and dependency resulting in greater insecurity by increasing the importance of international economic relationships and therefore increasing the opportunities for friction. This, in turn, leads to greater insecurity.[168]

Stratfor.com returns to the 1980s theme of increasing potential for U.S.-Japanese economical conflict. "The greater U.S.-Japanese integration, for example, the greater the need on the part of each nation to control the other's behavior.[169]

The growing use of "political means . . . to control economic relationships" does not necessarily lead directly to military conflict. However, it sets the stage for such conflicts to eventually develop between the major economic powers. "Prosperity and instability—as we saw from 1900–1914—frequently go hand in hand. Thus, the paradox of the next decade will be that increased global prosperity will lead to increased global instability."[170]

Like the QDR 1997 report, Stratfor.com sees the actions of the world's greatest political-economic-military power as the prime driver of the international system. The fact that most nations want to be economically more like the United States does not guarantee an increasing harmony of interests.

> This happy economic picture does not face an equivalently happy political and military picture. That is not to say that this decade will experience a systemic, convulsive war like the Napoleonic Wars, World War I or World War II. Nor will it see a singular systemic confrontation, like the Anglo-French confrontation of the 18th Century or the Cold War. These will happen, but not in this time frame. Rather, the next decade will be a period of increasing disharmony both between nations and within nations. Underneath it all will be a singular political question: how will the international system cope with the growing power of the United States, and what will the United States do with its growing power?[171]

Regional Military Challengers

The threat that regional powers will challenge the U. S. militarily and seek to prevent the United States from projecting power into their regions is universally considered the primary challenge that U.S. foreign and defense policy will face in the first decades of the 21st century. "Regional dangers" is the term used over and over again to describe the potential for "the threat of coercion and large-scale, cross-border aggression against U.S. allies and friends in key regions by hostile states with significant military power."[172]

Initially, the prime regional threat was thought to be in Northeast Asia: predictable actions (or collapse) of North Korea, the world's last true Stalinist state. The second was, in Southwest Asia, the even more unpredictable actions of an unrepentant Saddam Hussein in Iraq, or—by implication—the simmering hostility of Iran toward its Arabian Gulf neighbors and the West.[173] This is the basis for the two MTW force posture adopted by the United States; as previously discussed, these threats are eminently plausible under current conditions.[174]

However, they do not necessarily represent the most demanding threats of the future in terms of capabilities. Clearly, those nations that have access to a large pool of trainable manpower and can sustain sophisticated defense industries and produce significant quantities of relatively modern weaponry would be the most difficult foes to face. From that perspective, there is clearly a rank order of potential (and current) regional military powers. Within this order, almost every futures assessment identifies Russian and China as having the greatest potential for regional dominance.[175] *As New World Coming* states: "Major powers—Russian and China are two obvious examples—may wish to extend their regional influence by force or the threat of force."[176]

In terms of strategic weapons systems, Russia remains the most formidable.[177] Despite the economic turmoil of its difficult transition to a market economy, it retains considerable technological expertise and industrial capacity for the development of highly sophisticated weapons systems, such as nuclear submarines, fighter aircraft, and tactical rockets and artillery.[178] Available manpower has been significantly reduced since the secession of the former Soviet republics; however, continuing conscription can supply a relatively large military force. As is evident from exercises and operations in Chechnya, training of regular units may be very weak.[179] However, Russian (former Soviet) doctrine has always emphasized that the use of special forces, and extensive training of small numbers of highly effective personnel is quite supportable.[180] Additionally, Russia retains access to a large space launch infrastructure, and is currently the only state capable of mounting a challenge to America's almost complete dominance of the military use of space.[181]

China is viewed in an analogous position as Russia—a regional power, but under current conditions, not absolutely dominant within its region. Just as expansion of Russian power could be checked by NATO, Chinese expansion could be stymied by a loose alliance of economically strong Asian nations backed by the United States.[182] In the past, China has viewed itself as ringed by potential opponents, from Japan to India.[183]

However, unlike Russia, China is viewed as having considerable economic potential that could fuel an extremely robust military expansion.[184] Some sources suggest that China could have the world's largest gross domestic product (GDP) by 2025.[185] While other sources view such a forecast as unrealistic, the fact remains that the world's business community views China as a vast future market and emerging economic power, based primarily on its tremendous population. At the same time, China is committed to the rapid absorption of advanced technology, particularly military technology.[186] Chinese interest in the debate concerning an information-based RMA has been noted.[187] Whether or not Chinese military effectiveness grows at the alarming rate some suggest, it is obvious that China's military potential will grow.[188]

China also appears to have the greatest likelihood among the current military powers of sparking a regional conflict to achieve its political aims.[189] The future of Taiwan is not simply an unresolved irredentist claim, but—in the perspective of the mainland—a continuing challenge to the legitimacy of the Beijing government.[190] Even though Beijing has been successful in diplomatically isolating Taiwan and has been recognized in all international forums as the government of China, Communist party cadres will never consider their revolution complete until Taiwan, the last bastion of the Kuomintang, submits to their authority.[191] Ironically, formal Taiwanese declaration of independence from the mainland—which would end any pretext of Kuomintang rule under the "one China" policy through the simple recognition of reality—is viewed as a greater threat than if Taiwan remains an unconquered part of China.[192] In the circumstance of formal independence—or if it appears that Taiwan is unable to put up significant resistance—it is likely that Beijing would act on its stated policy of conducting a military assault on the island.[193] Unless the United States were to ignore its history of support for Taiwanese self-determination, and give up the pretext of preventing international aggression, the result would be a regional war.[194]

Fueling the potential for regional war is the Chinese Peoples' Liberation Army (PLA) view of the United States as their foremost military opponent in the future security environment.[195]

India, which demographically and technologically is the dominant power of South Asia, has long attempted to reduce U.S. (and other Western) influence in its region.[196] However, with the collapse of its client relationship with the Soviet military-industrial complex, India has had to back away from its pseudo-hostility toward American power. Although conflict with Pakistan appears a constant possibility, the situation differs markedly from the Cold War, when the United States supported an anti-Soviet Pakistan.[197] A regional war involving the United States and India would be an unlikely occurrence, as there are incentives to warmer relations.[198]

The European Union (EU), Japan, and Australia could be viewed as regional powers. However, all are American allies—although, as previously noted, there is potential for future economic or even political tensions, particularly with Japan.[199] Other potential or de facto regional powers, such as Israel, Egypt, Saudi Arabia, and South Africa, have positive relations with the United States and lack any significant issue of contention that would cause them to challenge the United States militarily.[200]

Several additional rogue states, such as Iraq, Iran, and Libya, have the potential of becoming military powers in their region, particularly through the acquisition of weapons of mass destruction.[201] Rogue state scenarios are considered the basis for two MTW planning.[202] However, it is also likely that rogue states would seek to use terrorism or other deniable means, rather than confront the United States directly.[203]

Consensus View

It is likely that one or more of the rogue states (North Korea, Iraq, Iran, Libya) may seek to militarily challenge the United States in the near term.[204] Such an assessment is based on current hostilities, plans or desire for regional dominance, propensity for aggressive military action, or a pattern of anti-U.S. military activity. In a longer-term view, the potential for conflict with a major regional power may grow, with Russia or China as the most difficult potential military opponents. This assessment is based on the historical experience of the international system, and multipolar and balance of power international politics.[205] However, there is no consensus as to which regional power or rogue state is likely to take action at any particular time. As noted, the staying power of the North Korean regime and Saddam Hussein has contradicted previous forecasts of their demise.[206]

Contrary View

Among the sources surveyed, there are no significant arguments that a regional conflict is unlikely before 2025. However, there is a perception that effective United States actions, along with a well-trained and technologically superior military, could deter such conflict. Likewise, astute management of relations with Russia, China, and India may prevent the development of hostilities.[207] Other sources argue that hostile states are simply too weak to mount a credible military threat to the overwhelming power of the Armed Forces.[208] However, a pessimistic view of the constant potential for regional conflict has settled in, primarily as a result of intellectual disappointment with the short tenure of the euphorically proclaimed "new world order."[209]

More Failing States

The terms *failed state* and *failing state* have been increasingly used to describe nations that cannot provide law, order, or basic human necessities to their populations. Such states may be wracked by civil war, tribal divisions, ideological or ethnic hatreds, or other conflicts that prevent the central government from providing internal security or promoting general prosperity.

While the internal consequences of such disorder have long been recognized, the external effects within the international environment have not always been considered a security threat to distant, stable nations. However, with growing industrialization, the stability of sources of raw materials and markets became important to the world's major powers, largely precipitating the age of colonialism. Although the colonial age has ended, increasing economic interdependence and the ubiquitous nature of information have ensured that stability of peripheral states remain critical to the core industrial/informational nations.[210] Instability in the economic periphery can cause direct effects in the economic core, from energy and resource shortages to monetary flight. This interdependence is forecast to continue. The U.S. Commission on National Security/21st Century highlights, for example, the importance of stability in oil-producing regions: "American dependence on foreign sources of energy will also grow over the next two decades. In the absence of events that alter the price of oil, the stability of the world oil market will continue to depend on an uninterrupted supply of oil from the Persian Gulf, and the location of all key fossil fuel deposits will retain geopolitical significance."[211]

The QDR 1997 report identifies failed and failing states as potential future security challenges for the United States. As the report states, "failed or failing states may create instability, internal conflict, and humanitarian crises, in some cases within regions in which the United States has vital or important interests."[212] Identifying countries ranging "from Albania to Zaire," the report postulates a continuum of results from failed governments that includes the "massive flow of migrants across international borders," and even prompting "aggressive action by neighboring states or even mass killings."[213]

However, the question of exactly where the United States has vital or important interests fuels the argument that American efforts to restore order in failed states is largely a humanitarian effort that does little to increase U.S. national security. And indeed, U.S. interventions in Somalia and Haiti during the Bush and Clinton administrations were largely justified on humanitarian grounds. Most telling is the precipitous withdrawal of U.S. forces from Somalia following the ambush of U.S. Rangers and the resulting public debate. Presumably, such a precipitous withdrawal would not have occurred if the Clinton administration considered the stability of Somalia a vital, or even important security interest of the United States.[214] Likewise, the current political and economic drift of Haiti—even after the restoration of elected government by U.S. military forces—does not seem to have sparked much debate concerning the vital nature of American interests in that unfortunate state.[215] Efforts to promote democracy—a significant component of foreign policy in the early Clinton administration—appear to no longer be justified on the basis of increased international security.[216] However, there are still compelling arguments for American intervention to stop genocide or massive loss of life.[217] Such arguments contributed to the American decision to prompt NATO intervention in Kosovo. But given the nature of democratic politics, such intervention ultimately remains discretionary.[218]

Consensus View

The consensus of the sources appears to mirror the above debate. On the one hand, the future international system is seen as containing an increasing number of failed states, while the effects of the collapse of the Soviet empire, the legacy of colonialism, and increasing globalization all play out. As the U.S. Commission on National Security/21st Century describes it: "Fragmentation or failure of states will occur, with destabilizing effects on neighboring states."[219] Africa and the Middle East are seen as being particularly vulnerable to such destabilization.[220]

On the other hand, the cumulative effect of the occurrences of failed states is not seen as requiring intervention in order to protect U.S. national security, except in isolated instances.[221] In this scenario, the United States retains considerable discretion as to whether it should become militarily involved, even when pushed by reports in news media.[222]

One of the isolated instances would be the collapse of control by the Stalinist regime in Pyongyang. North Korea, with its population facing starvation and its diplomatic isolation, is categorized by many as already having failed.[223] However, the North continues to defy the once prolific forecasts of its imminent demise.[224] The most frightening scenario of a total failure in North Korea is that of a destructive, vengeful war against South Korea that could include ballistic missile attacks with chemical or even nuclear weapons.[225] America's security relationship with the South and the presence of U.S. military forces would irrefutably place this in the vital interest category.[226]

Yet, curiously and perhaps reflecting the ambiguity concerning the impact of failed states in the 2000–2025 time-frame, many of the future security environment assessments foresee a unified, perhaps nuclear-capable Korea (led by the South Korean government) as a greater threat to regional security than a collapsing, vengeful, and heavily armed North Korea that is capable of striking U.S. (and Japanese) forces in Japan.[227] Like earlier forecasts, Korean unification is seen as a given during the 2000–2025 period.[228]

Other problematic failing states would include the collapse of a key regional friend or ally.[229] However, forecasts on individual states are met with counter-arguments, prompting such key failures to be placed in the wildcard category rather than as part of an anticipated future.[230]

Contrary View

Few if any sources are willing to categorically forecast a future security environment in which significant numbers of failed states do not occur.[231] There are, however, optimistic scenarios that are envisioned, even in the case of Africa.[232] But even the most optimistic sources include caveats along these lines: "Central to this positive evolution will also be stemming the conflict and instability that has wracked so much of the region for so long."[233] While some sources suggest an increase in the desire to actively stem such conflict, others point to an increasing reluctance on the part of most nations to become involved. Additionally, arguments have been made that advocates of intervention underestimate the complexity of involvement, and that such involvement is often counter-productive.[234]

Unambiguously positive assessments of a future with fewer failing states are largely confined to normative prescriptions masquerading as forecasts.[235]

More Nonstate Threats

The term nonstate threats is used to denote those threats to national security that are not directly planned or organized by a nation-state. Today, foremost among these threats are acts of terrorism other than those sponsored by a rogue state. However, there is a loosely defined spectrum of nonstate threats, increasing in intensity from humanitarian disasters to mass migrations, to piracy, to computer network attack, to organized international crime and drug trafficking, to terrorism with conventional weaponry, to terrorism with weapons of mass destruction. The

National Defense Panel of 1997 referred to such activities as "transnational threats;" however, the latter term implies that such threats could be subject to multinational control. Indeed, the NDP report states: "Transnational challenges and threats, by definition, reside in more than one country and require a multipartner response."[236] This need for a multipartner response creates distinctions between the NDP report, other definitions of transnational threats, and those sources using the term, "nonstate threats." Although nonstate threats may cross boundaries, it is not assumed that a multinational response is the sole means of defense. Additionally, the term "transnational threats" can also be applied to dangers that are generated through nation-state action.[237] The subtle difference between the two terms creates a degree of analytical confusion when comparing the recommendations of the NDP to those of the 1997 QDR or other sources. The 1999 version of the National Security Strategy simply states "transnational threats include terrorism, drug trafficking and other international crime, and illegal trade in fissile materials and other dangerous substances."[238] For the purpose of this study, transnational threats will be viewed as a subset of nonstate threats.

The term nonstate can also apply to international organizations, nongovernmental organizations, multinational corporations, and multinational interest groups. The degree that the activities of such entities are seen as threats to the security of nation-states varies according to philosophical views of the world system. Those holding the belief that an international system dominated by nation-states is the cause of war have long advocated multinational or nonstate solutions. During the 1970s and 1980s, numerous scholarly sources postulated, with varying degrees of support or condemnation, that the international system was soon to be readjusted and that the power of the nation-state would severely decline, with the void filled by international organizations, multinational corporations, and NGOs.[239] This was fueled by perennial forecasts/advocacy of an increasingly effective UN organization, world federalism, or other multilateral arrangement for governance that would supercede the sovereignty of individual nation-states.[240] To some extent such multilateral arrangements have superceded national sovereignty on a regional basis, the most apparent success being the developing European Union. However, the speed at which such arrangements have emerged has not kept pace with the optimistic forecasts. And for every effort at multilateral institutions that appears to succeed, other institutions fail or become weaker, such as the waning influence of OPEC or the weakness of the Organization of

African Unity (OAU) in completing peace keeping missions on the African continent.[241] At their core, multilateral arrangements are still dependent on the voluntary compliance of member nation-states.[242]

Alarmist predictions that nonstate actors, issues and threats would overwhelm and break the abilities of most nation-states to deal with them have simply not materialized.[243] Nations that have collapsed into anarchy have largely been victims of civil wars, a phenomenon that long precedes the current definition of nonstate threats.[244] Many of these civil wars have been fueled or supported by foreign parties, international actors, or other nations. To that extent, nonstate or transnational threats do contribute to such internal collapse, but in ways that have been relatively consistent throughout history.[245] Thus, as most of the sources that identify a growth in the number of nonstate threats in the future generally acknowledge, the development of nonstate threats to the national-state systems appears as an evolutionary, rather than an exponential rise.[246]

Nation-states are as vulnerable as the choices they make—such as for greater commercial dependence on the Internet or for wider ranging free trade agreements—require or permit them to be.[247] As a commercial phenomenon, globalization has tied the economies of advanced states tighter together, but such ties are not historically irreversible, and it is unclear what the effects of a major downturn in the global economy might be on the process of globalization itself. Individually, some states will choose greater degrees of autarky than others, cutting their vulnerability to certain nonstate threats. For example, states that erect significant physical barriers to immigration will be less vulnerable to the effects of mass migrations than those that do not.

Likewise, the growth of nonstate actors will likely continue, but does not necessarily threaten the independent powers or national security of nation-states.[248] To some extent, the increasingly public roles of NGOs are recognized as matters of convenience; they are performing missions or functions that states do not choose to do, or can save resources by allowing someone else to do them. Humanitarian NGOs are the most notable in carrying out missions that provide for the public good, but that no one state is responsible or can necessarily afford. At the same time, many humanitarian NGOs are becoming increasing dependent on governmental funding for their activities, an issue that is being debated within the traditionally independent NGO community.[249] This reinforces the arguments that NGOs function as surrogates rather than supplants.

Even the most aggressive issue-oriented NGOs have found limits to their ability to challenge national sovereignty.[250] On issues in which popular opinion is at odds with governmental policy, it is recognized that NGOs can galvanize opinion to change national policies, or even affect international policies by promoting a degree of discomfort for a certain state. A prime example is the Greenpeace-led campaign to change Japanese and Russian policy toward whaling. However, when a Greenpeace chapter attempted to prevent the U.S. Navy from conducting an underwater test launching of submarine launched ballistic missiles by positioning a vessel in the launch area, they were rammed, towed, and arrested without a flutter in popular opinion.[251] Likewise, Greenpeace opposition to the deployment of U.S. forces to the Persian Gulf in support of Operations *Desert Shield* and *Desert Storm* caused such a significant loss in contributions in the United States that a number of local chapters quickly backed away from that position. In such cases, considered matters of national security, governmental power was in no way diminished.

Internet interest groups are another form of NGO that has been identified by some sources as having the potential to reduce the loyalty of individuals toward national identity. As the U.S. Commission on National Security/21st Century finds: "New technologies will divide the world as well as draw it together."[252] Their finding suggests the development of a "cyber-class of people" consisting of educated elites with "greater mobility and emigration."[253] However, the existence of such sub-cultures is not without precedent, and does not necessarily presage the development of an increasing array of alternative loyalties. As *New World Coming* concedes, an anti-technology backlash is conceivable.[254] It is also conceivable that members of the new cyber-class may be more competitive than cooperative. Psychologists have suggested that the anonymity of Internet users can lead to an increase of anti-social behavior.[255]

Critics of economic globalization have pointed out that the Internet may allow more corporations the opportunity to avoid taxation by transferring operations to those nations with more favorable tax laws.[256] To some extent this can be seen as a nonstate threat to security. However, it is likely that advanced states will find a host of legal remedies to prevent significant effects.

The U.S. Commission on National Security/21st Century has identified the evolutionary nature of nonstate threats through the juxtaposition of two of their findings. The growth of nonstate and transnational threats is acknowledged by the observation that: "All borders will be more porous; some will bend and some will break." But at the same time, the resilience of the nation-state in retaining its role as primary international actor is recognized by the finding that: "The sovereignty of states will come under pressure, but will endure."[257]

Consensus View

The consensus of the sources is that nonstate threats will increase in number and intensity in the future. However, this anticipated increase parallels vulnerabilities that are by-products of the evolutionary process of globalization. There is not enough evidence to suggest that states cannot take measures to reduce their vulnerability, if they so choose. Logically, the technologies that fuel globalization, and presumably are the heart of increasing vulnerability, should be able to solve as many nonstate problems as they create. Other nonstate threats such as terrorism and international crime may seem more potent due to the advantages modern technologies may bring to the perpetrator. However, the same or other modern technologies can be used to strengthen defenses. The wave of increasing nonstate threats will likely be closely followed by a wave of technologies to defeat them. But it must be admitted that this does not solve the near-term problems of terrorism, particularly if terrorist groups come in possession of WMD.[258] An occurrence of this nature is such an obvious legal and security threat that most sources assume increased levels of vigilance and effort by law enforcement agencies and the armed forces are needed to deter, defend against, and react to such threats.[259] The consensus view is not sanguine about the near-term potential for terrorist incidents. Yet, the level of current and future vulnerability of societies to terrorism is still hotly debated.[260]

Similarly, the majority of sources view the influence of NGOs as increasingly important, though only indirect affecting international security. The treaties and understandings they have traditionally fostered and supported cannot guarantee security without voluntary enforcement by sovereign powers. Efforts to ban the use of land mines, like previous efforts to ban the use of submarines or poisonous gas, ultimately rely on the self interest of supporting states. The consensus remains that, although NGOs may become more ubiquitous, their power will not supplant that of nation-states in the 2001–2025 timeframe.

Contrary View

There are no sources that are willing to maintain that nonstate threats will not increase in the 2001–2025 time frame. However, some sources do view the rise of these threats as exponential in nature, and they indicate more alarm than the consensus view might imply. Of particular concern is the possibility of terrorism with WMD, also known as "catastrophic terrorism."[261] However, since terrorist attacks can be part of an overall military attack by a hostile state, this threat straddles the line from nonstate threats to asymmetrical attacks, which are the subject of another consensus point.[262] It is assumed that development of WMD or information warfare would be easier for a nation-state and its physical infrastructure and resources than it would be for a nonstate terrorist group.[263]

Military Technology

Diffusion of Technology

The category of advanced military technology is rather broad and constitutes a spectrum of technologies or innovative uses of technology developed during the last few decades. This spectrum, arrayed in terms of the destructiveness of the products of advanced technology, ranges from emerging biological weaponry and other weapons of mass destruction, to new forms of nonlethal weapons including information operations using mass media.[264]

Because of the dynamism of technological development, "advanced" remains a relative term. Yet, in discussing military capabilities, it is possible to identify technologies within the reach of only a few of the world's armed forces. Initially, the resulting advanced weapons are often produced in small quantities because of difficulty in manufacture. However, they may later proliferate as technology advances and cheaper techniques are developed. Currently, such advanced weaponry includes highly accurate ballistic and cruise missiles, fourth-generation aircraft (complex surveillance, detection, tracking and targeting equipment), surface-to-air missiles, nuclear powered submarines, and numerous other relatively high-cost systems.

Some of these systems can be readily purchased from the manufacturers, although most nations place export controls on their front-line weapons. However, a cash-strapped Russia has recently sold advanced weapons systems that it would not transfer during the Cold War, such as the SS–N–22 Sunburn (Russian: *Moskit*) anti-ship missile.[265] Advanced weapons are sometimes sold illegally. Other dual-use (military and commercial) technology has been legally transferred under the guise of commercial contract. The controversy generated by the sale of U.S. computing and satellite launch technology to China, which the Chinese are reputed to have used in enhancing their ballistic missile lethality and accuracy, is but a recent example.[266]

Development (and to some extent, use) of advanced military systems requires a mastery of diverse technologies, from missile and satellite guidance to high-energy power sources. However, much of the underlying scientific knowledge can be obtained from readily available open-source literature. Most states have at least a small indigenous intellectual infrastructure capable of translating scientific advances into technical applications. More importantly, the university systems of the advanced nations are generally open to students of all nationalities, allowing the diffusion of scientific and engineering knowledge throughout the world. Thus, nations seeking to apply older, available technology to new military system generally have or can gradually obtain an indigenous knowledge base from which to proceed. This indigenous base can be extended by the hiring of foreign scientists, technologists or engineers. Hence, the frequently expressed concern about the post-Soviet collapse hiring of Russian technologists by rogue states.[267]

When an indigenous or hired knowledge base is applied to the improvement or upgrade of weapons systems already available on the world market, the results can be the development of an advanced system that outclasses other regional militaries. Both North Korea and Iraq, along with other states, were able to extend the range of ballistic missiles originally sold to them by the Soviet Union. This indigenous capability, with its relatively low cost, is a factor in the assessment that ballistic missiles (and cruise missiles) will be "weapons of choice" in the 2001–2025 timeframe.[268] Both India and Pakistan were able to translate their civilian nuclear power capability, by means of secret programs and, possibly, outside assistance, into nuclear weapons. There is the significant potential that less technologically advanced nations can convert commercial-off-the-shelf (COTS) into military capabilities through use of unique or unexpected applications, a process for which Paul Bracken has coined the term "sidewise technology."[269] In addition, considerable military electronic technology has become commercialized. A primary example is the Global Positioning System (GPS), an aid to navigation that was used extensively by the United States and the allied coalition in the Persian Gulf War, but was unavailable to the Iraqis.[270] GPS is now commercially available, although not necessarily with military standards of precision. However, these standards could be reverse-engineered.

Consensus View

The consensus of the sources is that advanced military technology will continue to become more diffuse through sales, modification of dual-use systems, and indigenous weapons development programs. Although international export control regimes may exist for certain types of advanced weapons, such as the Missile Technology Control Regime (MTCR), these agreements appear to be as easily circumvented as enforced. The U.S. Commission on National Security/21st Century points out that Iran, Iraq, North Korea, Pakistan, and India have all effectively foiled the MTCR.[271] Thus far, control regimes appear to have slowed potential nuclear weapons development by rogue states. However, Iraq—a nation that suffered such a crushing military defeat—continues to play cat-and-mouse games with the international inspectors mandated by the peace treaty. Evidence indicates that there are other covert proliferation efforts.

At the same time, the scientific knowledge that forms the basis for many military technologies flows freely.[272] To some extent, it is inherent in the freedom of information in modern democracies. But it becomes even more difficult in a more globalized and Internet-linked international environment to keep genies in their bottles. That does not mean that nations will not attempt to control their technological secrets, particularly precise details in the manufacture of advanced weapons. But it does mean that knowledge can be focussed so as to replicate these secrets. Such focusing requires considerable financial resources, which is why not every nation can replicate every technology. But it is possible that certain nations, particularly rogue states, might choose to focus their resources on a particular technology, thereby being able to duplicate or supercede the most advanced systems of the advanced states in that particular niche.[273]

Contrary View

Although there are sources that endorse greater efforts to negotiate and strengthen weapons control regimes, none argue that military technology will not continue to become more diffuse in the 2001–2025 period. In fact, it is the alarm at which military technologies are spreading that prompts the more urgent calls for international controls. Under current circumstance, proliferation of advanced systems appears to be but a matter of time and resources.

Commercially Available Intelligence

Information is the prime necessity for military operations with high-technology weapons. The precision attacks demonstrated in the

Gulf War could only be achieved by real-time, targeting-quality information gathered by a sophisticated network of intelligence, surveillance, and reconnaissance (ISR) sensors. In the case of the United States, this capability is largely a byproduct of the national technical means (NTM) developed during the Cold War to detect nuclear attack or significant conventional force movement by the Soviet Union.

The end of the Cold War allowed the United States to reorient portions of the global NTM network and combine it with operational and tactical military ISR systems in order to provide combat forces with a more complete view of potential battle spaces. NTM still remain a prime element of U.S. nuclear deterrence, its application has broadened to the point that separation between strategic and tactical information has begun to dissolve. At the same time, corresponding Russian global ISR capabilities have generally eroded, allowing the United States to develop an unprecedented information advantage over possible antagonists. Although NATO ISR is nominally independent—and other U.S. friends and allies have developed their own, albeit limited, ISR systems—the reality is that these systems either rely on support from U.S. ISR or are unable to provide a real time picture beyond their own immediate regions, or are focused solely on potentially opposing strategic nuclear forces (such as those of Russia or China). In the near term, real time global information suitable for military targeting is primarily an American commodity.[274]

The availability and quality of commercial satellite imagery, however, continues to increase. SPOT Image Corporation, for example, can provide digital imagery of 10-meter resolution for much of the world.[275] Although this information is rarely real time, due to the expense of permanent satellite coverage, the use of commercial information for military planning before the start of hostilities makes perfect sense. If the number of commercial remote sensing and digital imagery satellites increase as predicted, the cost of their products should logically decrease, putting them within the range of even nonstate actors.[276] The U.S government has actively encouraged remote sensing commercialization as a cost effective method of providing non-real time military information.[277] But it is also possible that an increased number of dedicated satellites could provide real time imagery for customers other than the U.S. military.[278] Militarily important imagery could also be covertly obtained by weather and environmental monitoring satellites.

Yet, satellite imagery is but one portion of the U.S military ISR effort, a network that includes land-based radars, manned and unmanned reconnaissance aircraft, and intelligence gathering by submarine and other platforms. Although the great increases in computing power makes the fusion of multiple source information faster and more affordable, it would be difficult for a potential opponent to develop an ISR network of the scope of the U.S. effort. Admittedly, an opponent would not necessarily need a system for global reconnaissance, and might opt for one focussed on the immediate region. But a regional system would not be effective in detecting and tracking U.S. forces before their entry into the region, thus, allowing the United States a capacity for surprise. Use of commercial systems monitoring North America or other regions might eliminate this capabilities gap.

The issues of when real-time imagery will become commercially available, and whether commercial interests would continue to sell imagery to a rogue state or other nation at war against the United States or American allies, are contentious. Even if real-time imagery were available, the commercial interests involved would likely be Western-led corporations with greater ties to the United States and allies than any other states. Under such circumstances, it would be natural for these corporations to cut off information to states conducting a war against the United States. However, critics have argued that we cannot assume that multinational corporations would retain a sense of national loyalty, and they might find the trade in wartime imagery particularly lucrative.

Consensus View

Given the current trends in space launch and commercialization, the consensus is that operational intelligence—primarily satellite imagery—will become more and more commercially available. The potential for such a market is growing. The U.S. Commission on National Security/21st Century predicts that: "Due to the wide availability of commercial sources of space-supported information, by 2025 the United States will no longer enjoy a monopoly in space-based C4ISR" [command, control, communications, computing, intelligence, surveillance, and reconnaissance].[279]

Yet, reflecting the consensus view, the commission forecasts that the United States "will, however, maintain a preponderant edge, using its technical systems to produce timely and usable information."[280] The infrastructure necessary is simply too difficult to create except through the obvious expenditure of considerable resources.

At the same time, the consensus view concerning militarily-significant commercial information is that it would be available to a potential aggressor until the commencement of hostilities, but would be voluntarily or covertly shut down upon the initial attack.[281] It is hard to conceive of a circumstance where even the most independent of multinational corporations would care to jeopardize future contracts with the United States or American allies. Actions by the IRS or by civil lawsuit round out the less forceful end of potential incentives.

But the fact that operational intelligence would not remain available during conflict may be of little consolation, since the information obtained during pre-hostilities would be sufficient to target fixed sites, such as land bases, in advance. The use of WMD might also make the need for real-time targeting information moot.

Contrary View

None of the sources surveyed suggested that operational intelligence will not become commercially available in the 2001–2025 timeframe. Opposition to the consensus view revolved around two points: (1) that satellite information is largely irrelevant to the most likely threats the United States military will face—Third World anarchy and tribal warriors, and (2) that a cutoff of commercial imagery during hostilities cannot be presumed.[282]

U.S. Lead in RMA

The concept of an ongoing RMA dominates the work of the Office of Net Assessment and propels advocates to make wide-ranging proposals for the transformation of U.S. military forces.[283] But the debate over what exactly constitutes an RMA still ongoing, and there are numerous skeptical voices.[284] Yet, there are a number of advances in military technology that are frequently cited as evidence that an RMA is underway, and even skeptics concede that these advances have had a tremendous effect on warfighting. Advances in information processing and command and control are cited most frequently, with digitalization of the battlefield and more availability of real-time information at the command level being the expected results. When this advanced information processing capability—referred to as battle management—is combined with advanced sensors, particularly space-based sensors, command and control of military forces are significantly enhanced. Some proponents claim that new ISR technology and battle management systems have dispelled the fog of war that has previously prevented the commander from having a thoroughly accurate picture of the battlefield.[285]

Another class of systems frequently linked to the RMA is precision weapons. The significant increase in accuracy of cruise missiles and air-launched ordnance has indeed increased the lethality of modern striking power, in turn, reducing the number of platforms and weapons required to achieve a desired effect. This was quite evident from the earliest stages of Operation *Desert Storm*. At the same time, advances in stealth technology have made strike platforms more survivable against air defense systems. Combining precision strike and stealth, along with the continuing development of stand-off systems (weapons that can be fired from beyond the reach of the defender) creates an exponential increase in the ability of modern platforms to strike previously difficult targets with great accuracy. The advances in ISR and battle management allow for greater detection of these targets, and efficient processing of information from sensor to shooter.

Other technological advances, from biological weapons to highly miniaturized weapons, or nanosystems, are also taken as indicators of an RMA.[286] These new technologies are frequently seen as pushing modern warfare away from the bloody killing fields of ground combat.[287]

Critics of the RMA concede that the importance of the advances in military technology have greatly increased the striking power of modern militaries. However, they argue that such advances have not changed the fundamentals of warfare, and that victory ultimately requires closing with the enemy and occupying territories or destroying centers of gravity.[288] Even the U.S. Commission of National Security/21st Century, which provides general support for the argument than an RMA is underway, acknowledges that "the essence of war will not change ... [and will include] casualties, carnage and death; it will not be like a video game."[289]

Whatever the particulars of the RMA, it would seem natural for militaries to increase their capabilities vis-à-vis potential opponents through mastery of emerging technology. There are historical examples of the rejection of advanced military technology, the abandonment of musketry by the Japanese Shogunate being one such case. Arms control agreements are also direct or indirect inhibitors of the advancement of some military technologies. However, the history of warfare—like the overall history of humankind—reflects a thirst for technological advancement. Potential opponents seek to gain advantages over each other, and qualitative technological advancement generally appears to be the most effective method. If, in fact, the U.S. military is in the midst of an RMA that is making the weaponry of potential opponents obsolete, it seems logical that these potential opponents would seek to grasp the fruit of the revolution and seek to find areas in which they can exploit new technologies to counter U.S. advantages.

But pursuing an RMA requires resources. Most, if not all, potential opponents of the United States and its allies cannot afford to devote the level of financial resources that the world's largest gross national product (GNP) can provide.[290] Either they must attempt to uniquely capitalize on technological information made available to them, or must concentrate their resources on a technological niche in which they can gain at least a temporary advantage.[291]

Both attempts hold some potential for providing temporary advantages. COTS equipment now dominates digitalization. Such systems can be purchased even by countries that lack a sophisticated technological infrastructure. Through "sidewise" innovation, it would be possible for less technologically-advanced states to develop unexpected weapons. Likewise, it is possible to outspend the United States or other advanced nations in a particular area of military technology, particularly if developments in that area do not appear promising to the United States. Advanced, long-range cruise missiles are now seen as systems that provide the United States with a considerable military advantage. Often forgotten is that the United States largely abandoned cruise missile technology in the early 1960s, in order to pursue more promising advances in ballistic missiles.[292] Even while seeking to match or surpass the United States in ballistic missiles, the Soviet Union attempted to exploit the advantages provided by their continued cruise missile development in the 1960s and 1970s.[293] For a while, they did hold a lead in the category of anti-ship missiles.

However, it would seem very difficult for potential opponents to challenge the overall technological lead of the United States and its allies.[294] Arguably, the one significant past attempt resulted in bankruptcy for the potential opponent. Part of the reason is the commercial push present in the advanced countries that encourages across-the-board development in technology.[295] Although the results of research and development (R&D) can be spread through globalization, the United States maintains the largest technological infrastructure as well as the higher education system that trains most of the world's advanced technologists. Increasing amounts of commercial computer code may be written in India and other less overall technologically-advanced nations, but it is largely at the direction (or at least economic sufferance) of Silicon Valley. Even U.S. allies, whose scientific skills match those of the United States, find it difficult to keep up with America's in fielding high-technology military systems.[296]

Consensus View

Potential opponents may pursue the RMA through the development of advanced weaponry, but—barring an economic disaster in the West—they cannot surpass the overall U.S. lead in advanced military technologies in the 2001–2025 timeframe. Certain niche technologies, such as advances in chemical and biological warfare or the development of nanosystsem weapons—which would be easier to transport and deploy in space or on earth—could provide a temporary technological lead in specific areas.[297] Developing a niche, such as in WMD, could literally provide a state with limited resources more bang for the buck, but it would be unlikely that such a specific development would make the entire U.S. arsenal obsolete, or completely paralyze national level decisionmaking. At the same time, the overall U.S. technological lead would likely facilitate the development of defenses against these advantages, or at least methods of mitigating the threat.[298]

Contrary View

While conceding America's current overall lead in military technology, several sources point to alarming trends. From their perspective, the United States is not producing enough American engineers and scientists to maintain the knowledge capital to retain the overall technological lead.[299] Worse, from this perspective, the American university system is educating technologists loyal to potential opponents.[300] Eventually other states could take technological leadership.

Other sources argue that the United States is not taking the RMA seriously and, therefore, is squandering our technological lead.[301] In this view, the Department of Defense continues to spend money on legacy systems, but, at the same time, underfunds both basic and advanced R&D, and experimentation.[302] This combination gives opponents an opportunity to leapfrog over the capabilities of our formidable arsenal and make our overall technological superiority moot.[303]

Technological Surprise

Following on the consensus view concerning America's overall lead in commercial and military technology is the perception that it is unlikely that a technological surprise—a completely unexpected invention or discovery—could occur in a way to give military superiority to a potential opponent. In a sense, this is a refutation of the belief that the ongoing evolution (or revolution) in military technology could be leapfrogged. However, this point of consensus is more narrowly focussed on the general nature of technological development, rather than on the potential to capitalize on new discoveries.

An unanticipated technological surprise is, by definition, unforeseeable, so its future occurrence cannot be completely dismissed. However, there is such a myriad of public forecasts concerning every conceivable category of science and technology that the truly unanticipated seems to be crowded out. Predictions from "our future as post-modern cyborgs" to "the future of God," would seem to leave little room for developments that are not being examined or, at least, contemplated.[304] Advocates for scenario-based planning recommend seeking out the thoughts of "remarkable people," some of them on the fringes of society, for incorporation in futures analysis.[305] Science fiction is also advocated by some as a source for the examination of unanticipated developments.[306] It would seem that an unanticipated technological development would be much rarer than anticipated developments that never come to fruition.

Nevertheless, it is possible that the prodding of development in a niche of technology could provide a rather startling product. But, again, the tremendous commercial push of the advanced economies, and the technological infrastructure and knowledge capital of the United States and friends and allies would point to the product being developed first or quickly replicated in the West. A resurgently hostile Russia could conceivably reconstitute its military technology infrastructure to pursue technological surprise, and other states might do likewise in niches. But even during the technological race at the height of the Cold War, breakthroughs had relatively short half-lives as the contestants sought to counter offensive advantages with defensive, or other offensive developments. It is more likely that a contestant simply cannot afford to compete than be surprised by developments of which it was unaware.

Consensus View

A consensus of sources examined indicates that a truly unanticipated development in military technology is unlikely in the 2001–2025 period. But if such were to occur, the consensus view holds that it would most likely be the product of Western or advanced-state development—a nation not hostile to the United States. If a technological surprise were to occur in a hostile state, it is likely that it could be quickly replicated somewhere in the West. Infrastructure, knowledge base, and commercial incentive appear to be the drivers of new, surprising technologies. These are indeed centered in the democratic capitalist states.[307]

Contrary View

The sources surveyed do not suggest the likelihood of a technological surprise. But among those assessments of the future security environment that identify potential wildcards, a major technological surprise was listed as an occurrence of potential concern.[308] Khalilzad and Lesser identify it as a specific event to hedge against, proposing that "the Department of Defense can and should take steps to avoid future catastrophic technological surprise."[309] Their study, reflecting its funding source, suggests that "the U.S. Air Force in particular might consider developing a technology warning system" that would enable it to flag both evolutionary and revolutionary advances of particular salience."[310] Arguably, such is the overall goal of DOD R&D efforts. Placing technological surprise in the context of other wildcards, the RAND study also suggests that the "military could assemble a small, joint, planning cell responsible for sketching the basic outline of possible responses to unexpected challenges."[311] Although other authorities might concur with this suggestion, their wildcard focus is primarily on political events.[312]

Proponents of the concept of RMA routinely express concern over the military effect of a technological leapfrog over U.S. capabilities. From their perspective, an unanticipated technological development can be considered a subset of the potential for strategic military surprise. Yet, the majority of specialized studies in strategic and operational surprise again identify political factors, rather than technology as the driver of potential Pearl Harbors.[313]

Opposing Strategies

Control of the Seas and Air

Even if America does have a propensity for being operationally surprised, it often emerges from the event militarily stronger. Such is indeed the legacy of the Pearl Harbor attack of 1941, and its effect remains apparent in U.S. sea and air dominance.

The current overwhelming naval strength of the United States is as much a product of the World War II as the Cold War, for it was during war in the Pacific that the art of war at sea reached peak intensity.[314] The conceptual and doctrinal basis for modern naval warfare—defense in depth, combined undersea-sea-air-land operations (and now space)—were largely perfected through this trial of combat. What has happened over the past fifty years is a continuing evolution of naval technology that has vastly increased the reach of naval forces onto land. The collapse of the Soviet Navy through the dissolution of the Soviet Union has allowed U.S. naval forces to shift to a landward focus because there is no longer a fleet capable of challenging the United States in the open oceans.[315] This situation, the lack of opposing fleet, allows for the use of naval power in a direct and joint fashion against the littoral battle space and targets deep ashore.

When combined with the overwhelming size of our transoceanic Navy, such naval dominance is self-reinforcing.[316] Attempting to protect land targets from naval strike reduces the resources of a potential opponent available for building an ocean-going fleet. The size and strength of the current U.S. fleet—as well as that of the fleet mapped out in the future defense program—makes the construction of the few vessels affordable to an opponent appear militarily ineffectual. A quick assessment of comparative strength in ocean-going fleets as of March 2000 is evident in the table below.[317] Of note is the fact that the majority of fleets capable of global operations are long-term U.S. allies.

Richard Danzig has argued that the quantity and quality dominance of U.S. naval forces has a *dissuasive* effect on potential opponents.[318] They are dissuaded from investing resources in naval construction because of the difficulty of ever catching up with America's maritime investment. Operationally, dissuasion also influences their calculus of the outcome of challenging the U.S. dominance in the open-ocean. Such effort would appear futile.

Likewise, the evolution of U.S. air power has traveled an historical course to overall air dominance. Roots of this dominance grow from the World War II experience, in which both strategic and tactical uses of air power were vital elements of victory. The early era of the nuclear age was largely a competition in the design and construction of increasingly more capable air platforms (including missiles). While Russian construction of new generation aircraft has continued beyond the collapse of the Soviet Union, the result of the collapse of the Soviet armed forces is a vast quantity, quality, and operational lead for U.S. air power.[319] The rapid achievement of absolute air supremacy in Operation *Desert Storm* was an unprecedented feat in combat involving modern military forces. As difficult as it would be to defeat U.S. air power in regions where basing is available for it to operate from, it would seem impossible to challenge American land-based and sea-based forces in the long-range fashion that

Comparative Ocean-going Naval Strength (August 1999)

	United States*	China	Russia	India	Japan	United Kingdom	France	Italy
Carrier	12	0	0	0	0	0	1**	0
VSTOL Carrier	0	0	1**	1	0	3	1	1
Cruiser	29	0	7	0	0	0	1	1
Destroyer	50	18	17	7	9	11	4	4
Frigate	28	0	10	13	46	20	34	24
SSBN	18	1	21	0	0	3	4	0
SSN	65	5	19	0	0	12	6	0
SSGN	0***	0	9	0	0	0	0	0
SS	0	64	16	16	16	0	2	8
Large Amphib	12	0	0	0	1	1	2	0
Amphib	26	17	25	9	5	7	7	3
Mine Warfare (Ocean Going)	11	34	15	12	30	21	22	13
Underway Logistics	39	3	28	3	3	9	5	3
Other Support	26	33	36	3	10	10	9	8
Total Ships****	316	141	175	64	130	97	98	65

Source: International Institute for Strategic Studies; numbers are for comparative purpose and may not be exact.

Notes: * U.S. numbers do not include ocean-going U.S. Coast Guard ships, many of which would be considered naval combatants by most other nations.

** These units are judged to be currently nonoperational or still in sea trials.

*** Many SSNs are capable of firing anti-ship or land attack cruise missiles from vertical launch tubes or torpedo tubes even if they are not designated as SSGNs.

**** Total ships do not include nonoceangoing vessels, such as patrol combatants, and may not reflect official fleet totals.

was envisioned during the Cold War. Although the table below indicates the relative sizes of world air forces, it does not quite capture the significant qualitative advantage that U.S. air power currently enjoys.

As with maritime forces, the scope of American air power may have a dissuasive effect on direct competition. That is not to say that potential opponents will not attempt to challenge U.S. air power within

Comparative Land-based Combat Air Strength* (August 1999)

	United States*	China	Russia	India	Japan	United Kingdom	France	Italy
Carrier	12	0	0	0	0	0	1**	0
Long-Range Strike/ Attack (Bombers)	178	120+	150	0	0	0	0	0
Tactical Fighters/Strike	1594	1500+	1455	693	270	261***	372	266
Reconnaissance	57	40+	135	16	20	45	45	30+
C3/Electronic Warfare	40	UNK	20+	12	15	10	4	5
Transports**	853	380+	280	175+	30	60+	87	38
Tankers	596	45+	20+	6	0	20	11	8

Source: International Institute for Strategic Studies; numbers are for comparative purpose and may not be exact.

* U.S. numbers do not include aircraft in storage or shorter-range transports; Chinese, Russian numbers include only modern aircraft comparable to U.S. aircraft, absolute numbers are much higher.

** Some transports have dual-use as tankers.

*** Does not include naval aviation assets.

their region. Certainly, it appears that such is probable. But challenging U.S. air power on a global basis would seem impossible absent the combined air power of a coalition of opposing states. Potential opponents interested in increasing their military power would likely direct resources to weapons that could negate American advantages within their own regions, developing missile and other WMD-capable platforms to target the supporting infrastructure that U.S. naval and air forces would use in the event of a regional conflict. This would constitute an indirect or asymmetric challenge to American sea and air dominance, rather than a direct force-on-force challenge.[320] "The world's commons"—the sea and air spaces that are international and not legally subject to any state—would appear likely to remain both accessible to and dominated by U.S. military power.

However, forecasts of continuing U.S. sea and air dominance assume that the United States will seek to maintain the relative size advantage it has today and will continue to modernize its naval and air forces at a pace that keeps it abreast of critical technological developments.[321]

Consensus View

The consensus of sources is that the size and operational experience of the Navy and Air Force make it nearly impossible for potential opponents to mount a serious challenge in the waters and air space over the world's oceans.[322] This is likely to continue until 2025. Even if potential opponents do not remain dissuaded from direct competition against these American strengths, it would take at least 20 years for any competitor to build to the numbers and sophistication of the U.S. naval and air fleets. That is not to say that an opponent would not seek to contest U.S. sea and air control in their own region, or even undertake force-on-force engagements outside their region. However, the investment needed to challenge the United States on a global basis in areas where the United States has long maintained operational advantages is staggering. The investment in shipbuilding and aircraft construction may be a less difficult challenge than achieving the training and experience required to conduct extensive maritime and aerospace operations.

It is likely that certain competitors will seek to build or purchase fourth-generation platforms and the most modern ocean-going warships, but in relatively small numbers.[323] These could be used to dominate regional opponents. If they are used in combat operations directly against the U.S. naval and air fleets, it is likely they would operate as a high-tech guerrilla force, attacking areas of perceived weakness until they were destroyed or securely hidden from U.S. response. Victories against individual U.S. platforms could be significant morale factors in the opponent's will to fight, not unlike the effect of individual ship engagements on the United States in the War of 1812. However, U.S. ISR capabilities would likely curtail such operations in relatively short order.

Contrary View

No source suggests that the U.S. naval and air fleets could be decisively defeated, and particularly not within the global commons in the 2001–2025 period. However, concerns are frequently expressed that the United States could become complacent with its current margin of superiority and elect not to replace aging systems with more technologically advanced first line platforms. Over the long term, the cumulative effect of a procurement holiday might make the bulk of U.S. naval and air forces obsolete.[324] To some extent, that is the logic of the proponents in recent debates over acquisition of the F–22.[325] The concept of block obsolescence for legacy systems also appears in the arguments of proponents of transformation.

That advanced capabilities—along with better training, spirit, and morale—can beat size is a fact of military history. And, indeed, complacent powers often are defeated. However, the technological push of the U.S. private sector appears to be a considerable influence in encouraging military modernization. It is often pointed out that the U.S. military is no longer the driving force in scientific R&D that it was before the explosion in information technology. If, indeed, warfare of the future will be primarily focussed on information, the commanding lead in platform numbers seems of even greater significance, rather than less.[326]

Critics of American complacency also point to the continuing development of high tech weaponry for export by technologically-advanced nations. Russia, with its economic woes, has considerable incentive to continue production of advanced systems for foreign sale.[327] This includes platforms as well as systems, as is evidenced by the recent Russian sale of an aircraft carrier to India and four *Sovremenny*-class destroyers (armed with SS–N–22 antiship cruise missiles) to China.[328]

Navies and air forces are trappings desired by nations that view themselves as emerging great powers. This produces an arms race dynamic, at least to some degree, as other states seek to protect themselves from the threat of military force from these emerging powers.[329] The result may not be a challenge to American naval and air dominance by any one state; but it could allow for a powerful force if a military coalition of hostile states developed. Historically, this was a concern of Great Britain in the era in which the Royal Navy dominated the seas, resulting in their attempt to maintain a two-power standard in naval forces. Arguably, the United States has an effective two-power standard force. However, critics argue that it will be unaffordable to keep such an advantage throughout the 2001–2025 period. If so, the overwhelming American advantage in sea and air forces will gradually dissipate during this period.

Additionally, there are sources that argue that general American dominance of sea and air is largely irrelevant in dealing with the more likely future threats of terrorism, chemical, biological and information warfare, and failing states, as well as against the prepared antiaccess or area-denial strategies of regional opponents.[330]

Antiaccess/Area-Denial Strategies

The concept of antiaccess or area-denial strategies for use against American power projection capabilities has been a focal point of research in the Office of Net Assessment since at least the mid-1990s.[331] The genesis of the concept lies in a series of anti-Navy studies designed to examine the capabilities of post-Cold War militaries to prevent the Navy from operating with impunity off their immediate coastlines.[332] These studies were viewed not only as a means to test the ability of the Navy to carry out its ... *From the Sea* strategic vision, but also reflected the reality that, with the collapse of the Soviet Union, there were no potentially hostile blue-water navies capable of engaging the Navy at sea. According to this construct, if there were to be threats to U.S. naval operations, they would come from weapons systems designed to deny American passage through maritime choke points or the ability of the Navy to conduct operations near land.[333] Such weapons, seen by both the Office of Naval Intelligence and the Office of Net Assessment as proliferating throughout the world, include ballistic missiles, cruise missiles, diesel-electric submarines, sophisticated naval mines, and fast patrol craft.[334]

In the logic of the antiaccess approach, a potential opponent would not seek to engage the Navy at sea, where the United States holds absolute dominance. Rather, it would seek to prevent U.S. maritime forces from entering their littoral waters by massive attrition attacks by the proliferated asymmetric weapons.[335] However, the anti-Navy core of these studies was soon expanded to include all U.S. overseas presence and power projection forces.

As previously noted, sustained long-range power projection is both a unique strength of U.S. military forces and a requirement for an activist foreign policy and forward defense. The Office of Net Assessment work on the RMA and studies of ballistic missile proliferation led to an intellectual linkage between the proliferation of military technologies—particularly the production of indigenous ballistic missiles—and the desire of potential opponents to blunt U.S. capabilities of projecting power into their regions. The implicit assumption is that ballistic missile attack—particularly with WMD—provides the fastest and cheapest method of area denial.[336]

The obvious first step in such an area-denial effort would be to neutralize any existing lodgment of U.S. forces in the region. This would entail destroying U.S. forward presence forces while simultaneously attacking the regional infrastructure that would allow for the flow of follow-on power projection forces. The Office of Net Assessment has used ballistic missile development as an indicator of a potential opponent's capacity to carry out this first step.

Another step would be to attack the ports and airfields of embarkation of forces in the continental United States. However, that is generally beyond the anticipated conventional capabilities of most regional powers.[337] Arguably, a strike against the U.S. homeland would strengthen U.S. resolve to prosecute the conflict rather than discourage the effort—the Pearl Harbor effect.[338] Because of range limitation and the uncertain psychological effect, it is likely that the regional opponent would focus on closing access through regional straits of choke points, rather than expending limited resources on a CONUS attack. However, the use of terrorism, information warfare, or other asymmetric means remains a distinct possibility. And, as previously discussed, ample evidence exists that a number of rogue states seek to develop extended range ballistic missiles.

These antiaccess efforts are most evident in use of relatively low-cost maritime forces in blocking the attempts of U.S. and allied navies to re-enter the region. Antiaccess maritime platforms would include quiet diesel submarines, sea mines, cruise-missile carrying patrol boats and light combatants, and other fast attack craft, as well as land-based aviation and cruise missiles.

With regional land bases destroyed and maritime access denied, the potential regional opponent would effectively extend its defenses out to the entry points of its region. The United States would find itself in the position of having to undertake costly forcible-entry operations. This would be the modern equivalent of the D-Day invasion of Nazi-occupied Europe, but with both sides having access to high-tech weaponry.[339] Even in this war of attrition, it is likely that the United States would eventually breech the antiaccess defenses, particularly through the use of stand-off weapons stationed outside the region or in CONUS. However, the real goal of an antiaccess strategy is to convince the United States and/or its allies or coalition partners that the cost of penetration is simply too high.[340] Hostilities could thereby be ended via a diplomatic agreement that granted the regional power its wartime objectives. Such an agreement would be encouraged by international organizations that traditionally advocate negotiated peace.

Enhancing the desirability of the antiaccess strategy for regional powers are the perceived lessons of the Persian Gulf War. While it was a crushing victory for the coalition forces, critics point out that it took six months for the United States and its partners to build a logistical "iron mountain" in the theater. Iraq had no capacity to counter this build-up nor prevent American entry into the Gulf. If Iraq could have blocked the Straits of Hormuz or shut down the supporting ports and airfields in Saudi Arabia, the argument goes, it is unlikely that the coalition could have retaken Kuwait, or could have done so only at high cost in casualties. Because of their massive and often lingering effects, weapons of mass destruction could have given Iraq the capability of denying U.S. access, through the destruction of Saudi ports and airfields, as well as any forces entering the narrow confines of the Gulf, or through the mere threat of use, which might have caused the Saudis to withdraw permission for the stationing of U.S. forces on their soil.[341]

The perception that other nations have noted these lessons is reinforced by an apocryphal report that a former chief of staff of the armed forces of India, General K. Sundarji identified weapons of mass destruction as an integral ingredient of any "keep America out" strategy. According to the report, Sundarji said: "One principal lesson of the Gulf War is that, if a state intends to fight the United States, it should avoid doing so until and unless it possesses nuclear weapons."[342] Although it is possible to develop and antiaccess strategy through conventional means alone, it is well evident that the possession of weapons of mass destruction makes any such strategy more potent. The ability to threaten targets outside the region, or even in the continental United States, increases this potency. However, as discussed previously, long-range targeting is a more difficult problem than targeting within the region.

Consensus View

The consensus of sources surveyed is that an antiaccess or area denial is the most likely campaign plan for an opponent of the United States to adopt, and thus the likely strategic U.S. power projection forces would face in a major theater war. This conclusion is based not only on the proliferation of ballistic missiles and other suitable weapons, but on the underlying logic of the strategy itself.

The Greek attempt to prevent an invasion by the numerically superior Persian force at the pass of Thermopylae in 480 BC, and the subsequent Greek concentration on the destruction of the Persian fleet, is but the first recorded example of an antiaccess style strategy.[343] The Greek city-states perceived that they could not defeat the Persian land army if it were free to forage the Hellenic interior and attack the city-states one by one. Militarily inferior states have attempted similar anti-invasion strategies throughout history, Hitler's *Festung Europa* being a more recent unsuccessful attempt. Armed with the means of carrying it out, the antiaccess strategy remains a historically-proven means of making the costs of intervention too high for the more powerful state to bear.[344]

The proliferation of ballistic missiles and WMD and the perceived willingness of rogue states to use such weapons make antiaccess an even more likely strategy for a regional aggressor to adopt.[345]

Contrary View

None of the sources surveyed maintain that the antiaccess approach is an unlikely strategy for a potential opponent to adopt in order to prevent the United States from intervening to stop regional cross-border aggression. If such a major theater war were to occur, an antiaccess strategy would appear the best—perhaps only—method to blunt U.S. power projection strength. However, a number of sources see the occurrence of cross border aggression and major theater war as much less likely than the chaos of failed states and internal civil strife. These sources would not necessarily agree that U.S. military forces should focus their efforts on developing the tactics and weapons systems to break potential antiaccess strategies.

Among the sources that accept antiaccess strategies as the most likely methods of conflict adopted by regional aggressors, there are differing perceptions concerning the ability of such aggressors to carry out regional closure in the 2001–2025 time frame.[346] In contrast to the forecasts of the Office of Net Assessment, several sources suggest that, before 2025, most potential opponents will be unable to use ballistic missiles effectively against moving targets, allowing U.S. air and naval forces opportunities to attack the weak points of an antiaccess campaign.[347] Other sources suggest that the ability of rogue states to coerce potential American allies into denying U.S. access to their territory has been overstated.[348]

WMD in Large-Scale Combat

One of the most controversial consensus statements is that large-scale combat in the future is likely to include weapons of mass destruction. This controversy is not rooted in assessments, but in the popular reaction to "thinking the unthinkable." For over the fifty years of the Cold War, nuclear weapons were perceived as qualitatively different than conventional weapons and were designated as elements of strategic deterrence and weapons of last resort. The concept that nuclear weapons, along with other weapons of mass destruction, could be used in conventional military operations was considered dangerous and destabilizing, at least by American decision-makers and military planners.[349]

However, there is a growing awareness of the efforts of many states to obtain the components of weapons of mass destruction and the means of delivery. The extensive efforts of the UN weapons inspectors in Iraq following the Gulf War were based on the perception that Iraq continued to actively seek to build a WMD arsenal. Recent testing of nuclear weapons by India and Pakistan gives testimony to the fact that the nuclear nonproliferation regime has not completely eliminated the desire of emerging regional powers to possess a nuclear arsenal. At the same time, the general disregard of the international law of conflict by the rogue states implies that future use of WMD may not be inhibited by the norms of Cold War behavior. Iraq's use of chemical weapons in its war against Iran may be the best documented case of WMD use, but there is evidence of other rogue states using such weapons in internal conflicts.[350] Terrorist groups also appear interested in purchasing or developing WMD. Preventing Osama Bin Laden from obtaining chemical or biological weapons was one of the U.S. Government's justifications for the Tomahawk strike on a pharmaceutical plant in Sudan in 1998.[351]

Combining the desires of certain states for WMD arsenals, the rate of proliferation, and a seemingly growing disregard of the laws of armed conflict with the lessons aggressors can draw from the Gulf War provides a portrait of the potential integration of WMD into classical military operations.[352] Most sources assume that proliferation will continue in 2001–2025. Many of the international control regimes seeking to prevent the spread of WMD are expected to break down, or at least be consistently ignored by states unhappy with the international status quo. As discussed previously, underlying technologies, particularly dual use systems such as nuclear reactors that could generate power or enrich uranium, are becoming available to potential aggressors and provide cover for weapons development. Humanitarian NGOs persistently report that the law of war appears to be devolving, with scant distinction made between attacking military forces and civilian noncombatants. The sum of these developments points to the likelihood that tyrannical regimes facing potential removal by outside forces would use WMD in combat.

Consensus View

The majority of sources surveyed view the likelihood of use of WMD during large-scale conflict in the 2001–2025 period as being quite high. The consensus is that chemical or biological weapons use would be more likely than nuclear war, but many sources view WMD use as the *primary* future threat to American security. Disagreement remains as to whether such weapons would be used in the initial stages of a major theater war, particularly in an antiaccess scenario, or whether even the most desperate of opponents would reserve WMD use for the prevention of regime change in case their aggression was successfully opposed. But there seems to be agreement that, in the case of certain rogue states, if weapons of mass destruction were available, they would be used for survival of tyrannical regimes.

Since the United States possesses the ability to project power into warring regions with apparent success, it is natural for U.S. forces to be a primary potential target for WMD. The warning not to fight the United States without possession of nuclear weapons is advice on how to neutralize the power projection advantage, whether by deterrence, coercion, or employment. Although the U.S.-led coalition chose not to force the removal of the Hussein regime in Iraq and did not send forces toward Baghdad, there is a wide perception that the whole element of choice would be taken away in a similar future scenario if WMD use is threatened.[353] In such a scenario, potential aggressors could maintain a sanctuary of their own territory. In the antiaccess scenario, WMD use could create a de facto sanctuary of the whole region.

The potential of WMD in the hands of terrorist groups has already been discussed, and is considered a more frightening situation by many sources. Terrorist attacks, like state attacks in conventional conflicts, could obviously be directed against civilian populations as well as military forces. Arguably, the civilian populace—if it can be reached—is a softer target than military forces that would be more likely to possess personal protective gear. The perception that this soft target would be more attractive to potential opponents than an attack on U.S. military forces is the prime concern of sources focused on identifying the growing vulnerability of the U.S. homeland to WMD.

Contrary View

Although conceding the likelihood that potential opponents would seek to leverage the possession of WMD as a counter to U.S. actions, there is also a perception that use in conflict can be deterred.[354] Obviously, the United States retains a most formidable nuclear arsenal. Given current arsenals, a nuclear exchange between the United States and a state other than Russia would be a horrendous, unmitigated disaster. But it would not destroy American society. Contrariwise, the large American arsenal could literally lay waste to most rogue states, removing all instruments of power. While nuclear arsenals are forecast to increase in the 2001–2025 period, the rate of increase does not suggest that more than a handful of states, perhaps no more than two or three—or potentially none, if the United States developed an effective national missile defense—could threaten mutual destruction. Because chemical and biological weapons are routinely categorized along with nuclear weapons as

WMD, there is, by definition, ambiguity as to whether chemical or biological use would naturally provoke nuclear use. From this perspective, it is possible that the use of WMD against forces in large-scale armed conflict with the United States would be deterred by the American WMD arsenal, which consists solely of nuclear weapons.

Sources that view chemical and biological weapons as the significant threats of the 2001–2025 period do not necessarily dispute the deterrent effect of the U.S. nuclear arsenal, or even the deterrent effect of conventional power projection forces. Rather, they argue that it is possible to use WMD on American soil or against U.S. forces in a manner than could render their source unidentifiable.[355] If it appeared that WMD use constituted a terrorist attack, state opponents might successfully attack the United States without legitimate retribution.[356] Or a state could use seemingly unsponsored terrorist groups as proxies in a WMD attack designed to paralyze American response to regional aggression. Other sources argue that technology (and the American psyche) renders such attacks ultimately attributable, mitigating the attractiveness of such a reckless course of action.

Sources that see WMD as a potential combat threat do recognize that the United States has and continues to develop means of force and theater protection.[357] Several are willing to suggest the increase in the ability of U.S. forces to engage in counter-proliferation or counter-WMD action, such as the "Scud hunt" of the Gulf War, greatly reduces the possibility of WMD during conflict.[358] An additional deterrent might be U.S. theater ballistic missile defenses. If positioned before the outbreak of conflict, such defense might act as a deterrent to WMD use in the initial stages, or perhaps the entire conflict.

It has also been suggested that a U.S. declaratory counter-proliferation policy of pursuing regime change in the event of WMD use, or threats of use, would have also have considerable deterrent effect. If the likely end result of any WMD-laden confrontation with the United States or ally would be the decapitation of the aggressor, rogue states might reconsider any potential tactical advantages of WMD use. In any event, if a potential user of WMD perceives that it has more to lose in the long run, the attractiveness of WMD employment in combat appears to be reduced.[359] As proponents of this view might argue, even Hitler decided to respect the moratoriums on the use of poisonous gas against enemy troops.[360]

Homeland Vulnerability

The perception that the U.S. homeland will become increasingly vulnerable in the 2001–2025 timeframe can be traced to the National Defense Panel report of 1997. It has subsequently become an almost universal forecast by defense analysts.

The NDP argued that: "Threats to the United States have been magnified by the proliferation of, and the means to produce and deliver, weapons of mass destruction."[361] However, the NDP also linked its call for homeland defense to an increase in other state and nonstate threats, such as terrorism, information warfare, attacks on critical infrastructure, and transnational threats. This typology, along with the perception that greater efforts are needed to combat such increasing threats, has been incorporated into the National Military Strategy, National Security Strategy, Presidential Decision Directives, and other planning documents.[362] In 1999, the U.S. Commission on National Security/21st Century echoed the prevailing perception that "America will become increasingly vulnerable to hostile attack on our homeland, and our military superiority will not entirely protect us."[363] Their forecast goes as far as to suggest that in event of a future conflict, "Americans will likely die on American soil, possibly in large numbers."[364]

From the perspective of recent history, the perception that the American populace is in increasing danger may appear counter-intuitive.[365] During the Cold War, literally thousands of nuclear warheads were targeted on the American homeland. Some argued that alert procedures put a massive nuclear attack on a hair-trigger basis. With the end of the Cold War and the agreed de-alerting of nuclear forces, along with reductions in overall U.S. and Russia nuclear arsenals, it would appear that the American populace is much less directly vulnerable than they have been in at least thirty years.[366] However, proponents of the increasing vulnerability view point to the balance of terror that made a nuclear war between the United States and Soviet Union irrational. Rogue states, they argue, are less likely to be deterred from making asymmetric attacks on the U.S. homeland in the event of a conflict.[367] Indeed, asymmetric attacks may be the most useful—perhaps only—military tool in the hands of potential opponents.[368]

Additionally, acceptance of the forecast that nonstate threats are increasing leads naturally to the belief that such threats, along with the proliferation of WMD, increase the vulnerability of the U.S. homeland.

The days in which the broad expanses of the Atlantic and Pacific Ocean were assumed to provide sanctuary seem long gone.[369]

Consensus View

Despite some skepticism that the U.S. homeland is more vulnerable than it was during the Cold War, the consensus remains that the U.S. homeland will become more vulnerable to new threats, particularly chemical and biological weapons in the hands or rogue states and terrorist groups.[370] The ability to transport such weapons in small packages and devices that can be easily smuggled is often cited as a contributing factor. In addition, it is obvious that rogue regimes, such as in North Korea, are attempting to develop ballistic missiles capable of reaching the continental U.S. Although these intercontinental missiles probably would be optimized for nuclear attack, those states cut off from possessing fissile material would likely opt for chemical or biological warheads.

Realization that the United States forward defense posture allows for but limited defense of the U.S. coastline and airspace has increased among individuals who had ignored this concern during the Cold War.[371] At the same time, the Internet and the ubiquitous nature of computer control seem to have made America's infrastructure more vulnerable to nonexplosive attack, such as information warfare. Although computer network defenses are possible, they bear both a financial and social cost.

However, the consensus position differs from more alarming forecasts on questions of the degree of future vulnerability. While the rhetoric of many homeland defense advocates would suggest an exponential, almost insurmountable rise in new threats, the majority view is that such threats are evolutionary, rather than exponential. As use of the Internet continues to penetrate society, vulnerability to disruption increases. However, this is to be anticipated, and, as more users become dependent, it is more likely they will demand redundant and protected systems. Likewise, globalization may cause a rise in transnational or nonstate threats, such as massive migrations. However, by providing a worldwide increase in employment, the benefits of globalization may mitigate such threats to the homeland. Meanwhile, the United States appears to be taking initial steps to deal with the catastrophic terrorism and infrastructure attack, potentially matching the threat increases of the 2001–2025 time frame. From this perspective, measured responses match the measured increase in anticipated vulnerability.[372]

Contrary View

Few sources argue that there is not a myriad of emerging threats. However, contrary positions exist on both sides of the argument concerning the degree of vulnerability in 2001–2025. Sources suggesting that we are essentially less vulnerable today, and will remain so, argue that American society can absorb such isolated attacks, and that, because such attacks are not militarily significant, they are relatively unlikely. Supporting this view is the belief that potential opponents recognize the Pearl Harbor effect and are reluctant to sponsor a catastrophic attack that would arouse a significant response by a militarily-superior United States.[373] Advocates of national missile defenses postulate that, with such defenses, America would become less vulnerable to nuclear weapons in the future, potentially making such weapons obsolete. Others would argue that the American populace has always been considerably vulnerable, particularly during the 1970–1989 period, but refused to recognize that fact.

On the other hand, several sources suggest that the developmental rate of future threats—fueled primarily by the malicious use of new technologies—is indeed increasing at an exponential rate. From this perspective, increasing homeland vulnerability is inevitable, particularly if active defenses, interagency cooperation efforts, redundancy, and reconstitution do not receive substantial funding increases within the U.S. defense budget.

Information Warfare

At least two distinct facets characterize information warfare.[374] The first is the use of various measures to attack the information technology (IT) systems on which a military opponent may depend.[375] The systems under attack may be providing ISR or command and control capabilities necessary for the conduct of modern, high-technology warfare. But the attack could also be an asymmetric strike on the civilian infrastructure of the opponent's homeland.

Concern for the IT infrastructure of the U.S. homeland is based on the expectation of a continuing explosion in computer technologies and communication systems, and of a growing increase in the influence of mass media.[376] In particular, the Internet is seen as creating—along with its obvious scientific and commercial advantages—new vulnerabilities to the U.S. economy.[377] In addition to the indirect vulnerabilities caused by the disruption of corporate business, concern focuses on the potential for direct attacks on computer-controlled public utilities, such as water facilities and the power grid. In recognition of this potential, the U.S. Government adopted Presidential Decision Directives 62 and 63, which set in place responsibilities and interagency procedures for protecting critical infrastructure and "the national information structure" that provides for the flow of control information.[378]

The second facet of information warfare is the control and manipulation of the information available to the civilian populace of an opposing state.[379] This modern use of propaganda has obvious historical parallels and is a natural aspect of interstate conflict. However, there is a perception that the ubiquitous nature of modern news media has made control of information—when it can be achieved—more effective in changing popular attitudes.[380] Likewise, it is perceived that continuing growth in information technology also increases the value of information control and manipulation.[381] Dependent on information to run society, the populace is less likely to be able to discern real from manipulated information, and, at the same time, can bring more immediate pressure to change U.S. Government policy.[382] To some extent, this public relations war would have a less lethal and more indirect effect on the populace than computer infrastructure attack. However, as seen in the Vietnam War experience, it may have a more direct effect on the willingness to prosecute a war.[383]

With recent efforts, the U.S. Government has taken strides in computer network defense (CND) and critical infrastructure protection, but in the face of an emerging and somewhat indistinct threat, defense necessarily lags offense.[384] An aspect of concern to some is the potential anonymity of attack and the possible use of information warfare by non-state actors, particularly terrorist groups. The mechanism of the Internet is such that both hackers and terrorists could use multiple paths of entry to disguise their identities and intentions.[385] Although it is possible to trace these paths to a source, such efforts take time and resources.[386] The question remains as to whether a hostile state could mask an information attack to such an extent that the United States would be unable to determine the source and take timely defensive or retaliatory actions.[387]

The fact that American society is so open to information (via Internet and more traditional media) does allow exposure of its populace and infrastructure to information warfare.[388] On the other hand, the fact that it is open allows for exposure to multiple sources of information, which makes it difficult for the message of a hostile attack to remain unchallenged. While it is relatively easy for an opponent to disrupt the normal sources of information, it would seem very difficult for them to monopolize all sources. In the vernacular of the Internet, it is possible to clobber an account with spam, but it is harder to convince the recipient that it is more than annoying junk mail. Metaphorically, it is difficult to convince anyone that spam is filet mignon, unless they have never tasted filet mignon. This is not necessarily true of closed societies, where control of a single source of information may, in fact, provide an information monopoly. In a real sense, America's vulnerability to information is also a strength.[389]

In classical military terms, the use of information is an attempt to lift the fog of war that envelops the battlefield. Commanders have always tried to acquire accurate information; what is different is that modern IT appears to provide a greater opportunity to clear away the fog than ever before. Thus, it is natural for U.S. forces to strive for information dominance or knowledge superiority in any conflict.[390] The fact that there are more tools to make more information available would naturally imply that information has become more important to victory, although, conceptually, information dominance has always been an element of success.[391] At the same time, this growing importance of information also implies that deception, disinformation, and the use of media are also of increasing value as military tools.

Consensus View

The consensus of sources is that information is increasing in importance as information technology increases in reach and capacity. In modern combat operations requiring precision strike and limited collateral damage, it is said that information dominates the battlefield. Because information can act as a force multiplier, increasing the lethality of existing units, denial of information to the enemy has always been a critical element of warfare. But with the existence of long-range sensors and high speed computing, the future struggle for information dominance appears to be almost decisive in itself.[392] The maneuver of information, some would suggest, is becoming almost as important as the maneuver of troops—possibly more important in many circumstances,.[393]

At the same time, the growing dependence on precise information for combat operations raises greater opportunities for deception. Technologically superior armies, like open societies, appear more vulnerable to denial and deception than less interconnected forces or closed societies. In the absence of a personal encounter, information—whether correct or incorrect—creates reality for those dependent on it. Another apocryphal story, this one concerning French defenses against the German *Blitzkrieg*, is that, of all the French units, the colonial infantry put up the most resistance to the German invasion of 1940 because they did not have radios and therefore did not know that they were being defeated.[394]

The consensus viewpoint stresses the need for a future balance between ISR systems, information denial capabilities, power projection, precision strike, force protection, trained and motivated personnel, and inspiring leadership.[395] While information remains a common link, it is not an end in itself, nor a decisive element in every situation.[396]

Contrary View

While there is no direct disagreement with the proposition that information will be a critical element in future warfare, there is disagreement with the consensus view over the extent to which information—and, by extension, information warfare—will be the dominant element.

On one side is the view that information was always important and that the current focus on information dominance blinds us from the realization that the other elements of warfighting, such as maneuver and overwhelming force, are just as important.[397] This view is one of concern that we could forget that war is not simply about gathering information, but is about killing people and breaking things.[398] Proponents of this view argue that the fog of war cannot be lifted completely, and that many potential future enemies, such as third world warlords, are simply too unsophisticated to be significantly vulnerable to information warfare.[399] An additional factor is that the human brain simply cannot process the mass of information being made available to the decision-maker, creating its own fog in stressful situations.[400] If the focus on information warfare dominates U.S. thinking and causes us to abandon both redundancy and less-sophisticated, less vulnerable systems, U.S. forces would be *less* prepared for future contingencies.[401]

An opposing viewpoint is that modern IT *does* ensure that the fog of war can be lifted, and suggests that the U.S. military must be radically transformed in order to optimize its capabilities in an information warfare-dominant future.[402]

Chapter Six

Divergence and Contradictions

nalysis of the survey sources reveals a number of diverging views on
certain aspects of the future security environment. Unlike the
points of consensus, there appeared no one dominant view on these
particular issues. Rather, there seemed to be opposing schools of thought.

For the purpose of simplification, these alternative assessments of
the future are posed in the accompanying table (Diverging Views) as either-or statements. But it must be clearly noted that this depiction is a
simplification; there are varying degrees of agreement, and the either-or
statements generally represent the alternate ends of this range. Depending
on categorization, multiple schools and many variations could be identified. However, to describe every variation would be an involved process,
too lengthy for the task of identifying substantial divergences.

It should also be noted that these statements do *not* necessarily
represent a fifty-fifty split between sources. And like the points of consensus, no single source would necessarily agree or disagree with any
particular set or combinations of statements. The point is to capture the
range of views.

Like the points of consensus, the either-or statements are categorized, this time by nature of conflict (which replaces military technology), threats, and opposing strategies. However, there is much overlap
between categories. For example, "future wars will be more brutal" may
be an assessment of the future nature of conflict (indiscriminate attacks
on civilians), but when applied to external conflict, could also describe
an opposing strategy. Its antithesis is a view on how developments in
military technology will mitigate such a strategy. It is the juxtaposition
between technology and strategy that led to changing the category to nature of conflict.

Diverging Views

Nature of Conflict:

- It is unlikely that two major theater wars (MTWs) would happen simultaneously, *or* two near-simultaneous MTWs will remain a possibility.
- Future wars will be more brutal with more civilian casualties, *or* information operations and precision weapons will reduce the lethality of warfare.
- Chaos in the littorals or panic in the city are more likely contingencies than major theater war, *or* major theater war will remain the primary threat to security.
- Space will be a theater of conflict, *or* space will remain a conduit of information, but not a combat theater.

Threats:

- A near-peer competitor is inevitable over the long term (and preparations must be made now), *or* preparing for a near peer will create military competition (thus creating a near peer).
- Overseas bases will be essentially indefensible, *or* future capabilities will be able to defend overseas bases.

Opposing Strategies:

- Current (legacy) U.S. forces will not be able to overcome antiaccess strategies except at high cost, *or* techniques of deception or denial of information will remain effective in allowing legacy systems to penetrate future antiaccess efforts.
- Nuclear deterrence will remain a vital aspect of security, *or* nuclear deterrence will have an increasingly smaller role in future security.
- Conventional military force will not deter terrorism or nonstate threats, *or* U.S. military capabilities will retain considerable deter or coercive effects against terrorism and nonstate threats.

For the purpose of conducting a defense, an identification of the contending positions on the future security environment is the prelude for making deliberate choices on how to prepare for an analytically uncertain future. But that does not mean that these decisions must rely on either end of the either-or positions. They could, instead attempt to hedge toward a future that could go either direction along the range identified.

Nature of Conflict

Two Near-Simultaneous MTWs

A divergence of views on the likelihood of two near-simultaneous MTWs lies partly hidden in the background of most future security environment assessments. Yet, it appears primarily in the form of assumption, rather than analytical argument. There seems to be little effort to prove the validity of either position.

A number of critical assessments—some of which are linked to a recommended strategy or force structure different than the current posture—discount the possibility of two MTWs occurring nearly simultaneously. Preparing for two such overlapping contingencies is dismissed as unsupportable, worst-case thinking. Yet, despite dismissive rhetoric, few detailed logic as to why this could not occur. Taking a cue from the NDP, many analysts find the two-MTW construct inconvenient to their recommendations for transformation, since readiness for the simultaneous scenarios requires considerable expenditure of resources and the maintenance of considerable standing forces. If defense budgets remain at current levels, it is difficult to fund considerable transformation activities while still paying a high bill for readiness and current operations. The NDP report puts the argument plainly:

> The Panel views the two-military-theater-of-war construct as a force sizing function and not a strategy. We are concerned that this construct may have become a force-protection mechanism—a means of justifying the current force structure—especially for those searching for the certainties of the Cold war era.... The two-theater construct has been a useful mechanism for determining what forces to retain as the Cold War came to a close. To some degree, it remains a useful mechanism today. *But, it is fast becoming an inhibitor to reaching the capabilities we will need in the 2010–2020 timeframe.*[403] [emphasis added]

The NDP report recommends accepting "transitional risk" while moving away from a two-MTW posture. As discussed earlier, the panel discounts the demands of the two traditional theaters of Northeast and Southwest Asia, at least for the near term. Recommendations proposed by the NDP to the Secretary of Defense and Congress are seen as emphasizing long-term security. The implication is that the United States needs to prepare now for future near-peer competitors, although the NDP report does not state so explicitly, positing diffused future capabilities as the threat. However, this appears more a policy recommendation than a forecast. Obviously, Congress may legislate that U.S. forces not prepare for two near-simultaneous conflicts, but Congress cannot legislate that two near-simultaneous major world crises do not occur.

Despite the NDP implications, when assessments of potential regional conflicts are combined, the possibility of crises or conflicts developing near-simultaneously in two or more regions seems quite plausible. Sources point out that there are both historical precedents and strategic logic for a potential regional opponent to make aggressive moves when conflicts arise in other parts of the world. Presumably, the distraction or resource challenges of responding to the first conflict or contingency would make the objectives of an opponent in a second conflict easier to achieve. A patient aggressor could wait until the United States was fully committed to intervention in the first conflict. This would not necessarily require collusion on the part of the two aggressors, although a loose alliance could develop.

To some extent, that is what occurred during World War II. Although Nazi Germany and Imperial Japan were nominal allies, at no time did they attempt to coordinate their strategies.[404] Yet both appear to have assumed that the other would attract the primary attention of the United States.[405] The Japanese already knew that the attention of the United Kingdom and France was focussed elsewhere; if the United States intended to support them against Hitler, considerable resources would be required. On the other hand, Hitler waited until after the dramatic Japanese attack on Pearl Harbor to declare war on the United States It may be mere speculation to suggest that his underlying assumption was that America's forces would focus against the enemy that struck such a direct blow. However, the timing of these actions bare considerable logic in attempting to over-stretch the response of the Armed Forces.[406]

Obviously, dealing militarily with two conflicts in the 2001–2025 time frame would appear a strenuous situation, and there is no guarantee of a swift and overwhelming victory as in Operation *Desert Storm*. In fact, the reality may be that preparing for two near-simultaneous wars is unaffordable at current levels of defense spending.[407] Then again, preparing for such conflicts might be considered affordable if one were to accept the fact it would not be on a come-as-you-are basis, that American society would have to accept some economic pain in order to mobilize sufficient resources, or that one theater operation would essentially be a holding action. The point is that two near-simultaneous theater conflicts are not unlikely simply because they are not affordable.[408] Arguably, it may make them more likely. If history is to be used as evidence, it should again be pointed out that the World War II was, indeed, two near-simultaneous theater wars (or three or four, depending on how military theaters are delineated).

It has become common to describe recent NATO actions against Serbia—presumably a smaller-scale contingency—as constituting an MTW's worth of Allied air forces.[409] If SSCs occur at a near-continuous rate, it is almost inevitable that two or more will occur near-simultaneously, simply based on the law of averages. The United States may not choose to involve itself in more than one SSC, but if it did choose to handle two, the inevitable question is, at what point do they require two MTW's worth of effort?

The two-MTW construct may indeed be designed as a force-sizing tool, and it is certainly not predictive. To become involved in two conflicts would, ultimately, be the choice of the United States. But, many assessments would indicate that near-simultaneous occurrence of two large-scale world crises is quite possible, even if the construct itself is not a recommended policy option. Thus, there remains a divergence in the sources surveyed.

Lethality of Warfare

The question of whether future wars will be characterized by greater brutality and greater civilian casualties or by more discriminate attacks and fewer civilian casualties emerges from debates concerning the existence and effect of an RMA and the importance of information warfare.

At one end is the view that the trend toward a world of warriors—in which much of the youthful population of the less economically-developed world is involved in ethnic, religious, or tribal conflict— naturally creates more brutal forms of warfare, in which the international laws of war are rarely observed.[410] Sources point to the ethnic cleansing of Bosnia and Kosovo (along with a myriad of civil wars)—conducted largely by paramilitary terror squads whose primary skills involved the killing of unarmed civilians—as true representations of the future of war.[411] Discrimination between combatants and noncombatants is observed arbitrarily, if at all. Victory consists of complete destruction of the lives and property of the enemy.

At the other end is the vision that precision weapons and information warfare, the natural forms of warfare for a growing "third wave" global economy, will make warfare both less likely and less bloody. Kosovo is also used as an illustrative case—this time as an example of how precision bombing, with considerable effort to spare civilian lives and property, was able to win a modern war and reverse ethnic cleansing. Because such precision strikes rely on accurate intelligence, surveillance, and reconnaissance (ISR), the processing of information is a dominant feature of this style of war. Extrapolating from this fact, proponents of information warfare argue that the manipulation of information may, in itself, preclude physical combat in future conflicts.[412] Under perfect conditions, it is argued, the manipulation of information will prevent a populace from going to war by projecting images that indicate the war is unjustified or is already over, or by turning the populace against governments intent on war.[413]

Somewhere in between these views is the argument that future wars will not necessarily be more brutal, but precision strike and information warfare does not presage an era of "immaculate warfare." The U.S. Commission on National Security/21st Century, while generally enthusiastic about the precise effects of emerging military technology, expresses this middle ground in its findings:

> Despite the proliferation of highly sophisticated and remote means of attack, the essence of war will remain the same. There will be casualties, carnage, and death; it will not be like a video game. What will change is the kinds of actors and the weapons available to them. While some societies will attempt to limit violence and damage, others will seek to maximize them, particularly against those societies with a lower tolerance for casualties.[414]

The strongest statements concerning the growing brutality of modern war come from NGOs and relief agencies. Oxfam, in particular, has sketched a future in which the majority of wars—fought primarily, but not exclusively in the developing world—will focus on the civilian as target and will flout the existing laws of war. The end of the Cold War has meant that these wars will not be proxies in the struggle between ideologies, but will be fought over the distribution of resources within or between states. Globalization presumably magnifies the effects of these struggles throughout the international system.

Within these conflicts, the line between soldiery and banditry becomes blurred, and victory consists largely of replacing one unrepresentative and exploitative government with another unrepresentative and exploitative group.[415] Features of this type of warfare include ethnic cleansing, genocide, mass movement of refugees, famine, torture, and rape. In this milieu, the weapons used can range from the primitive to the merely unsophisticated. While armored vehicles, artillery, and shoulder-held anti-air missiles may be used, the dominant platform is the individual warrior—possibly under the age of twelve—and the small arms carried. The use of commercial GPS and cellular phones are useful, but not essential for operations.

The implication is that the sophisticated precision weapons, along with the information systems, that characterize the Armed Forces have relatively little effect against such an enemy.[416] There are simply no enemy systems to spoof, little communication to disrupt, no common picture to manipulate, and no center of gravity to attack (with the potential exception of the controlling warlord leader—an approach unsuccessfully adopted in Somalia).[417] Thus, it is argued that advanced weaponry cannot prevent ethnic cleansing. The only option is to close with the enemy, a style of warfare that the RMA and information operations have presumably made obsolete.

Another implication is that a considerable investment in RMA-type systems represents overkill. Humanitarian NGOs, which have traditionally argued for the developed nations to spend less on arms and more on aid to developing states, see investments in high tech weaponry as a waste that does little to deal with the real problems of future warfare. If the likelihood of MTW-like cross border aggression is low, as one side argues in the two MTW debate, then it is plausible to suggest that future military systems should be tailored to dealing with a lower-technology threat.[418] A priority would be to tailor military forces so as to be able to intervene early in low-intensity conflicts. Collective wisdom has been that high-tech systems may be useful tools in low-intensity conflict, but that, ultimately, small unit tactics conducted by lightly armed, but well trained personnel are needed to defeat guerrilla-like opponents.[419]

Those arguing that RMA systems and information warfare can create a less brutal style of warfare, would counter the above argument with two separate strands of logic. The first is the forecast that new information systems will make even the dirty wars and low intensity conflicts more transparent, so that combatants, but not civilians, can be targeted. At future concept seminars sponsored by U.S. Joint Forces Command, the prospect for developing personnel identification systems—in which the population of whole countries could be tracked and identified on a real-time basis—was discussed.[420] Even if this particular proposal might seem unlikely, the general tenet of those seeking to apply the RMA to SSCs and low-intensity conflict is that advanced technologies, such as nonlethal weapons, could be used in situations so as to prevent prolonged brutal civil wars.

A second assertion made by some of the high-tech future warfare forecasters is that civil wars are not real wars, and in any event, they are not the sort of wars in which the United States should be involved.[421] And if we choose to become involved, we should certainly not involve our ground forces. The argument is made that the American people are so casualty-adverse that the U.S. military is now (or should be) confined to "post-heroic warfare."[422] Instead of exposing itself to possible casualties by closing with the enemy on the ground, the United States will use stand-off attacks enabled by high-technology to halt potential aggression by systematic destruction of enemy assets, such as armor, trucks, artillery, missile launchers, and air defenses. The objective is to contain the crisis and role back enemy gains at an acceptable cost, without seeming to engage in wanton slaughter.[423]

Presumably other developed nations will also adopt this post-heroic style of war, ensuring that any war fought between developed states—in the unlikely case they were not deterred or self-deterred—would indeed be the high-tech affairs envisioned by the less brutal school. Technology (and technical prowess) would be pitted against technology in a manner that could minimize death and destruction.

If the United States cannot avoid becoming involved in a brutal ethnic conflict, and stand-off warfare cannot achieve at least some of our partial aims, the post-heroic solution would be to enlist the cooperation of a friend or ally more willing to risk ground forces in a coalition response to the conflict. Conflicts fought under UN peace-enforcement auspices could rely on the ground forces from such lower-technology nations eager to gain international favor or perhaps compensation for its troops. The role of the United States would be to provide the supporting sea power, air power, lift and ISR capabilities.

A feature of the divergent views on the future brutality of warfare are the differing assumptions on why wars are fought, as well as maintaining a separation between military and civilian involvement in conflict.

The Future of Classical Warfare

The issue of the separation between military personnel and civilians, or combatants and noncombatants, underlies the question of where and how future warfare will take place. Classical warfare is assumed to take place between clearly identified armies in terrain suitable for direct engagements. History—replete with siege warfare, attacks on infrastructure, and massacres of civilian populations—may demonstrate that the ideal is an exception. However, there remains the popular impression that just war is, or at least should be, about defeating the cross-border aggression envisioned in the current MTW scenarios.

Of course, the Armed Forces are used for more than MTWs. Throughout its history, America has called on the military to deal with many contingencies outside formally declared wars. These contingencies have ranged from punitive expeditions to humanitarian interventions. Current wisdom is that the number of such SSCs has greatly increased since the end of the Cold War, along with a greater propensity on the part of American decisionmakers to intervene. Sources also point out the relatively rarity of American military involvement in major theater warfare against cross-border aggression. From this perspective, *Desert Storm* is an exception rather than a rule.[424] Given the apparent increase in the number and frequency of nonstate threats and the potential for asymmetric operations, it has been suggested that the primacy of the DOD focus on preparing for classic MTWs is a mistake. The threats of the future, according to this view, will be significantly different and will require a different emphasis in preparations.[425]

One perspective is that future conflicts—particularly those within failed states—will present little opportunity for firepower-intensive warfare. There will be no front lines or rear areas, and in some cases no clearly identifiable enemy force. Rather, there will be an overall atmosphere of chaos in which the primary mission of U.S. forces will be to establish order and quell violence in the most humane way possible. Often referred to as a police function, establishment of order in a chaotic situation without a functioning government or court system is more similar to anti-guerilla operations or wartime occupation duty than policing. But obviously the rules of engagement and the military skills required are different than those of force-on-force combat.

A major proponent of the forecast of future warfare in chaotic environments has been a former Commandant of the Marine Corps, General Charles C. Krulak. During his tenure as commandant (1995–1999), General Krulak sponsored a series of seminars, workshops, and briefings concerning future operations of the Marine Corps, culminating in a briefing he frequently presented entitled "Ne Cras" ("not like yesterday"). Forecasts included the continuing urbanization of the world's population—a driver identified by many other sources—and the continued breakdown of failed states, leading to numerous tribal-like conflicts.[426]

Calling upon Marine and Army experiences in Somalia and similar contingencies, and adding insights from the then-popular chaos theory, "Ne Cras" and the other briefings postulate a world in which U.S. forces will be predominantly called upon to intervene in the chaotic conditions of the "three-block war," in which the U.S. military has to simultaneously perform three or more disparate, and perhaps contradictory, missions within the confines of three urban blocks.[427] As the example goes, on the first block, U.S. forces are conducting a full-scale urban engagement against aggressors or terrorists, on the second block, another part of the force is attempting to maintain a tenuous peace between warring factions, and on the third block, yet another part of the same force is conducting humanitarian operations in support of destitute refugees. The chaos of this ungoverned situation requires forces to make rapid decisions distinguishing threats from nonthreats and combatants from noncombatants, and whether to use force or remain disengaged. The implication is that forces designed for warfighting against a clearly defined cross-border aggressor—presumably trained to destroy targets as they appear—are not appropriately organized or prepared for the chaos of the three-block war.[428]

As befits a naval service, Marine briefs point to the fact that over seventy percent of the world's urban population are within operating range of a coastline, otherwise known as the littoral region.[429] "Chaos in the littorals" is shorthand for future contingencies in such regions.[430]

Spurred by the potential use of chemical or biological weapons in urban areas, a slightly different perspective can be termed "panic in the city." Proponents of this view are concerned that asymmetric or terrorist attacks could create similar chaotic conditions within the U.S. homeland.[431] The U.S. military would not simply have to stabilize chaotic conditions overseas, but would be expected to do the same at home. While many emerging strategy alternatives call for increased military involvement in homeland security, most assume that the military would merely play a support role to civil authorities, providing resources that may not be readily available in the civil sector. In contrast, those who view panic as the new weapon envision homeland security as the preliminary, even primary, mission of the Armed Forces. The implication is that civilians simply cannot face the physical or psychological aspects of the chemical and biological threats, and both precautions and responses should be military functions. Once the perception of homeland sanctuary is broken by an asymmetric attack, the American population would panic and flee toward areas of perceived safety, while demanding that their elected officials cease whatever foreign activities might have provoked such an attack.

In order to prevent such a scenario, sources argue, the military needs to refocus its efforts away from the less likely case—a classical military response to cross border aggression—and toward the more direct and more likely threats of asymmetric attacks against the homeland and the use of panic as a weapon of the globalized future.[432]

In contrast, a significant number of sources view MTWs as the most likely form of warfare in which the United States would become involved, and job one for its military. From this perspective, America's large-scale warfighting capability is the primary deterrent of both chaos and asymmetric attack. Unlike the "Ne Cras" view, future war may indeed be "not like yesterday," but it need not involve urban warfare under the conditions postulated by three-block war. This is a perspective that would support the development of some capability for military operations in urban terrain (MOUT), but would consider it but one among a number of key military missions—and certainly not the primary.[433] Likewise it would view involvement in chaotic conditions as a more discretionary situation than responding to a classical attack on an ally or regional pivot. Supporting friends and allies is viewed as a vital interest; intervening in chaos elsewhere is not. There is also a lingering implication that reversing cross-border aggression, which would presumably require more combatant forces, is a more demanding task than quelling tribal warfare in smaller-scale contingencies.

Panic in the city would also appear a less likely form of war than MTWs. For one thing, the United States does not have hostile states on its borders, and attacks on the U.S. homeland would either continue to prove difficult in the 2001–2025 period, or could be defended against by classical means, such as a dedicated national missile defense (NMD).[434] A second point would be that the American people historically have not exhibited much panic, so panic attacks are not a likely form of warfare. A third point is that the deterrent effect of classical warfighting capability makes asymmetric attack less likely. Though attempts at asymmetric warfare should be expected, these are best defended against by classical defensive means at home, combined with an overwhelming offensive in the opponent's home region.

The divergence of opinion on whether future warfare will *primarily* take the form of chaos in the littorals and panic in the city, or will mostly resemble the expected forms of MTW, appears to be related more to preferred prioritization of threats than to any conclusive forecast of wars to come. But there is evidence on both sides of the issue.

Militarization of Space

The question of the so-called militarization of space is particularly contentious. Space-based intelligence gathering, surveillance, and reconnaissance (ISR) are critical to U.S. military operations and gave such an informational and command and control advantage during Operation *Desert Storm*, that some have called the Gulf War "the first space war."[435] To a considerable degree, the United States has become dependent on space based assets to provide information and command connectivity to military forces in both wartime and peacetime. However, there are great distinctions between the military *use* of space, a war *from* space, and a war *in* space.[436] Every future assessment predicts increasing use of space assets by the military, but there are wide differences on whether war from or in space could occur in the timeframe to 2025.[437]

A number of sources are very certain of the potential for a force-on-force space war. The U.S. Commission on National Security/21st Century's "Major Themes and Implications" states explicitly: "Space will become a critical and competitive military environment. . . . weapons will likely be put in space. Space will also become permanently manned."[438]

This finding supports the view expressed by the commander-in-chief, U.S. Space Command (CINCSPACE), one of the joint unified commands that control U.S. combatant forces, who envisions the development of "emerging *space forces* missions" including ". . . defensive and offensive counterspace, and if directed by the NCA, a force application capability" (i.e., space-based kinetic or energy weapons) [emphasis in the original].[439] The implication is the inevitable development of space as a theater of combat because of the military and commercial value of satellite assets.[440] The CINCSPACE long range plan maintains: "It's difficult to project how much additional investment or how many satellites will be in service in 2020, the target time frame of our plan, but there is little doubt of the answer. *SPACECOM will be called upon to conduct space operations to protect U.S. investment and commercial assets, in addition to securing our other national interests in space.*"[441] [emphasis in original] This is portrayed as a response to the fact that: "*In 2020, if not sooner, adversaries will essentially share the high ground of space with the United States and its allies.*"[442] [emphasis in original] This forecast had also appeared in statements by previous SPACECOM commanders.[443]

An opposing viewpoint is the forecast that militarization of space is not likely to occur before 2025. This reasoning projects a continuing U.S. advantage in military space systems based on previous investment and infrastructure development. From this posture, "the United States is in a good position to win any ensuing arms race."[444] Even with increasing investment, it would be difficult for most nations—with the possible exception of Russia, which retains some of its previous space launch infrastructure—to produce, launch, and control indigenous military space systems. Those nations with sufficient technical capabilities are generally allies of the United States.[445] Although the use of commercial space assets by potential opponents is possible, and, as previously discussed, likely before hostilities, commercial systems do not possess offensive or defensive characteristics suitable for combat. Currently, commercial systems are not electromagnetic pulse (EMP) hardened, making them vulnerable to the long-range effects of exoatmospheric nuclear bursts.[446]

International treaties governing space activities are another potential inhibitor of space-based weapons.[447] A broad interpretation of the 1967 international "Treaty on the Principles of the Activity of States in the Exploration and Use of Outer Space Including the Moon and Other Celestial Bodies" and the 1972 U.S.-Soviet Anti-Ballistic Missile Systems treaty would appear to preclude the deployment of offensive weapons in space. However, a narrower interpretation is that these treaties ban only orbiting nuclear or other WMD in space, and systems designed to shoot down Russian ICBMs. Many types of anti-satellite (ASAT) weapons would not normally be considered WMD, nor would space-to-ground energy or kinetic kill weapons not designed for an ABM role fall easily into the WMD category. In the narrow interpretation, there is but minimal treaty restriction on space weaponry.[448] Whether or not the current treaties will remain in force, or more extensive treaties will be negotiated, is difficult to forecast.[449] Proponents of arms control point to the lasting affects of most treaty prohibitions; skeptics resonate with the oft-cited quote by French president Charles DeGaulle that "treaties last while they last."[450]

Skeptics of treaty prohibitions tend to share the inevitability view of the introduction of space weaponry in the 2001–2025 timeframe. As former Secretary of the Air Force Sheila E. Widnall argued: "We have a lot of history that tells us that warfare migrates where it can—that nations engaged in conflict do what they can, wherever they must. At a very tender age, aviation went from a peaceful sport, to a supporting function, very analogous to what we do today in space—to a combat arm. Our space forces may well follow that same path."[451] A similar argument is made by Major General Robert Dickman, USAF, who was the DOD space architect in 1997: "To hope that there will never be conflict in space is to ignore the past."[452]

Threats

Military Competitor

As discussed earlier, the development of a global military near-peer competitor to the United States before 2025 is unlikely. However, that forecast does not quell the debate on whether such a near peer is inevitable in the long term. Sources that view a near peer as inevitable base their argument on historical example; every aging leader is eventually challenged by younger, growing competitors. To ignore this is also to ignore the past. Even the Roman Empire fell.[453] In terms of the academic study of international relations, there appears always a struggle among states to become the hegemon that dominates the international system.[454] The struggle for hegemonic control can vary from long-term wars between empires or alliances or political imperialism, to economic competition or cultural imperialism. There are major diversions in the contending schools as to whether political, economic, or cultural dominance represents true hegemonic control. But even scholars who question the morality of hegemonic control—and in particular the position of the United States as the current hegemonic power—appear to believe that such a struggle is the natural order between states. Hence, the desire or expectation for some other political entity to replace the nation-state as the dominant form of international actor. This desire for or expectation—or opposition to and fear—of the increasing role of nonstate actors, including such nonstate threats as terrorist movements, is reflected in the discussion of the consensus point on the increase in nonstate threats.

If the struggle for hegemonic control is the natural order of the international system, it would also be natural that those responsible for the security of the United States—including its freedom, institutions, population, and prosperity—would prepare for such a struggle. Having achieved victory in a Cold War that took the form of an ideological struggle, it is said that the United States is now enjoying a strategic pause in which it can plan and position itself for survival and success in any future hostilities. The concept of strategic pause reflects an acceptance of the inevitability of future hostilities resulting from challenges of dissatisfied states that seek to overturn the stability of the current international order. While there may be a continuous debate as to which preparations are most appropriate—and how the outbreak of hostilities can be deterred in the near term—there seems to be agreement among many that a dissatisfied state could eventually build itself into a military near peer to the United States sometime after 2025.

The belief in the inevitability of a near peer is also reflective of the consensus point that "advanced military technology will become more diffuse." To be a near-peer competitor, the opposing state would presumably need to be able to utilize military technology on a par with the United States. It could be possible to develop different technologies, perhaps using "sidewise" methods, that could temporarily neutralize American technological dominance. However, even that would require some familiarity with the nature of current technological developments. Such would likely occur under conditions of high technological diffusion. As military technology becomes more diffuse, it appears inevitable that any American advantage in military technology would gradually shrink, creating de facto near-peer competitors.

There is, however, an alternative view on the inevitability of military near-peer competition. In this view, it is not the natural order for near-peer challengers to occur, but, rather, the actions of the leading power that *causes* such a competition.[455] Supporters of this view range from those who see a competitive international system as an anomaly of the capitalist world, to those who view gradual world democratization as eventually leading to a world free from major war—under the premise that democracies do not fight democracies. Others subscribe to the belief that near-peer competition is not inevitable as an unspoken corollary to their idea that a leading power can take actions that *prevent* such a competition from occurring. To some extent, such a view underlies the premises of a proposal by Ashton Carter and William J. Perry for a "preventive defense."[456]

The question of the inevitability of a near-peer competitor after 2025 is not merely an academic question. It ties directly to the choice of a future defense policy. If an inevitable conflict with a near-peer competitor is expected after 2025, it would behoove the United States to take distinct steps to develop a defense policy and force structure that would retain a measure of military superiority sufficient to dissuade, deter, or—if necessary—defeat a potential near-peer opponent.[457] Choices could include whether or not to forego near-term modernization in order to focus resources on the science, technology, and experimentation that would shape military force structure in the years beyond 2025. This might require a deliberate policy of avoiding military involvement in most failing states in order to preserve resources to prepare for the direct threat of a hostile near-peer competitor. Future military systems would be optimized for near-peer conflict, which might include a significant level of information and space warfare, at the expense of systems optimized for near-term intervention against nonstate threats, many of which might be resolved by other states.

However, if actual or proposed military preparations of the hegemon propel other states to seek parity, it may be in the interest of the United States to break the cycle of increasing military expenditures in order to prevent the development of a near peer. Specific policies could be adopted—along the lines of preventive defense—that seek to co-opt or manage a potential near peer by allowing a degree of American vulnerability in order preserve the current balance, which appears in favor of the United States.[458] Part of this logic parallels the action-reaction paradigm that underlay Cold War-era arms control theory. By foregoing the choice of maintaining or increasing the current massive level of military superiority, the United States might be able to channel more resources into failed state and humanitarian intervention, thereby preventing the development of more dissatisfied states. Proponents also point to increasing globalization as creating the sort of economic interdependence that would dissuade hostility among world powers. Such a view implies that the primary role of U.S. defense policy would be to prevent the outbreak of major conflict until such time as globalization and interdependence would lead to a more peaceful world. The force structure selected under such a policy could be vastly different than that designed to prepare for a military near peer.

Between the inevitability and the preparation-as-cause views are a range of perspectives that seek varying degrees of hedging against the rise of a military near peer and its prevention through military policy and diplomacy.

Defense of Overseas Bases

The reach of opponents into space, along with the adoption of other techniques of antiaccess or area-denial warfare would have a damaging impact on the overseas bases upon which America's current power projection forces appear to be dependent. If the 2001–2025 period is indeed one in which potential opponents strengthen their anti-access capabilities, then the threat to overseas bases would appear to increase. This forecast is commonly accepted.[459] However, there is a debate among the sources as to whether the nature of the future security environment will conspire with the laws of physics and the diffusion of technology to make an overwhelming threat to fixed land bases permanent.

In the eyes of the bases-will-be-indefensible school, defensive measures simply cannot keep up with the offensive threat that places fixed military forces at grave risk.[460] In this perspective, the action-reaction phenomenon of military technological development naturally favors offensive systems. This is similar to the argument against NMD that such defenses can *always* be penetrated by massive attacks or fooled by decoys, and even if one missile, presumably armed with nuclear warheads, were to penetrate the defense, the resulting destruction would be massive.

Hence, a defensive system is quite pointless. Even some sources favorable to the development of NMD consider overseas bases nearly impossible to defend.[461] For one thing, they are closer to potential aggressors and can be targeted by short- or intermediate-range ballistic missiles, both of which are easier to develop than the intercontinental ballistic missiles (ICBMs) that could threaten the homeland of the United States. In that sense, defending against an ICBM attack on the continental United States could be easier than defending a fixed base in or near a region of conflict. Such overseas bases could be attacked with WMD by other means of delivery, such as cruise missiles, attack aircraft, or artillery shells.

At the same time, political vulnerabilities may make overseas bases, particularly those within the sovereign territory of a host nation, much more difficult to defend. The host nation may seek to placate a potential aggressor by insisting that defenses be kept to a minimum in order to maintain the current strategic balance. If the base relies on the movement of mobile defense into the theater, such as the arrival of Patriot missile batteries, it is vulnerable to preemptive attack or coercion. The host nation may decide not to let the United States use its base facilities, lest such permission provoke an attack by a regional aggressor.

Because of the continuing development and proliferation of commercial imagery and satellite navigational aids, fixed bases appear to be increasingly easy to target with more precise weapons. The targeting solution for a fixed position—which would rely primarily on the simple input of latitude and longitude into a guidance system—is so many orders of magnitude easier than attempting to attack moving targets that fixed bases would appear to be the most cost-effective targets in any conflict.

Interpretation of all of these factors lead some sources to argue that it will be nearly impossible for the United States to successfully defend overseas bases in the 2001–2025 period from any significant regional threat.[462] This has considerable implications for American defense policies and the expenditure of defense resources. If, as the studies of the Office of Net Assessment suggest, the threat to fixed positions will only continue to increase, despite U.S. efforts to develop theater ballistic missile defenses (TBMD), then, logically, resources should be channeled to long-range or stand-off weapons and platforms that do not rely on overseas bases. A concurrent reduction in such systems as short-range tactical aviation and logistics-heavy ground units would also be logical. Sea-based and space-to-ground weaponry might also prove more desirable as replacements. The power projection forces of the United States—capabilities which mark the U.S. monopoly on global military power—would have to be reshaped to eliminate any dependence on theater-based logistics, such as the need for land-based pre-positioned equipment. All this would make mounting a power projection campaign considerably more difficult.

It may be a reaction to the implications for American power projection that cause other sources to insist that overseas bases could be successfully defended in the 2001–2025 time-frame. To admit the growing vulnerability could cause undesirable revolutionary changes in the allocation of defense resources. However, the bases-can-be-defended view also argues that emerging military technologies can make defenses against WMD more effective. Weapon technology is not necessarily biased toward the offensive. While force protection may be difficult, it may not pose a greater difficulty than that facing the aggressor in his efforts to stage a coordinated attack. The continuing and natural lead of America and its allies in emerging military technology, as identified in consensus points noted above, cause some to conclude that defenses can match offenses, particularly when backed by the eventual triumph of qualitatively (and possibly quantitatively) superior U.S. power projection.[463] Likewise, the regional use of WMD may be deterred by the vast U.S. nuclear arsenal, use of which might be provoked by significant casualties of U.S. military personnel or host nation civilians.

Other sources argue that overseas bases can be defended by sea-based or space-based systems. Naval TBMD systems might prove especially valuable in defending littoral bases, since their mobility makes them a more difficult target.[464] If shorter-range ballistic missiles can be destroyed in the launch or boost phase by space systems positioned overhead, the ballistic missile threat to overseas bases may be reduced. There is the potential for continuing development of such sea-based and space-based systems in the 2001–2025 period.

Additionally, there is the argument that vulnerability of land bases actually works to the advantage of the United States. If an attack on overseas-based U.S. forces occurs, it is likely that the United States would be reinforced in its determination to pursue the end-state of a regime change. This perception could deter a regional aggressor from launching such a strike. Also, the vulnerability of the host nation's territory to an aggressor might provoke the host nation to seek greater, rather than lesser military cooperation with the United States. As previously discussed, certain sources also argue than any host nation that could be coerced to restrict U.S. access to bases threatened by the regional aggressor's WMD is simply not an ally worth defending.

Opposing Strategies

Legacy Systems and Antiaccess Strategies

The debate on the defensibility of overseas bases has a parallel concerning the continuing effectiveness of power projection forces. Supported by the same data concerning the growing development of antiaccess systems and strategies, a number of sources suggest that the power projection forces of the United States, as currently constituted, will have increasing difficulty in penetrating antiaccess defenses in the 2001–2025 period. This would appear an evolutionary effect of the diffusion of advanced military technology, but with a reversal of the offenses-will-lead-defenses argument. There seems a bit of irony in the fact that the same sources that argue that overseas bases cannot be effectively defended also argue that offensive platforms will have great difficulty in penetrating antiaccess systems. However, their premise is that overseas bases are critical to the lodgement and sustainment of U.S. power projection forces entering a contested region. The vulnerability of overseas bases, therefore, is but the initial aspect of growing strength of antiaccess strategies directed toward prevention of U.S. intervention in a regional conflict.

The proponents of this view, however, do not necessarily see these developments as an evolutionary challenge to which the United States can modify and adapt its current forces. Rather they see this as a revolutionary development that is enabled, in part, on foreign adaptation to the RMA. Several of these sources disagree that the United States will retain the overall lead in technology. But even sources that see an overall U.S. lead, argue that temporary advantages in niche technologies may allow regional powers to strengthen their antiaccess networks. Strengthening antiaccess systems would appear quite logical as a reaction to the Gulf War lesson that the only way to defeat the United States is by keeping its forces from entering the region. In any event, the proponents argue that relying on current systems—as superior as they may be in direct combat—will eventually doom the U.S. ability to project its power.[465] Continuing to spend resources on maintaining and upgrading current military systems and platforms—somewhat disparagingly called "legacy systems"—is seen as a sure path to military impotence. This position could lead to radical changes in the U.S. defense posture, some of which are advocated by the transformation school. Indeed, the perception of the growing strength of antiaccess strategies is a major impetus to the calls for defense transformation.

In contrast, there remains a body of literature that characterizes antiaccess strategies as natural aspects of war that require incremental improvements in American power projection forces, but are not a revolutionary development requiring radical change. As previously discussed, the modern version of antiaccess efforts can be seen as attempting to conduct the traditional mission of coastal defense using higher technology weapons. This view argues that current developments, particularly in theater missile defense and stand-off and precision weapons, allow U.S. power projection capabilities to keep pace with antiaccess systems.[466] The Army vision of a "strategically responsive" force that is less dependent on heavy equipment and multiple air- and sea-lifts contributes to the perception that U.S. power projection forces may become even more effective in the 2001–2025 period.[467]

Conceptually, antiaccess strategies rely heavily on ISR assets in order to target approaching forces and coordinate defense efforts. ISR can be a weak link if not hardened against attack. Space-based assets, especially commercial imagery, could be particularly vulnerable to American counter-measures. Thus, there is a growing argument that blinding an antiaccess opponent by initially attacking and destroying ISR assets could quickly make the area-denial effort ineffectual and allow for the effective use of many of the so-called legacy systems in the U.S. inventory.

A divergence of views on the penetrability of antiaccess defenses in the 2001–2025 period underlies a divergence of defense policy recommendations, particularly concerning the pace of transformation.

Nuclear Deterrence

Throughout the Cold War, nuclear deterrence was considered the ultimate defense of both the homeland of the United States and the integrity of NATO. This perception was based on a self-fulfilling pattern of logic that considered both the United States (and the NATO alliance in general) and the Soviet Union to be rational actors who did not want to see their respective societies destroyed in a spasmodic nuclear war. Nuclear deterrence was a focal piece of international diplomacy and, in large measure, defined the limits within which choices on American defense policy could be made.

With the collapse of the Soviet Union and significant reduction of the immediate nuclear threat to the American homeland (and, therefore, Russian homeland as well), many of the assumptions concerning the workings of nuclear deterrence would seem open to challenge. Recognizing that it had more to lose in a tactical nuclear exchange, the United States had already begun a phase-out of much of its tactical nuclear inventory in the mid-1980s, particularly in naval weapons.[468] To some, these developments have brought into question the future effectiveness of the nuclear deterrent and the validity of the whole concept of nuclear deterrence. Who was the U.S. nuclear arsenal to be directed against? Given a world in which nuclear arsenals will continue to be reduced, what exactly would prompt a liberal democracy to retaliate with nuclear weapons? And if the potential opponents were rogue states with less rational decisionmakers what exactly would nuclear weapons deter?

Sources are split in their assessment of the importance of nuclear weapons and the validity of traditional nuclear deterrence in the 2001–2015 period. On the one hand are those who see nuclear weapons as less effective in deterring war.[469] On the other are those sources who concede that nuclear weapons may have a different role than they had at the height of the Cold War, but that they remain the ultimate deterrent with considerable effect on the actions of even rogue states.[470]

The argument that nuclear weapons will no longer be significant elements of military strategy brings together some strange bedfellows.[471] Many who state a moral opposition to nuclear weapons have translated their desires into forecasts of a globalized world in which nuclear deterrence no longer makes sense. With greater economic interdependence, this argument runs, even the so-called rogue states will be reconciled to the international order, renouncing or reducing their overt or covert nuclear arsenals. The major nuclear powers of the United States and Russia will continue to reduce their own arsenals to very low numbers, and China will be forced by world opinion to follow suit. By 2025, according to this vision, nuclear weapons will be all but outlawed.

Sources that view future conflict as consisting primarily of brutal civil wars in undeveloped states—and Western intervention to prevent suffering and injustice—simply see no utility in nuclear weapons. Since nuclear weapons cannot solve any of the real issues of conflict and appear to have no obvious deterrent effect on the outbreak of such ethnic wars, nuclear deterrence will play a much smaller role in conflict. While nuclear weapons may not be completely abolished, they will remain in the far background along with the potential for major interstate war.

From a considerably different perspective, some suggest that the RMA has simply passed nuclear weapons by. If information operations will be the dominant form of conflict in an Internetted world, the use of nuclear weapons would seem merely suicidal. Nuclear effects, such as EMP, hold the potential of destroying much of the technical access to information on which both war and international society are dependent. Again, there would seem to be no utility in nuclear warfighting, so nuclear deterrence is confined to a background role.

Others who focus on the potential for RMA advances to make national missile defenses effective argue that a defense-dominant world will eventually lead to the abolition of nuclear arsenals. Indeed, this was a stated objective of President Ronald Reagan's Strategic Defense Initiative (SDI). In this vision, the reliance on nuclear deterrence as ultimate protection gives way to the reliance on active defense during the 2001–2025 period.

Additionally, some sources argue that nuclear deterrence simply has little effect on irrational rogue regimes and terrorist groups, the two threats that are most likely to attempt asymmetric attacks on the U.S. homeland.

In opposition to this composition of views stand those sources that view nuclear weapons as retaining considerable deterrent effect, even on rogue regimes. Since, it is argued, active defenses can never be one hundred-percent effective, the potential for nuclear destruction will remain.[472] Nuclear deterrence, therefore, retains a considerable role in protecting the homeland from weapons of mass destruction.[473]

A few sources suggest that a world in which there are more nuclear powers is a world in which interstate conflict is much less likely.[474] Peace would thereby be even more dependent on nuclear deterrence than it is today. The dominance of the United States, and the relative quiescence of Russia in the realm of nuclear weapons, currently make the world safe for conventional war and increases the value of conventional over nuclear deterrence. However, such a condition may not last, as other states follow the lead of India and Pakistan in demonstrating nuclear capability. This change would again make nuclear deterrence the centerpiece of defense policy.

Other sources would argue that rogue regimes are much more rational than popularly portrayed. Although their objectives are widely divergent from the goals of liberal democracies, rogue regimes approach these objectives through a train of logical decisions. Since they have no desire to be decapitated, rogue regimes would remain cautious in provoking a disproportionate response from the United States, an idea that is further developed below. America's nuclear deterrence is what keeps such rogue regimes—or states of concern—"in the box."

Finally, sources suggest that the inherent logic of nuclear deterrence continues to be intellectually robust and retains considerable impact on international decisionmaking. Due to the collapse of the Soviet Union, nuclear deterrence may have ceased to be a front page news story, but it remains about as important to American security, no matter the inventory levels of the Russian and American nuclear arsenals.

Divergence of views on the importance of nuclear deterrence in 2001–2025 would seem to presage a debate on that portion of future American defense policy.

Conventional Force versus Nonstate Threats

Sources that focus intensely on the increasing vulnerability of the U.S. homeland and on the potential for asymmetric attack tend to doubt the ability of conventional military force to deter such attacks. Although there is not necessarily a direct correlation with specific views on the validity of nuclear deterrence, many of these sources tend to downplay the role of nuclear weapons and assume that potential opponents would concentrate on developing chemical or biological weapons of mass destruction, rather than expend resources on developing an extensive nuclear arsenal. Biological weapons, in particular, are frequently assumed to be immune to deterrence by conventional military forces—and possibly by nuclear weapons as well.[475] The logic is that opponents who would be so irrational or immoral as to use biological weapons (particularly against civilian populations) would not easily be swayed by the threat of extensive damage to their own people.[476] More importantly, terrorist groups—having no state or population to protect—do not necessarily present the vulnerabilities of a traditional military opponent. If there is an inherent difficulty in determining the perpetrators of a biological attack, there may be no apparent target for conventional (or nuclear) forces to attack.

An opposing viewpoint is that there are always vulnerabilities than can be attacked—even for terrorist groups.[477] Presumably, terrorists act for causes that have overt elements. For example, Al Fatah terrorists demanded an independent Palestinian state, and the Irish Republican Army claimed to fight for greater political power for Catholics in Northern Ireland. For many years, Israel and the United Kingdom utilized conventional military and police power, as well as special operations units, to attack the terrorists directly. These actions were successful in preventing these movements from gaining power until they adopted peaceful means. States less respectful of international law and morality have used less discriminate means of deny-ing terrorists their objectives. Given the human emotions that propel re-venge and retribution, it is difficult to say what reaction use of WMD by terrorist groups might provoke. And contrary to the most alarmist specula-tions, effective terrorist groups tend not to be crazy or self-destructive.[478]

Proponents of the deterrence-is-possible position point to the ex-ample of the 1986 *Eldorado Canyon* reprisal against Libya, which ap-peared to cause Muammar Qaddafi to reduce his support of terrorist ac-tivities.[479] At the time, Libya was judged a significant threat to peace, with tremendous military potential—at least on paper—and ongoing WMD programs. By the time of the Gulf War in 1991, Libyan activities as a rogue state seemed greatly reduced.[480] With a combination of intelligence, overt reprisal, covert reprisal, effective law enforcement, and some degree of consequence management preparations, it would seem possible that terrorist activities—particularly with weapons as sophisticated as WMD, which are extremely difficult to obtain or utilize effectively—could be prevented, dissuaded or deterred.

The question of whether information warfare is a facilitator of or deterrent to terrorism hinges on the assumption of whether defenses will always lag behind offenses. Presumably, terrorist groups with never be able to outspend the United States government or commercial sector in information technology. Therefore, terrorist use of information will al-ways be dependent on the vulnerabilities that are built into the informa-tion systems themselves. Could systems be designed to function some-thing like reactive armor on a tank? If launching an information attack were to lead to an immediate counterattack, would such attacks be de-terred in the same ways as nuclear or conventional deterrence? It would seem quite possible for such a deterrent to be developed. Likewise, it ap-pears possible that protective defenses could be developed that may not be one-hundred percent leak-proof, but that can be supplemented with an offensive counterstrike capability. It is this combination of defense ca-pabilities with the overwhelming offensive strength of U.S. forces that makes terrorist groups vulnerable to an effective American response.

The nine points of divergence described above are based on dif-fering assumptions concerning the implications of previously identified consensus points. It is possible for opposing points of view to accept the plausibility of any or all of the consensus points and yet advocate sub-stantially different defense policies. While that seems to make the creation development of baseline expectations that American defense policy will need to fulfill to maintain security in 2001–2025. From this baseline, alternative policy options can be explored.

The identification of divergent viewpoints helps to frame the more contentious issues of the defense debate. It also suggests that there may be developments that future defense policies may need to hedge against. If reputable, well-informed sources differ as to the future impact of chaos and urban warfare, or the future role of nuclear deterrence, it may be prudent to develop policies that are effective under multiple alternatives. This leads back to the concept that the validity of any particular policy is derived from its ability to adjust—relatively intact—to a changing future, rather than to be optimized for a particular future alternative.

Another element that suggests the need for hedging strategies is the identification of outliers and wildcards.

Chapter Seven

Wild Cards

This is my prediction for the future—whatever hasn't happened will happen and no one will be safe from it.

—J. B. S. Haldane[481]

Defense planning is primarily a matter of risk assessment. However, there are some risks to national security which, by their very nature, can be conceived, but not predicted or fully anticipated. Because they cannot be anticipated, such events are very difficult to plan for effectively. At least two reasons apply. First, by their very nature, these events alter the international system by their reversal of significant trends, thereby undermining the facts upon which future planning is built. Second, many of these events fall outside the scope of traditional or permitted defense planning.[482]

Events that cannot be fully anticipated are characterized in futures studies as wild cards. Although individual sources may forecast wild cards as if they were anticipated events, such singular forecasts are analytical outliers concerning topics that generally have not been addressed by the main body of future security environment literature. Other wild cards are not forecast by any source and remain on the edge of plausibility. However, the prospective effects of these outliers/wildcards can be so devastating to American security that their consideration in creating hedging strategies is of vital importance.[483] While anticipating the unanticipated may seem a contradiction, this is indeed a primary purpose in constructing alternative futures and, ultimately, forms the basis for comprehensive planning. The survey of sources identified the seven outliers/wildcards below as having potential effects on defense planning.

Assessing the potential effects of wildcards may bring one to the point where imagination overtakes research. Nevertheless, sketching the outlines and prospective impacts of such unanticipated events helps to identify the alternative against which hedging strategies may be appropriate.

Outliers/Wildcards

■ Creation of a standing UN military force that will supplant U.S. influence
■ Congressional repeal of restrictions on direct U.S. military involvement in domestic law enforcement
■ Worldwide economic collapse
■ Cascading environmental disasters
■ Development of a military near peer sooner than expected
■ Failure or hostile takeover of a key U.S. regional ally
■ Rise of neo-facism or ethnic hatred as potent ideologies

Standing UN Military Force

According to the vision of its founders, the fundamental purpose of the UN is the prevention of war. This was intended to be done through encouragement and offices for the pacific settlement of disputes (UN Charter, Articles 33–38) as well as collective self-defense under the auspices of the Security Council (Articles 39–51). Article 42 of the UN Charter empowers the Security Council to "take such action by air, sea, or land forces as may be necessary to maintain or restore international peace and security." To achieve this, Article 43 requires all members to "make available to the Security Council, on its call and in accordance with a special agreement or agreements, armed forces, assistance and facilities, including rights of passage, necessary for the purpose of maintaining international peace and security." Article 45 specifically requests members to "hold immediately available national air-force contingents for combined international enforcement action." Control of these forces would be exercised by the Security Council through a Military Staff Committee consisting of "the Chiefs of Staff of the permanent members of the Security Council or their representatives" (Article 47).

As a practical matter, the Cold War division between the Soviet Union and the other members of the Security Council ensured—with one exception—the ineffectiveness of the collective security Articles.[484] The Military Staff Committee has remained moribund. Instead, peacekeeping operations have largely been conducted under the auspices of the General Assembly and through the personal efforts of the Secretary-General, whose de facto powers have greatly expanded.

Proponents of world government have championed the increase in General Assembly-sponsored peace enforcement as an alternative to the domination of the Security Council's great power Permanent Members. Though the end of the Cold War appeared to bring the potential for a renewal of Security Council efforts at collective security, proponents have continued the effort to divorce UN military actions from great power influence. Calls for the creation of a standing UN military force that would not be under direct Security Council control have continued throughout the 1990s.[485]

Many of these proposals have taken on the form of forecasts, although the practical hurdles to the establishment of an independent UN military force would seem near insurmountable. Few nations seem willing to give up direct control of their military forces, the possible exceptions being smaller states that view peacekeeping actions—in which their soldier's salaries are paid from UN funds—as a source of revenue and expanded international influence. Secondly, command and control of sizable multinational forces, with their differing weapons systems, doctrines, and organization, is extremely difficult. It was the dominant size of the U.S. effort—rather than tight coordination—that ensured the success of the *Desert Storm* coalition (which was supported by UN sanctions, but without direct UN involvement). It is unlikely that a UN-appointed commander could achieve a similar success without a lead nation being "more equal than others."

Nevertheless, the creation of a standing UN military force could have both positive and negative impacts on U.S. national security efforts. On the positive side, a UN military force could relieve the United States of much of its humanitarian intervention and international peacekeeping efforts, reducing the operation tempo and conserving the resources of U.S. forces. This, in turn, would allow the United States to focus military preparations on MTWs and defense of the homeland, ensuring high readiness for both missions.

On the negative side, it is possible that a standing UN military force under the control of the Secretary General or General Assembly— and not the Security Council in which the United States retains a veto— could be used to oppose U.S. interests. The worse case might be a scenario in which UN troops were deployed to prevent U.S. military actions, whether as peacekeepers interspersed between U.S. forces and an aggressor, or as a directly opposing force. What, for example, would have been the result if a UN peacekeeping force had been deployed to the Saudi-Kuwaiti border as an effort to ensure that peaceful negotiations between the invading Iraqis and the exiled Kuwaitis took place without outside interference? Guided by a principle of absolute sovereignty for all member states, could a standing UN force have been used to oppose U.S. intervention in Panama or Grenada, however justified such intervention might be?

Although a wildcard, the potential for the creation of a standing UN military force in the 2001–2025 time-frame is worth some modest planning consideration. Policy choices for Washington would range from attempting to politically preclude its creation, to wholehearted support as a means of ensuring U.S. influence over its use.

Domestic Law Enforcement

One of the fundamental principles of American democracy has been the absolute and unquestioned subordination of the military to civil authority. Part of this tradition, stemming from a consistent interpretation of the Constitution, includes prohibitions on the use of the military for domestic law enforcement. These prohibitions are largely confined to the United States and a number of constitutionally-governed nations. In contrast, many if not most states routinely use their military forces as gendarmerie or a national police force. This is particularly true in Africa, where many of the national armies have been primarily organized for the quelling of civil unrest. Indeed, the inability of the Iraqi armed forces to put up much of a battle against coalition forces, yet their relative ease in massacring Kurds and other domestic opponents, has made public the fact that the primary enemy of the so-called professional military of the authoritarian states are actually the civilian citizens of their own state.

Fear of the possible imposition of a military dictatorship and of the potential alienation of the military from civil society have been the twin drivers of Constitutional prohibitions. The early American colonial experienced the frequent quartering of British troops in their homes, spurring greater support for independence. America's significant experience of the use of Federal troops in domestic law enforcement was during the Civil War, primarily—but certainly not exclusively—in recaptured areas. This prompted enough legal and political opposition to make President Lincoln and his administration—although facing a bloody and divisive rebellion—show considerable restraint. The Union military leaders likewise appear to have avoided, as much as possible, involvement of their troops with law enforcement. This historical reluctance to involve the military in maintaining domestic order has evolved into a unique separation between the regular Army, Army Reserve, and National Guard. The National Guard, primarily consisting of reservists, has been the military element used for domestic law enforcement in extenuating circumstance, and usually only under state—not Federal—authority. This system has insulated regular, full-time active duty members of the Armed Forces from having any involvement in *posse comitatus.*[486]

It is conceivable, though counter to the American tradition, that Congress could seek to void the prohibitions on military use in domestic law enforcement. The most likely circumstance would be widespread terrorism or violence internal to the U.S. homeland. Catastrophic terrorism with weapons of mass destruction would seem to be the potential trigger for an internal military response. Sources suggesting panic in the city as the result of the threat or use of WMD on U.S. soil, paint a picture in which the American people might demand that the U.S. military be used for internal security. Whereas many of the identified homeland defense functions—such as national missile defense—do involve action against a foreign military force, internal security performed by regular military components would seem a fundamental break from current concepts governing U.S. military policies and organization.[487] Support for domestic authorities, when it involves consequence management or disaster relief, is one thing. The arrest, detention, or interrogation of American citizens by soldiers would be quite another thing—a drastic change akin to a wildcard event. The regular U.S. military is not structured, trained, or predisposed to internal security, and such a legal change would require a near-complete reorganization of the Department of Defense.

A non-wild card aspect of homeland security would be the transformation of the National Guard into an organization completely dedicated to the homeland defense mission. This is, in fact, an active proposal articulated in political and military literature. However, there is still an unarticulated assumption that these homeland defense functions would remain primarily military in nature, or supportive of civilian agencies. Law enforcement functions utilizing National Guard troops, such as for temporary riot control, would still remain under a separate chain of authority primarily controlled by state governors. In these functions, the National Guard essentially performs as a militia rather than a military service.

Economic Collapse

It is our natural preference to believe that economic security is a human birthright. And, in fact, universal economic improvement—in the long run—is a historical fact. In selected periods, however, economic downturns have been the cause of both personal suffering and domestic and international conflict. The most widespread interpretation of the rise of fascism and communism in Europe, along with the eventual cataclysm of the Second World War, is that it was fueled by the economic deprivation caused by a growing worldwide depression that was not felt in the United States until 1929.[488]

The great depression and World War II were defining experiences for a whole generation in the United States, Europe, and Asia. However, this is a generation that is reaching the end of its life span, and the concern they held toward a repeated economic collapse appears to be faded. In fact, the current, repeated rhetoric of mainstream economists, national governments, and the financial industry is that a world wide economic collapse is an impossibility. Investor disinterest in the gold market is but one point of evidence that the possibility of a persistent economic downturn is discounted.

Yet, if globalism is the dominant phenomenon of the international system, it stands to reason that one of its effects would be the transmission of local economic difficulties into the overall world economy. As previously discussed, greater interdependence means the greater vulnerability of individual nations. If historical patterns remain, cascading economic downturns could easily lead to wars as individual nations scramble to protect themselves and ensure access to critical wealth-producing resources. Contrariwise, many globalists argue that the international system will eventually become so interdependent that no nation would be able to make war. However, this forecast carries with it the echoes of the European socialist movement circa 1914.

Other sources, however, argue that the world economy is largely regionalized and—like the European Union—becoming more so. In a regionalized world system, certain regions can prosper even while others might decline. In fact, a globalized financial market might even promote greater regional disparities as it becomes easier for capital to flee distressed regions for more stable ones, making the stable regions even more prosperous. It may also mean that conflict fueled by economic crises may affect only certain regions. This regionalization theory is one of the more frequent explanations of why the downturn in Asian economies in the

1990s had unexpectedly slight effects on financial markets in the United States and Europe.[489]

Whether through regionalized or global effects, the potential economic collapse would hold several implications for defense policy. The first is one of the employment of forces: if economic crises leads to greater regional conflict, it is more likely that the Armed Forces would be involved in regional conflict.[490] To some extent, the threat consists of failed states, writ large. But what exactly could U.S. defense policy do for a failed *world*? Intervention in multiple simultaneous regional wars is a scenario that could quickly overtax American military capabilities, leaving the United States vulnerable to a type of conflict that most prefer not to contemplate—the starving have-nots of the Western hemisphere versus the North American haves.

But another implication is the shifting of resources away from defense as a reaction to strains in the U.S. economy. Congress could decide that the United States simply cannot afford a robust defense, and particularly not one based on high-technology and power projection. It is possible that the United States could adopt a neo-isolationist policy that eschewed any overseas military involvement while the nation healed its own economic wounds. The resulting effect in the international system is not something current defense policies envision.

Even if desired, formulating plans to hedge against this wildcard would be extremely difficult. First, a defense policy based on the potential for economic collapse would certainly not be a confidence builder in the domestic economy. Likewise, it would be at odds with current policies on world trade and investment. It would be difficult for most administrations to exhort popular faith in economic growth at the same time its Defense Department appears to be planning for economic collapse.

Secondly, an economic collapse could put current friends or allies of the United States into the have-not camp. It would not appear prudent for the Department of Defense to construct formal plans for defense against our current friends and allies—at least, not if we want them to remain friends and allies.

Thirdly, an economic collapse could mean considerable reduction in the defense budget. How, exactly, could the Defense Department hedge against that? It could purchase less sophisticated weapons that cost less to operate and maintain. But that seems in considerable conflict with policies that emphasize full spectrum dominance, precision weaponry, and information systems. Likewise, a policy of financial investment that could create an endowment for the Department of Defense to spend in lean times does not seem like prudent policy for a democracy. Nor can defense reinsurance policies be purchased to indemnify national security in a coming economic collapse.

Such are the true characteristics of a wildcard—plausible, but unlikely, unpopular to contemplate, and nearly impossible to prepare for.

Environmental Disasters

Futures assessments conducted by environmental-issue NGOs have consistently pointed to an increase in pollution and environmental degradation, particularly as lesser-developed nations seek to expand their industrial capacity. While environmental issues have yet to lead directly to international conflict, access to resources that are sensitive to environmental conditions—such as cod fisheries—has been the source of skirmishes and potential military confrontation. Fossil fuels have also been the source of ongoing conflict and military build-ups; currently, a potential conflict over territorial claims entailing oil rights in the Spratly Islands of the South China Sea pits China against the Philippines, Malaysia, Vietnam, Indonesia, and Taiwan. Another possibility previously noted is the prospect of conflict over water rights in much of Asia, Africa, and Latin America.

In addition to conflict over individual environmental resources, there is indeed a future potential for hostilities over pollution and other environmental degradation. This possibility would be particularly acute if a cascading environmental disaster involving a multitude of nations were to occur.

Although generally optimistic about the potential for change, most assessments of the future of the natural environment will *not* rule out the prospect of a global economic disaster that puts much of the world's population at risk.[491] Ozone depletion, deforestation, and destruction of ocean resources, such as reefs, are but three environmental blights that could have worldwide effects, even if they occurred in but one region. If a series of cascading environmental disasters were to occur, it is possible that both civil and international wars would ensue as individuals, groups, and states scrambled for access to remaining resources. Action to prevent further degradation might foment violence; it is not inconceivable that states or alliances might invade other states for the express purpose of preventing them from polluting.

Other states may attempt to turn environmental degradation into a direct weapon of war. Saddam Hussein's troops set fire to oil wells and opened pipelines that spilled oil into the Persian Gulf, nominally to disrupt coalition military operation, but more likely as yet another form of international blackmail. Weather control weapons have been a staple of science fiction novels and movies.

But is a cascading environmental disaster something that should be inserted into defense planning? Can military power act as a hedge against its development? Clearly the Department of Defense could prevent its own participation in growing environment degradation by being a good steward of its resources.

On the other hand, through the expenditure of ordnance, fuels, other toxic substances, war and the resulting physical destruction of combat is a source of pollution—an obvious fact that environmentally oriented, anti-war activists proclaim with great solemnity. But the environmental results of all of the wars of history do not equal any of the routine effects of industrial production. And it is unclear exactly how defense policy could hedge against further environmental disasters unless the United States identified regional or international pollution as a cause for intervention.[492] Currently, such a policy would seem as much of a wild card as a cascading disaster itself.

Military Near Peer

With the consensus indicating that a military near-peer competitor is unlikely in the 2001–2025 timeframe, the possibility of an unexpected peer becomes a wild card. But if the rise of a military near peer is indeed inevitable in the long run (sometime beyond 2025), it would be a wild card of somewhat higher probability.

Preparation for global conflict with a near peer was the posture of the U.S. military throughout much of the Cold War. The United States retains many of the power-projection capabilities developed throughout that era. Thus, from a conceptual point of view, shifting from today's focus on regional conflict to a global conflict focus would not pose a great difficulty—it would not be a voyage in uncharted waters.

But such preparations would also require an increase in U.S. defense expenditures in order to maintain the overall force structure and level of readiness at a global war level. Two major theater wars do not equal a global war against a military near peer.

Hedging—that is, taking some modest preparations that could be rapidly expanded if the wild card occurred—is a much more affordable course. Arguably, preparations to fight two overlapping MTWs is already a considerable hedge against sudden emergence of a near peer. From a force structure viewpoint, a solid base for rapid expansion is already present. However, conflict against a military near peer would imply the use of state-of-the-art, complex, military systems. A more significant requirement for hedging effectively may be an increase and expansion of weapons modernization and organizational transformation. And that is exactly the argument of many military transformation opponents: we need to take steps now to prepare for the inevitable competitor—and those preparations cannot wait until 2025.

Collapse of Regional Ally

A hostile regime change in a key U.S. regional friend or ally is certainly not a completely improbable event. Obviously, it has happened in the recent past, the fall of the Shah of Iran being the most notable example. But it is a difficult event to prepare for, since the requisite preparations may counteract the very policies intended to maintain the friendship or alliance.

Arguably, maintaining the support of regional allies is even more important to today's regionally-focused military posture than it was during the Cold War. If the expected conflict is one against a regional competitor, the implication is that the United States is intervening to support a regional ally and that access to the region is facilitated by that ally. And, indeed, a key element of antiaccess or area-denial strategies is to remove—through coercion or the application of force—support for U.S. intervention. Thus, the collapse of such a key regional ally—an occurrence very difficult to predict—would be a defining event for U.S. military regional posture.

As a hedge against a collapse or hostile regime change, the United States could simply increase the level of engagement with the state at risk, hoping to sustain pro-democratic forces. Or, it could seek to maintain multiple allies within the region in order to ensure access if any one ally faced domestic uncertainty. From this perspective, hedging against the collapse of an alliance with any one particular state is part of normal policy.

However, the collapse of a key regional partner is an event that could bring the premises of U.S. security policy into question. Libertarian groups have long argued that alliance relationships in themselves enhance the security threat to America, since few states would have cause to challenge the United States, if it were not involved in regional security. If the United States were to eschew regional entanglements, according to this logic, there would be no cause for conflict unless the U.S. homeland were directly threatened.[493] Though the libertarian position may not currently be a popular one, collapse of a key regional ally could bolster the prospect of an inward-looking or Fortress America defense policy. Arguably, such a collapse would indicate that the policy of engagement is failing and that the United States simply could not rely on regional allies. A variant of this argument is implied in discussion of the divergence point on the defensibility of overseas bases, namely, that a regional ally that refuses U.S. forces unfettered access to its bases and facilities is simply not worth supporting.

Neo-Fascism

The tragedy of ethnic cleansing and sectarian warfare in the former Yugoslavia has awakened much of the international community to the fact that ultra-nationalism is still an ideological force that can propel conflict. This came as a shock to many who envisioned the breakdown of ethnic barriers through globalization, and particularly the gradual strengthening of the European Union.[494] Though great violence and even genocide occurred in a number of places in the world during the 1990s, it was presumed that the defeat of Nazi Germany forever stilled the appeal of ultra-nationalism, ethnic hatred, and fascism in civilized and cosmopolitan Europe. The Cold War struggle was seen in terms of potentially coexisting ideologies and rival economic systems, and not in terms of ethnic struggle, even though some authorities pointed to the Soviet Union as the prison-house of nations. The fact that ethnic conflict resurrected itself as communism retreated hints of the impermanence of imposed ideologies.

But native ideologies are another matter. It is notable that ultra-nationalism seems to translate into ethnic conflict in states with neo-fascist government masquerading as pseudodemocracies. The current Serbian government of Slobodan Milosovic has become the archetypal case. But such governments have struggled against pro-democracy forces throughout post-communist Eastern Europe and the former Soviet Union, as well as post-colonial Africa and Asia. To some extent, they are a legacy of the inexperience of the newly liberated in representative government, but even more, they are the result of impatience with the gradual economic improvements resulting from democratic market systems—the danger identified in the 1998 National Security Strategy. Rising to power on waves of anger, disappointment, or disillusionment, such governments generally require continued outward-focused anger to sustain their power. And the best source of such anger remains the smoldering hatreds of past ethnic injustice that can be fueled by charismatic demagoguery.

The resulting conflicts are indeed a significant target of U.S. military planning for smaller-scale contingencies. The ethnic cleansing that resulted in NATO intervention in Kosovo has been formally identified as a threat to international security. But such events are seen as the sporadic and disconnected results of failing states, rather than as indicators of a growing ideological challenge to democracy. Even in the face of widespread ethnic violence, the dominant belief among Western intellectuals is that multiethnic societies can be equitably governed and are the preferred model for nation-states. Military forces have been used to support this preference, with intervention justified on humanitarian grounds.

However, history indicates that the rise of ultra-nationalism in the form of fascism can break down harmonious, multicultural societies. Although the consensus remains that there will be no world-wide ideological movement comparable to Cold War communism that will challenge democratic capitalism in the 2001–2025 period, the cumulative effects of ultra-nationalist movements in scattered nations could pose a challenge to the democratic peace.

The wild card event would be the development of an international movement that links ultra-nationalist governments across states. This anti-democratic alliance has always been the fascist ideal and would be a likely cause of international conflict. But could prevention of such an event by military means be planned?

In the general case, the answer is yes. The current U.S. military mission of engagement is intended to strengthen the support for democracy and subordination to civil authority in foreign militaries. The U.S. military—the world's most powerful—is held up as a model for foreign militaries, particularly those of emerging democracies. Presumably, adoption of the model would facilitate greater organizational interaction with U.S. forces, thereby increasing the effective strength of the foreign military. The message repeated to foreign military leadership is: if you are more supportive of democracy, you will become more militarily effective. At the same time, the United States has intervened against selected despotic regimes, including operations to restore democracy. Unfortunately, some of these operations have not been completely effective.

This leads to a realization of the limits of planning for this wild card. A policy of pro-democratic intervention could lead to increasing levels of military operations in a continuous democratic crusade. Such, support for international democracy could collide with support for international sovereignty, as it has in the past. Accepting a high probability of occurrence for this wild card carries the implication that the operational tempo of U.S. forces involved in smaller-scale contingencies would be significantly higher than today. Choices would have to be made as to whether to increase defense force structure or downgrade readiness of the overall force for major theater wars.

Hedging is not an unfamiliar method to military planning. Developing worst-case scenarios, often denounced as a justification for military gold-plating, is essentially a hedging technique. But whatever method is used to articulate the implications of unanticipated events, hedging needs to be integrated into the normal planning process if it is to have much value.

Yet, all wild cards are not of equal probability. A careful selection needs to be made as to which are the best candidates for further study. Among the best guides are the degree to which current plans could be adjusted quickly to a particular unexpected event and the relationship between the particular wild card and the dissenting arguments identified through the development of the consensus.

In the first case, events that cannot be adequately handled by adjusting current plans might require the acquisition of inefficient resources tailored solely for the wild card. Such resources can be thought of as building additional flexibility into current plans. But acquiring these resources, even in the relatively small numbers appropriate for hedging, may require decisions that contradict the standard requirement definition process. An appropriate rule of thumb would be to answer the question: would capabilities currently have any effect on neutralizing the wild card if it occurred? If the answer is no, prudence may suggest the acquisition of tailored resources.

In the second case, themes repeated in the dissenting arguments may indicate the probability of occurrence of a wild card. If, for example, dissent on the issue of a competing ideology grows strong, it may indicate that the occurrence of a related wild card is growing more likely.

Integrating hedging with normal planning carries with it the requirement for constant review of the accepted plan. In light of the dangers of unexamined assumptions, such as the British Ten-Year Rule, this required review technique may be the most important aspects of attempting to hedge, particularly if safety for that which has not yet happened is to be achieved. In developing a consensus scenario, the following chapter also attempts to identify practical hedges for the unexpected.

Chapter Eight

Toward a Consensus Scenario

If you wish to live a life free from sorrow, think of what is going to happen as if it had already happened.

—Epictetus[495]

The most difficult challenge for any defense review is not the development of a future security environment assessment in itself. The most difficult challenge is to create a path of logic that leads to practical strategies and defense policies and suggests the force structure to implement them. Such an integrated path would be the translation of an inherently academic exercise of formulating alternative future assessments into a process that directs actions and produces effects in the actual, as opposed to the theoretical, international security environment. This is the point of such intensive defense reviews such as the QDR conducted in 1997, and is tough work indeed.

Thus, there is a degree of irony in the gentle chiding found in a recent future security environment scenario assessment effort: "Even in the U.S. Government's Quadrennial Defense Review (QDR) process the emphasis is less on alternative futures in scenario development and more focused on the articulation of future force planning challenges."[496] As suggested in earlier chapters, it may be that comprehensive defense reviews do *not* need to develop a separate—presumably novel—process for developing alternative future scenarios. Obviously, there is no lack of ongoing alternative futures projects from which to choose. Rather, comprehensive defense reviews need to be able to utilize the results of these competing, and sometimes conflicting projects in a way that provides for common conclusions and, at the same time, permits—better still, requires—the consideration of alternative views.

Constructing a Consensus Scenario

Having identified the current points of consensus appropriate for consideration in the QDR 2001 process, the task is to present these findings in a useful format. Constructing a consensus scenario that identifies a baseline common view of the expected future to create a logical starting point. This new baseline would replace the QDR 1997 assumptions about the future. However, QDR 1997 is included as a source so that the new baseline can be seen as much as a revision as a replacement.

Upon this new baseline can be added the contentious issues and potential outliers/wildcards. The alternative views of the dissenters can then be used as conceptual excursions from the baseline. By means of these excursions, policy decisions based on the consensus scenario can be evaluated in terms of their ability to hedge against alternative futures.

The table below provides the outline for a baseline consensus scenario that incorporates both the points of consensus and common aspects of some of the points of divergence.

In 2001–2025, U.S. Military Forces Must Prepare for:

- Military challenges by a regional competitor
- Attempts by a regional competitor to attack the U.S. homeland utilizing asymmetric means
- Use of antiaccess/area-denial strategies by regional competitors
- Use of WMD by regional competitors as part of antiaccess operations
- Involvement in failed states and in response to nonstate threats at *discretion* of national command authorities, but *some* degree of involvement is inevitable
- Operations in urban terrain and under "chaotic" conditions, by *some,* but not *all* of the force
- Continual diffusion of military technology to potential competitors and nonstate actors
- High level of information warfare

Although broken into separate bullets, this baseline consensus can also be articulated as an integrated narrative scenario of the anticipated future. The 2001–2025 consensus scenario is one in which:

The most critical military challenge to U.S. Armed Forces will be the readily identifiable military forces of one or more regional competitors. These regional competitors will not have the global power projection capabilities of the United States and will not be able mount militarily significant operations outside their own immediate regions against U.S. Armed Forces. U.S. control of the global commons of sea and international airspace will remain relatively secure.

But, because they cannot compete as a global military peer, regional competitors will seek to increase their chances of success by developing the capabilities to conduct limited attacks on the U.S. homeland and by excluding U.S. forces from their immediate region using antiaccess or area-denial strategies and systems.

In peacetime, their intent will be to create an appearance that the United States would not have the means or will to prevail in a conflict in their region, thus neutralizing potential allied support for U.S. actions. In wartime, their intent will be more to achieve a political settlement favorable to their objectives than to inflict a decisive military defeat on U.S. Armed Forces. The threat of severe American personnel casualties is increased through the possession and use of weapons of mass destruction (WMD) against forward deployed U.S. forces and U.S. power projection forces entering the region, or the allied infrastructure that could support U.S. intervention. It will be increasingly difficult to defend overseas land bases from mass attacks. The likelihood of WMD use in these circumstances is high, although the weapons used are likely to be chemical or biological rather than nuclear.

WMD attacks would likely be focused on military forces or supporting infrastructure rather than U.S. or allied populations. This will not be the result of moral qualms, but rather an attempt to prevent the "Pearl Harbor" syndrome of an aroused United States (and/or ally) fighting for revenge. Another potential aspect of WMD use would be a nuclear-generated electromagnetic pulse (EMP) in an attempt to eliminate the U.S. advantage in intelligence, surveillance, and reconnaissance (ISR) and command, control and computer (C^3) systems.

As an adjunct to their antiaccess efforts, and in an attempt to sway U.S. public opinion toward a political settlement, the regional competitors will attempt to conduct a high level of information warfare. U.S. public opinion will be seen as a center of gravity. Information warfare—as well as overall antiaccess capabilities—will be facilitated by a continual diffusion of advanced military technologies throughout the world. This diffusion includes access to commercial imagery and communication via space systems.

However, the diffusion of military technology is not likely to cause a reduction in the U.S. advantage in military technology, which parallels overall U.S. economic and technological strengths. It is likely that major technological breakthroughs, generated through commercial efforts, will occur primarily in the United States or its economically developed allies. Regional competitors may be able to generate a temporary advantage in a particular technological niche, but the diffusion effect also ensures that such advantages will not hold for long. Likewise, the access to commercial *satellite systems is not likely to continue during hostilities against the United States.*

Increased military technology will also be sought by potential nonstate threats, such as terrorist groups, and in the myriad of civil conflicts erupting in an increasing number of failed states. Although not considered the primary mission (which will continue to be to "fight and win the Nation's wars," even as the anticipated operations of these wars change), military intervention against nonstate actors and in failed states will be expected missions for U.S Armed Forces. Such interventions or smaller-scale contingencies will continue to remain discretionary, and different political administrations may choose differing levels of involvement. However, some level of involvement appears inevitable and is to be anticipated. As part of these interventions (and possibly as part of regional war), some portion of U.S. Armed Forces will be expected to conduct operations in urban terrain and under chaotic conditions.

U.S. Armed Forces will be expected to utilize available assets in humanitarian assistance and in support for domestic civil authorities. Likewise, homeland defense—in response to asymmetric threats—will be an expanding mission. Evolving challenges in homeland defense will include limited ballistic missile attacks by rogue states and the potential use of chemical or biological weapons by terrorists. However, the majority of America's military will be required to remain organized to conduct power projection operations during regional conflicts, a posture conceptually similar to today.

Unlikely Events

If the above scenario represents a consensus view of the future for which U.S. military forces should be prepared, there is a corresponding image of which unlikely developments do *not* necessarily require extensive military preparations.

In 2001–2025, the Following Events are Judged to be Unlikely:

- Global war against a near peer
- Anti-U.S. alliance or ideology of military significance
- War in the open ocean or massed air-to-air engagements

The above table may appear simply as a logical result of the identification of the more likely cases of the consensus scenario, expressing the unlikely opposite conditions. However, to accept the validity of the statement requires the examination of significant implications for future U.S. defense policies or programs. For example, if global war is not an expectation, it is possible that some of the U.S. forces stationed or forward deployed overseas in selected locations are redundant. It is also possible that U.S. forces do not need to be maintained at the continuously high level of readiness as is currently required.

If an anti-U.S. military alliance or an ideology capable of propelling military conflict against Western-style democracy is not in the making, then the United States may be able to pursue the development of bilateral relations with potential rogue states by means of a unique blend of compellance and incentives. Without a major economic patron, states like Iraq will remain vulnerable to sanctions and embargo without an effective means of retaliation against U.S. interests. At the same time, globalization and the spread of market economics makes it even less likely that such rogue states would find powerful patrons. The U.S. may find it easier to use force against rogues in the future.

If war at sea and massed air-to-air engagements are unlikely, then there is considerable choice in the type of naval and air platforms that could be acquired in the future. Platforms could be optimized for other missions, or the United States could consider purchasing a high/low mix of capabilities, an acquisition strategy that was considered questionable in the latter periods of the Cold War. Likewise, the modernization of current systems—which has been done at the expense of early retirement of certain platforms—may be pursued at a more deliberate pace.

Events to Hedge Against

The effect of resource constraints on defense strategy always requires plans to identify—either implicitly or explicitly—those contingencies *not* planned for. Since the insurance aspect of defense planning requires hedges against the unexpected, it is natural for defense decisionmakers to forego, for as long as possible, divestiture of systems whose probability of use has faded. Changing conditions may make the recently divested capabilities of renewed importance. What some might view as unwarranted conservatism may be, in reality, a reasonable degree of prudence.

A potential solution for the divestiture problem may be the partial retention of legacy systems, or the development of significantly flexible or multipurpose replacements, that are specifically identified as hedges against an unlikely future. The first step is to identify exactly which alternative futures are worth hedging against. Obviously, the most critical criteria are the direct effects that alternative events would have on U.S. security. On the top of the list would be those events that hold the potential of a catastrophic defeat of the U.S. military. Following closely behind would be those alternative futures that would lead to an apparent long-term erosion in U.S. security.

Hedging strategies have limitations. First, of course, is that military means may not be the most appropriate response to some events. Other methods of hedging may not be appropriate elements for defense policy. From the two outliers identified, repeal of the restrictions on the direct use of the U.S. military in law enforcement is not a contingency that the Department of Defense could plan for under existing law (with the exception of the National Guard component in its state-assigned roles). DOD contingency planning for domestic law enforcement could also bring the American principle of military subordination to civilian authority into question.

Secondly, there are wildcard events that the U.S. military would not—under most circumstances—have the means to affect. A cascading environmental disaster may call for a military role in supporting domestic authority through the provision of transportation, construction, or security services. Military platforms could be useful for supporting civilian response teams to specific events, much like the use of naval vessels to stage clean-up crews for the *Exxon Valdez* oil spill off the Alaskan coast. However, there are no distinctly *military* capabilities that would seem particularly useful in preventing (rather than responding to) an environmental catastrophe. U.S. military consequence management teams—designed to respond to a WMD event—might be useful in environmental management, but they would not be optimized for such a mission. Obviously, good stewardship of resources by the Department of Defense—particularly the safe handling of nuclear material—could be seen as preventing the start of a cascading environmental disaster. Sources also suggest that U.S. space tracking systems and modified ballistic missiles could be used in preventing the collision of asteroids with the earth.[497] However, overall preparations for a worldwide environmental disaster would seem outside the scope of practical military planning for the 2001–2025 period.

Likewise, preparing for worldwide economic collapse is outside the scope of practical military planning. If conflict were to occur as result of economic collapse, U.S. armed forces would obviously be called upon to engage the enemy, as they would in a conflict caused by any other means. But steps taken to directly shield the defense budget from economic downturn—for example, by investing operating funds in precious metals or other marketable commodities—have not previously been considered appropriate and would be politically questionable.[498]

However, there are a number of wildcard or unlikely events that a prudent defense plan would consider as contingencies. These include the events listed in the following table, which is based on a review of the points of divergence, the outliers, and wildcards, as well as the unlikely events identified above. These events to hedge against have three criteria in common: (1) they are events for which preparations in military planning or force structure are practicable, (2) if they occurred, their effects would be magnified by the expected trends identified by the consensus security environment, and (3) they hold the potential to create significant danger for the United States.

Events to Hedge Against

- Eventual military near-peer competitor
- Potential alliance of regional competitors
- Attempts to leapfrog into space warfare
- Collapse of key ally or regional support
- Trend toward a world of warriors

A hedge against an unexpected event could take two forms. First, contingency plans could be developed and a select group of resources could be maintained in reserve in order to carry out the plans. It might be necessary, in that case, to maintain an inventory of systems that are optimized for the particular contingency, but may not otherwise prove useful in the emerging security environment. For example, if one accepted the contention that major theater war is an unlikely event, and that the majority of future military missions will not involve traditional land combat, then a large number of heavily armored vehicles current in the U.S. inventory might be considered candidates for divestiture in order to free operating funds for other systems. However, heavily armored vehicles might be the most appropriate weapons systems for combat with a military near peer, if one should emerge. A certain portion of the inventory (reserve capability) might be retained as a hedge against such a contingency.

Likewise, hedging against a suddenly emerging world of warriors may require the maintenance of forces that might not prove useful in a previously information-warfare-dominated security environment.

A second form of hedging would be the development of adaptive systems, which could operate under unexpected conditions as well as perform optimally in anticipated missions. For example, hedging against the use of EMP weapons in an antiaccess strategy might require shielded sensors, nondigitized systems, or concepts of operations in which low-tech forces might be deployed—the equivalent of the apocryphal French colonial infantry.

The following table identifies some measures for hedging against the unanticipated events.

Event	Reserve Capability	Adaptive Systems
Eventual emergence of military near peer	Strategic reserve capable of being rapidly expanded	Systems capable of being rapidly upgraded in terms of lethality and sortie rate
Potential alliance of regional competitors	Strategic reserve capable of being rapidly expanded	Systems capable of being rapidly moved between theaters
Attempts to leapfrog into space warfare	Hedging force of anti-satellite systems maintain in storage for force on demand	Hardening of current space systems against future increase in threats
Collapse of key ally or regional support	Multiple regional allies that could provide similar level of operational support	Long-range systems that are operable from bases outside the region
Trend toward a world of warriors	Expanded reserves of special operating forces and other highly-trained low-intensity warfare units	Detection and surveillance systems capable of identifying combatants from noncombatants

Hedging against unanticipated events requires deliberate choices that might not be evident under the premises of the consensus scenario. The point of suggesting that hedging should be a conscious part of defense planning—particularly during upcoming defense reviews—does not negate the importance of the consensus scenario as a baseline for decision-making. Rather, hedging strategies can be seen as a conceptual overlay by which to evaluate any adopted defense policy. The initial objective is an understanding of how flexible the adopted policy would be in *dealing* with unanticipated change or the emergence of an alternative security environment. The ultimate objective would be an evaluation of whether the adopted policy contains the means of *deterring* the emergence of an alternative—presumably more hostile—future security environment.

Chapter Nine

Conclusion: Effective Defense Reviews

To foresee a victory which the ordinary person can foresee is not the acme of skill. . . . The skillful commander takes up a position in which he cannot be defeated and misses no opportunity to master his enemy. Thus a victorious army wins its victories before seeking battle; an army destined to defeat fights in the hope of winning.

—Sun Tzu [499]

I n order to ensure future victories, the United States has routinely conducted assessments of its defense policies and force structure. The Quadrennial Defense Review in 2001 will be one in a long line of reports, all of which have attempted to identify the battle space that will be contested and the enemies who will contest it. Generally, such assessments attempt to go beyond the vision of the future as predicted by a team of experts and extrapolations made from the latest intelligence analysis. The result is a myriad of competing assessments, each inevitably reflecting the inherent biases of individual participants and sources.

This survey has attempted to derive a consensus concerning the probable outlines of future conflicts from the current group of competing assessments. Mindful of the potential for bias, it has also sought to identify dissenting viewpoints and potential wildcard events. The goal is to develop a baseline consensus of the probable future, but at the same time identify those unpredictable catastrophic events—or predictable but unlikely developments—against which hedging strategies could be adopted as a form of national defense insurance. Here is where the discordant views of the dissenters are most valuable; they lead to plans that can also cope with alternative futures. The dissenting viewpoints are tools against complacency. In the vernacular of the military pilot, they prompt us to continually scan our instruments throughout the flight, ensuring that conditions are indeed as they appear to the eye. Likewise, the sum of dissenting views and unanticipated wildcards cause us—like prudent navigators at sea—to check the track laid out on the chart. We look not just for the effects of set and drift in pushing us off course, but examine the validity of the chart itself. What uncharted features might suddenly appear to put all our planning at risk?

At the same time, it must be recognized that there are issues on which a consensus cannot be developed. These are the issues that need to be debated if any defense review is to be effective. For example, should the United States prepare now for the coming of a military peer competitor? The consensus is that one will not develop before 2025. Yet, history suggests that the appearance of a challenger for international dominance is just a matter of time. Through values, planning, and fortuitous circumstances, the United States has emerged from the 20th century as the sole superpower. It is not likely to do so at the end of the 21th century by muddling through or complacently following an unadjusted track.

Some are concerned that the choices made today are ones that could provoke the very competition we seek to avoid. Whether it is possible to develop cooperative defenses with potential military rivals may be an issue worth examining, even as we admit that there is a very narrow set of circumstances in which they could be applied. One size of international policy never fits all, as British Prime Minister Neville Chamberlain found at Munich, to the sorrow of the world. Perhaps prudent defense planning requires a blend of the two views in order to deal with a sudden change in circumstance—sort of a cooperation-plus-containment approach that seeks to encourage our fondest hopes at the same time it retains the means of prevailing in our worst nightmares.

Likewise, the future of space forces or information warfare—both points of contention—is worthy of open debate prior to the shifting of resources from overseas basing, forward presence forces, or any other legacy system or posture deemed vulnerable in an emerging world. Vulnerable does not always equate to unnecessary. Even though the consensus is that information warfare will become more important in future conflicts, it is not the *most* important or decisive element. The coming of information warfare may not be cause for celebration, if the United States and its allies remain the most vulnerable, and if conflicts consist primarily of ethnic atrocities carried out by low-tech means. It should be remembered that the worldwide media broadcasts of the body of an Army Ranger dragged through the streets of Mogadishu were a prime cause of the American withdrawal. But they had little effect on ending the civil war in Somalia.[500]

If the consensus proves true, and WMD and elaborate antiaccess systems become fixtures of the future battlefield, war will become more difficult, but not necessarily less likely. All the information systems in the universe may not prevent increases in casualties and destruction. In fact, information warfare may simply make WMD and other current technologies more valuable. A nuclear EMP burst could devastate the eyes and ears of any technology-dependent force and temporarily ground the entire inventory of long-range systems.[501] This realization should encourage a debate on the extent to which the United States should transform its military. Perhaps the United States should maintain a certain inventory of low-tech troops, ships, and analog systems that, like the apocryphal French colonial troops, could stand and fight while the electronic storm swirling around them blew over.

Other trends may require the expenditure of additional resources. But in the reality of defense resource constraints, the assignment of resources to take on a selected emerging threat means that there will be some threat not addressed. Perhaps, in accounting for risk, prudent defense planning requires the rejection of ever-increasing efficiencies. Not every trooper should be trained in urban warfare, even in the face of continuing urbanization. Not every corporal needs to be trained to the level of becoming a "strategic corporal" able to assume command of a squad under the most chaotic of conditions.

The debates that defense reviews engender are always messy. The media makes quite a sport of pointing out the conceptual disunity and lack of jointness among the "squabbling" services. Rarely mentioned is the fact that defense policy in a democracy was meant to be contentious and inefficient. To debate up until the very moment the guns sound was always considered a healthy thing. This is in clear contrast to the policies and procedures of authoritarian regimes. As Chinese Communist Party Chairman Deng Xiaoping advised his political and military strategists: "Don't debate . . . Once debate gets started, things become complicated."[502] But powerful militaries that don't debate, such as the German Wehrmacht or Soviet armed forces, seem to end up on the wrong side of history, defeated by a future they did not anticipate.

Americans like debate and generally view the future as complicated, even while striving to predict it. QDR 2001 will also be complicated, as will its successors. But one of the ways we can begin getting to the issues worthy of debate is to start from a consensus view of the characteristics we expect to find in the future security environment.

We can assess the likelihood of alternatives while remaining open to the discussion of the unlikely and unpopular. If this survey manages in some small measure to facilitate the assessment of the future security environment for QDR 2001, then it will have been well worth the effort. More importantly, if an assessment of the future security environment is taken seriously during the QDR in formulating defense policy and force structure recommendations—and not simply relegated to boilerplate in a report—the next presidential administration, and the Nation, will be well served.

We cannot predict all possible wars. But we must be able to survive them. And no one will survive without plans that include some comprehensive assumptions about the future security environment.

Primary Sources

Congressionally-Mandated

Department of Defense, *Report of the Quadrennial Defense Review*, May 1997. The section entitled "Global Security Environment" in the QDR report is summarized in chapter four of this survey (see especially pp. 32–36).

National Defense Panel, *Transforming Defense: National Security in the 21st Century*, December 1997. The panel was chartered to provide alternatives to recommendations of the QDR report, and reflected concern over defense transformation. The analysis provides a snapshot of defense requirements for 2020, and implicit forecasts appear throughout the report. However, a section of scenario-based hypotheses on security conditions in the 2010–2020 is also included (pp. 8–10).

Shaped Stability: The United States is engaged internationally with public support, and a high level of interagency cooperation. International economic cooperation increases global wealth. Cooperative security relationships are developed, and international law is generally observed. However, ethnic and nationalistic tensions, resource shortages, WMD proliferation, and demographic problems remain.

Extrapolation from Today: The global system is one of economic growth, but regionally uneven. Rogue states continue proliferating and posturing. United States remains the leading world power, but "its sustained political-economic-military dominance is uncertain."

Competition for Leadership: The resurgence of traditional balance-of-power with one or more powers (or an alliance) challenging the United States for dominance. New alliances and trading partnerships form; increased military spending and arms races develop. Humanitarian missions and peace operations dwindle in significance in comparison to readiness.

Chronic Crisis: The American public is preoccupied with domestic matters and perceives little chance of influencing the chaos abroad—nationalisms and ethnic hatreds, deteriorating global economic conditions, narcostates, etc.

Since the NDP's interest in fostering transformation appears to predate its futures assessment work, the linkage between the scenario building exercise and the force structure recommendation is not particularly explicit.

The U.S. Commission on National Security/21ˢᵗ Century, *New World Coming,* **September 15, 1999.** Largely the brainchild of then-Speaker of the House of Representatives, Congressman Newt Gingrich, the National Security Study (as it was orginally titled) was chartered by Secretary of Defense William Cohen in July 1998 using funding set aside in the FY98 defense budget. The study organization consists of two levels of participants. The commission members include fourteen prominent American leaders selected on a bipartisan basis. The original chairmen were former Senators David Boren and Warren Rudman. Before releasing *New World Coming,* Boren resigned and was replaced as co-chairperson by former Senator Gary Hart. A second level working group consists of noted scholars and subject matter experts as full time or part time professional staff. The executive director is General Charles Boyd, USAF (Ret.). The study is being completed in three phases: assessment of the future security environment (*New World Coming*), completed September 15, 1999; "seeking a national strategy," completed April 15, 2000; and "building for peace" (national security architecture recommendations), to be completed March 15, 2001.

The findings of the commission members are presented as "Major Themes and Implications" on pages 141–145 of *New World Coming.* The majority of the published text was prepared by the professional staff.

White House

A National Security Strategy for a New Century, **October 1998.** An annual report on the President's national security strategy was first mandated by Congress during the Reagan administration. It has since become the primary written public expression of the administration's objectives and actions in foreign affairs, and is intended to reflect the coordination of defense strategy, diplomacy, and international economic policy in maintaining national security. Drafted by the staff of the National Security Council, such a document is—as to be expected—used to highlight administration success and persuade Congress to support presidential policies.

The 1998 report reflected the conclusions of QDR 1997, and incorporated some of the QDR report language. Thus, the assumptions concerning the future security environment are similar in both reports. However, of interest is the blending of the Department of Defense perspective with those of the Departments of State, Treasury, Commerce, and other agencies involved with security issues. Unlike QDR 1997, assessment of the future security environment is not confined to a specific section, but is evident throughout the document.

A National Security Strategy for a New Century, **December 1999.** While espousing similar policy objectives, the 1999 version articulates a slightly modified vision in which the role of the United States as the mentor of international democratization is somewhat deemphasized and the positive effects of economic globalization (as an inevitable and relatively uncontrollable force) is asserted. Thus, the concept of the threat of potential disillusionment with slow-paced effects of democratic improvements in developing states is replaced by the fear of a growing backlash against economic globalization. Overall, the policies identified parallel the 1998 version, as would be expected late in the same administration's second term.

Intelligence Community

National Intelligence Council, *Global Trends 2010*, **November 1997.** *Global Trends 2010* represents the primary, unclassified, public consensus of the U.S. intelligence community. The National Intelligence Council includes 12 national intelligence officers drawn from the private sector as well as career intelligence officers, and is considered "one of the few bodies that can speak authoritatively on substantive issues for the Intelligence Community as a whole."[503] The assessment is the result of conference deliberations sponsored by NIC and the Institute for National Strategic Studies at National Defense University in 1996, as well as follow-on discussions chaired by Richard Cooper, then-Chairman of the NIC. The principal drafter was Barry Lowenkron. Original publication (limited to official use) was in February 1997.

Designed as the primary national intelligence input to QDR 1997's "The Global Security Environment" section, *Global Trends 2010* was released in an unclassified version in November 1997. The analysis combines estimates, trend-based forecasts, and some use of scenario building.[504] Implications of alternative trends are discussed, but the overall assumption is that there will be "no radical surprises."

The National Intelligence Council is currently embarked in development of a significant revision, *Global Trends 2015*, which is expected to be released before the start of QDR 2001.

Working papers, briefing materials and notes from "Alternative Global Futures: 2000–2015" workshops held September, October, and December 1999.[*] In preparing an update to *Global Trends 2010*, the National Intelligence Council has sponsored a series of three workshops bringing together selected scholars and mid-range government officials. Discussions were focused on futures scenario development based on the drivers of current and anticipated trends. In addition to briefing materials, over a dozen papers were presented by subject matter experts. A compilation of briefing materials, papers and personal notes were used for survey of this source.

Defense Intelligence Agency, *Alternative Futures in International Security Affairs, 2015: A Summary Study of the "Transformed World, 2015" Project* (prepared by Paul F. Herman), December 1997.[**] [Unclassified sections] Primarily directed by Paul F. Herman, a career intelligence officer, the project was a deliberate attempt to use intelligence assessments in constructing alternative futures rather than a futures estimate mode. The study bears a resemblance to Air Force 2025, particularly in the geometric expression of the intersections of alternative trends.

Office of the Secretary of Defense

Department of Defense, "The Projected Security Environment," from *Defense Planning Guidance Update for Fiscal Years 2001–2005* (Washington, April 1999): 4–7 [Unclassified section] The overall Defense Planning Guidance, which is the Secretary of Defense planning directive for development of the Defense program for resource allocation, is

---

[*] Global Trends 2015 project is still ongoing. Background and briefing material and discussion notes were used for the survey.

[**] Classified material from this project was not used by this survey.

classified Secret. However, "The Projected Security Environment" section is unclassified. The section identifies the following as security challenges the U.S. will continue to face in the future: (1) regional coercion or aggression, (2) proliferation of dangerous weapons and technologies, (3) terrorism and international crime, (4) threats to the U.S. homeland, (5) failed states and humanitarian disasters (expected between now and 2015), (6) asymmetric challenges, (7) wild cards (ranging "from the unanticipated emergence of new technologies to the loss of U.S. access to critical facilities and lines of communications in key regions, to the takeover of friendly regimes by hostile parties."), and (8) the potential for a global competitor (but not expected until after 2015).

Under Secretary of Defense (Policy), 1999 Summer Study Final Report, "Asia 2025" (Newport, RI: July 25–August 4, 1999). Assembled briefing slides and text of one of two summer studies by the Office of Net Assessment for 1999 focussing on future trends in Asia.

Under Secretary of Defense (Policy), 1999 Summer Study Final Report, "Maintaining U.S. Military Superiority" (Newport, RI: July 25–August 4, 1999). Assembled briefing slides and text of one of two Office of Net Assessment summer studies for 1999 focusing on the requirements needed to maintain U.S. military superiority.

Joint Chiefs of Staff/Unified Commands

Joint Staff, *Joint Strategy Review 1998 Report** (September 4, 1998). The Joint Strategy Review (JSR) produces an annual report intended provide the recommendations of the Director, Strategic Plans and Policy (J-5), to a series of joint strategic documents, including the Joint Staff-drafted National Military Strategy (NMS), the Chairman's Long-Range Vision (currently *JV2010*), and the Joint Planning Document (JPD)—which itself is the Joint Staff's official input to the overall DOD Defense Planning Guidance (DPG). Classified Secret, the report contains numerous Unclassified sections as well as an Unclassified transmittal letter. Traditionally, the JSR has been an update to the previous year's comprehensive look at potential security threats. However, recent reports have been specifically thematic in topic or methodology. The Joint Strategy Working Group was tasked

---

* Classified material from this project was not used by this survey.

with JSR 1998, which contained representatives from the services, CINCs, Defense Intelligence Agency, and Joint Staff, was directed to analyze the conclusions of the JSR 1997 report by creating five alternative future scenarios and testing their implications. This was the first time the JSR focused exclusively on scenario building, and reflected the fact that scenario building had come into vogue in DOD, as it had in contemporary corporate planning.

U.S. Joint Forces Command (J-9), "Futures Program" Briefs, November 1998–September 1999. U.S. Joint Forces Command (then known as U.S. Atlantic Command) was designated the Department of Defense executive agent for joint experimentation in 1988. As part of an effort to define the anticipated requirements for joint experimentation, the Commander-in-Chief, Admiral Harold W. Gehman, Jr., USN, directed the convocation of several workshops to assess future security threats and U.S. military responses. Workshops included representatives from the services, unified commanders-in-chief, and defense agencies. This "Joint Futures Program," facilitated by a defense contractor, resulted in a series of briefs and papers detailing desired operational capabilities for future systems useful in dealing with a series of regional warfighting scenarios. Primary focus was the assessment of future military technology and potential experiments that could facilitated advanced development of new systems. Since the program results are not contained in a single document, available briefing slides, conference notes, and concept papers were collectively surveyed.

National Defense University

Patrick M. Cronin, ed., *2015: Power and Progress* (Washington, D.C.: National Defense University Press, 1996). A product of the Institute for National Strategic Studies "Project 2025," this volume assessed the future security environment in terms of great power competition, environment degradation and resource scarcity, the formation of alliances and coalitions, and future trends in technology and warfare.

Institute for National Security Studies, *Strategic Assessment 1998: Engaging Power for Peace* (Washington, D.C.: National Defense University Press, 1998). This is the fourth volume in a series of annual assessments based on a particular theme of U.S. defense policy. The

---

* Classified material from this project was not used by this survey.

1998 study assesses the implications of the recommendations of the 1997 Quadrennial Defense Review (QDR), and is shaped along the concept of "Shape, Respond, Prepare." The "Alternative Futures" chapter forecasts: "Today's states are largely at peace with one another and likely to remain so through 2018. Nevertheless, militaries are designed for the exception, not the ordinary."

But the assessment "sketches a three dimensional space" of potential military challenges: (1) larger foes (a larger adversary than any current rogue state), (2) foes who have mastered nasty technologies, such as WMD or space and information warfare, and (3) "a profusion of messier situations" such as civil wars, ethnic cleansing, and politico-humanitarian disasters.

The study identifies "three transition states, China, Russia, and India," as possessing "the theoretical resources and sufficient independence of interest to become larger adversaries of the core states." However, "a *global* challenge to the United States is much less likely; that would take decades of military investment, practice in power projection, and a belief system that results in global interests—all of which no large transitional state possesses."

The study postulates that "nasty technologies of warfare" will spread faster due to globalization, will enhance area-denial strategies versus U.S. power projection, "could extract unacceptable casualties from military forces operating overseas," and could cause "potential threats against cities of core states, especially in North America, [to] have to be taken seriously." Nasty technologies can be defended against, but defenses could never be completely leak-proof. Information technology can be used to "undo the three pillars of the coalition victory in the Gulf: superior logistics, command-and-control warfare, and dominant maneuver." However the development of WMD or strategic delivery systems "is fraught with risks. The very activity gets one noticed and may lead to countermeasures by the United States and others before efforts have been completed."

The study emphasizes that "messier" situations/conflicts are manpower intensive and usually do not provide the opportunity for decisive victory.

Institute for National Strategic Studies, *Strategic Assessment 1999: Priorities for a Turbulent World* (Washington, D.C.: National Defense University Press, 1999). The fifth volume in the series, *Strategic Assessment 1999* adopts a somewhat more pessimistic tone than its predecessor, emphasizing (as suggested by its subtitle) the increase in failing states, potential regional competitors, and potential for chaotic world conditions. Emphasis is also placed on the effects of globalization.

Army

Army After Next Briefs on "Future Military Art." A series of briefings used to describe the expected future battlefield and military missions requiring Army transformation.

William T. Johnsen, *Force Planning Considerations for Army XXI* **(Carlisle, PA: U.S. Army War College, Strategic Studies Institute, February 18, 1998).** Provides an outline for the near-term (10–15 year) future security environment that influences the requirements for a modernizing U.S. Army.

Earl H. Tilford, Jr., ed., *World View: The 1998 Strategic Assessment From the Strategic Studies Institute* **(Carlisle, PA: U.S. Army War College, February 26, 1998).** An annual survey of current and future world trends. There was no version published in 1999.

Navy

CNO Strategic Studies Group XIV, *The International Security Environment to the Year 2005,* **study group final report (Newport, RI, June 1995).** The Strategic Studies Group (SSG) consists of 8–9 Navy and Marine O6's assigned for one year at the Naval War College, Newport, RI, to analyze a specific defense issue at the personal direction of the Chief of Naval Operations (CNO). The majority of SSG members are considered strong candidates for promotion to flag officer. The task given by CNO in 1994–95 was to consider "what elected leaders would ask the Naval services to do and how Americans expect it done" in the future.

As self-described, the study "departed from the customary practice of assessing extant trends, coupling them with new departures and melding them into a single predictive scenario." "Instead, the SSG relied upon methodology developed from corporate planning techniques (specifically, Royal Dutch Shell as articulated in Peter A. Schwartz, *The Art of the Long View*) to draw up scenarios for two alternative futures that plausibly bound the possibilities for the international security environment ten years hence."

Two alternative worlds were developed, X and Y. The X World is characterized as a "new Cold War" on a regional scale. The "dominating feature is the existence of clearly perceived threats from one of the great powers prompting defense planning and procurement to counter the threat." Worldwide, defense spending is a higher share of a lower GDP caused by lower growth and trade protectionism. Greater emphasis on regional balances of power; lower emphasis on north-south cooperation and environment. The Y World is characterized by lack of a great power threat, and increased multilateralism with "relative cooperation in the zones of peace but conflict in the zones of turmoil." Key features include: more open economic competition; greater economic growth; defense spending is a smaller portion of larger GDP due to lack of major power threat; and DOD is reliant on the civil sector for dual use technology while the defense industrial base is unprotected. "A permissive environment for transnational actors in terrorism and crime provokes international response, including an expanded role for international law." Environment and world development rise on the list of global concerns.

Richard Danzig, *The Big Three: Our Greatest Security Risks and How to Address Them* (Washington, D.C.: National Defense University Press, 1999). Written between his appointment as Undersecretary and Secretary of the Navy, Richard Danzig's "big three" security threats consist of: (1) a renewed major military competition along the lines of the Cold War; (2) the risk of traumatic attack using WMD; and (3) potential lack of domestic support for U.S. Armed Forces.

Marine Corps

Charles C. Krulak, "Ne Cras" ("Not Like Yesterday") Brief. When Krulak served as Commandant (1995–1999), this brief represented the Marine Corps view of the shape of future wars and its role in them. It takes its name from the reaction of Emperor Augustus to the complete loss of Quinctilius Varus legions to the Gauls while "hemmed in by forests and marshes and ambuscades."

Charles C. Krulak, "The Three Block War: Fighting in Urban Areas," speech presented at National Press Club, Washington, D.C. (October 10, 1997); published in *Vital Speeches of the Day* (December 15, 1997):

139–141. Remarks by Krulak to the National Press Club. In effect, it is a text version of the points of the "Ne Cras" brief.

Air Force

Joseph A. Engelbrecht, Jr., et al., *Alternative Futures for 2025: Security Planning to Avoid Surprise* (Maxwell Air Force Base, AL: Air University Press, September 1996). A significant effort at generating a complete range of alternative futures and describing their characteristics in detail. Alternative futures are discussed in a comparative format in terms of "plausible history;" nature of actors, international politics, U.S. national security strategy, humanity, technology, environment, the defense budget, U.S. military capabilities, and "implications." The six scenarios developed in detail are:

Gulliver's Travails: "a world of rampant nationalism, state and non-state-sponsored terrorism, and fluid coalitions."

Zaibatsu: "a world dominated by corporate economic interests" of multinational corporations.

Digital Cacophony: "a world completely enmeshed in technology" in which "the world struggles with rapid change and its effects."

King Khan: a world dominated by an Asian coalition led by China and including Singapore, Taiwan, Malaysia, Indonesia and Mongolia.

Halfs and Half-Naughts: a world in which turbulent, uneven economic changes have greatly magnified the gap between have and have-not nations.

2015 Crossroads: "a bridge designed to serve as a decision point from which the other alternative futures might be reached."

Federally-Funded Research Institutes

Zalmay Khalilzad and Ian O. Lesser, eds., *Sources of Conflict in the 21st Century: Regional Futures and U.S. Strategy* (Santa Monica, CA: RAND, 1998). Future security forecast developed on a region-by-region basis on contract to the U.S. Air Force.

Frederick Thompson et al., *Vision-21 Source Book Volume 1: The Process* (Alexandria, VA: Center for Naval Analyses, November 26, 1996). The Vision-21 project was conducted by the staff of the Center for Naval Analyses at the request of the Marine Corps. Additional participation was provided by the Marine Corps Combat Development

Command, Arlington Institute, and Applied Futures, Inc. Following a series of seminars and workshops involving 19 general officers, the Marine Corps adopted a vision statement that became a basis for their annual Commandant's Planning Guidance and Congressional confirmation testimony for the then-incoming commandant, General Charles C. Krulak. The deliberations of this project greatly influenced the "Ne Cras" briefing. Volume 1 outlines the assessment process and primary conclusions, as well as identifying the source material used in the deliberations.

Independent Research Institutes

Andrew F. Krepinevich, Jr., *The Conflict Environment of 2016: A Scenario-Based Approach* (Washington, D.C.: Center for Strategic and Budgetary Assessments, October 1996). Formerly known as the Defense Budget Project, CSBA identifies itself as an independent research institute that attempts "to make clear the inextricable link between near-term and long-range military planning and defense investment strategies." Krepinevich utilizes an alternative scenarios approach to develop four potential conflict scenarios for 2016: (1) great power competition between China and the United States and a blockade of Taiwan; (2) blockade of the Straits of Hormuz by Iran; (3) Russian pressure on Ukranian independence; (4) and the internal collapse of Indonesia.

Jacquelyn K. Davis and Michael J. Sweeney, *Strategic Paradigm 2025: U.S. Security Planning for a New Era* (Dulles, VA: Brassey's, 1999). *Strategic Paradigm 2025* stems from a series of three conferences sponsored in late 1998 by the Institute for Foreign Policy Analysis in association with the Fletcher School of Law and Diplomacy, Tufts University. The study identifies overall global trends, discusses individual trends, and assesses trends directly affecting future warfare. It then develops in detail four alternative paradigms (scenarios) of the world of 2025.

Paradigm A is a world in which a coalition of states has developed to oppose U.S. interests. Paradigm B postulates a world of multipolarity in which the United States does not have a direct military opponent, but competes economically and politically with five or six great powers. Paradigm C is a weak unipolarity system in which the United States remains the world's sole superpower without a direct competitor, but with five or six great powers in the background. Unlike in Paradigm B, the great powers have developed along democratic lines and are not openly hostile to U.S. interests. Paradigm D is a world of chaos in which the United States as sole superpower faces a world of increasing numbers of failed states and anarchy.

Davis and Sweeney conclude with a series of general observations and direct recommendations for future American security policies. As noted, the study is dismissive of the value of assessing wild cards in long-range planning.

Nongovernmental Organizations

Allen Hammond, *Which World? Scenarios for the 21st Century* (Washington, D.C.: Island Press/Shearwater Books, 1998). A scenario-based approach, *Which World?* analyzes resource and economic trends on a regional basis out to the year 2050. Under the motto "global destiny, regional choices," Hammond, a staff member of the World Resources Institute, identifies "trajectories," or alternative scenarios, for regional trends (demographic, environmental, economic, political, social, technological, and security-related) that lead to three alternative worlds:

Market World: A new age of overall global prosperity based on economic reform, technological innovation, and regional integration; but with same havenots along with the haves. This could be characterized as benign globalization.

Fortress World: Global economic downturn, cascading environmental problems, and social ills lead to regional instability, breakdowns in social order, and international conflict. Wealthy nations are generally able to protect themselves (as fortresses), but they too suffer effects due to negative aspects of globalization.

Transformed World: Positive social, political, and environmental conditions are achieved due to wise policies, the sharing of international power, new social organizations, and effective issue-based coalition building.

Which World? is designed to promote aspirations for a Transformed World, and is representative of the overall views of NGOs specializing on environmental and international social issues.

Edmund Cairns, *A Safer Future: Reducing the Human Cost of War* (Oxford: Oxfam Publications, 1997). Sponsored by Oxfam, Cairns' study is representative of the views of many humanitarian NGOs concerning the increasing brutality of warfare. Unlike forecasts of future high technology wars with less collateral damage, Cairns identifies a trend toward civil and internal wars in which civilians will be the primary targets and casualties. Cairns maintains that "modern conflict—if that is what we should call it—challenges the very distinction between war and peace... Many modern wars are fought in order not to change the government within an existing state, but to carve out a new state or quasi-state on behalf of only one particular ethnic group; or to cleanse the state of all but that group, usually for the benefit of a comparatively small elite within that group." The study implies that the ability of high technology militaries to intervene in preventing such atrocities may be limited, and recommends international reinforcement of the laws of war and imposition of international sanctions as possible approaches.

Michael Marien, ed., *World Futures and the United Nations* (Bethesda, MD: World Future Society, 1995). Described as "an annotated guide to 250 recent publications," Marien's volume is a survey and compilation of futures study work sponsored by the United Nations, UN-related agencies, and nongovernmental organizations supporting UN objectives or focused on the future of the United Nations. The publication is co-sponsored and published by the World Future Society, the largest public membership association on futures study in the United States. Marien is editor of the World Future Society's monthly *Future Survey*, generally accepted as the most thorough guide to current futures literature.

Independent Commission

Graham T. Allison and Robert Blackwill, lead authors, *America's National Interests* (The Commission on America's National Interests, July 2000). The Commission on America's National Interests, consisting of 23 prominent Americans, receives funding from the Hauser Foundation and institutional support from Harvard's Belfer Center for Science and International Affairs, the Nixon Center, and RAND. Similar in concept to the U.S. Commission on National Security/21st Century, this commission has greater academic representation among its principals, along with political leaders with specialized expertise in national security issues, such as former Senator Sam Nunn and Senator John McCain. For the purposes of their study, national interests are primarily defined in terms of foreign policy objectives. Six "cardinal challenges" for future American presidents are identified: (1) strengthen our strategic partnership with Japan and with European allies; (2) "facilitate China's entry onto the world stage without disruption;" (3) prevent loss of control over nuclear weapons and WMD proliferation; (4) prevent Russian authoritarianism or collapse; (5) maintain U.S. global leadership; and (6) marshal resources to promote freedom, peace, and prosperity throughout the world. The primary concern is that the "U.S. is in danger of losing its way" in foreign policy in the future security environment, becoming reactive and driven by the media and special interests.

Political Candidate

George W. Bush, "A Period of Consequences," speech delivered at The Citadel, Charleston, SC, September 23, 1999 (text from website). Texas Governor George W. Bush's speech at The Citadel is considered one of the significant statements of defense policy during the 1999–2000 presidential campaign. Outlining anticipated security threats of the 21st century, the speech emphasizes a greater need for homeland defense initiatives as well as a requirement for defense transformation in light of a coming "revolution in the technology of war." Governor Bush also articulated his view of a policy for selective engagement in order to reduce the operational tempo on the current military structure and reverse its negative effects on personnel retention and the lives of military families.

Private Business

www.stratfor.com, "Decade Forecast—Decade Through 2005," December 24, 1994 (remains currently available on website). The international affairs consulting and forecasting firm of Stratfor, Inc., better known as Stratfor.com, has been the most aggressive of web-based forecasters, providing daily assessments of world events and weekly assessments of political and economic conditions of various regions. Subscriptions to their breaking news-related forecasts are free and advertised as "delivering news at the speed of television with the depth of print."

The company is heavily influenced by the work of George Friedman and Meredith Lebard, focusing on the political-military implications of international economic competition, and regionalization as a force opposing globalization.

In addition to yearly forecasts and continuously updated information on international political and economic trends, Stratfor.com maintains a decade-long forecast, of which the 1994 version was the first. The 1994 version was included in the survey because of its relationship to the 1999 forecast, which is essentially an update.

www.stratfor.com, "Stratfor's Decade Forecast 2000–2010: A New Era In A Traditional World," December 20, 1999 (remains currently available on website). Current updated ten-year forecast. Themes include the question of how other countries can limit American power and control, the search for equilibrium in the international system, and global economic desynchronization.

Individual Contributions

Paul Bracken, *Fire in the East: The Rise of Asian Military Power and the Second Nuclear Age* (New York: HarperCollins, 1999). Paul Bracken, a professor at Yale University, former researcher with the Hudson Institute, and author of an influential Cold War-era book on the command and control of nuclear forces, has served on defense advisory boards, such as the Chief of Naval Operations Executive Panel. He has been a frequent participant in future security workshops. *Fire in the East* presents his research on the rise of Asian militaries, emphasizing the development of antiaccess strategies, weapons of mass destruction, and unique applications of older military technologies.

Ashton B. Carter and William J. Perry, *Preventive Defense: A New National Security Strategy for America* (Washington, D.C.: The Brookings Institution, March 1999). A book-long version of the "preventive defense" recommendation of two prominent former defense officials, this volume has had significant influence on the current national security debate. Former-Secretary of Defense Perry and former-Undersecretary Carter identify four dominant future threats to American security: a potentially hostile China, a potentially authoritarian Russia, WMD proliferation and "loose nukes," and WMD terrorism on U.S. soil.

Ralph Peters, *Fighting for the Future: Will America Triumph* (Mechanicsburg, PA: Stackpole Books, 1999). A recently retired Army officer, Ralph Peters is a novelist and a prolific commentator on military issues, often presenting what would be considered contrarian views. Peters has frequently made presentations at numerous futures workshops, including those sponsored by the U.S. Commission on National Security/21st

Century and National Intelligence Council. His writings emphasize a future world of warriors in which high-technology military platforms may have limited applicability, but may require greater assets for human intelligence collection (HUMINT) and a reinvigorated military ethos. *Fighting for the Future* is a collection of interlocking essays previously published in military policy journals, such as *Parameters*, focused on the question of whether U.S. military forces are optimized for future threats.

Donald M. Snow, *The Shape of the Future: World Politics in a New Century,* 3[d] ed. (Armonk, NY: M.E. Sharpe, 1999). Donald M. Snow is currently a professor at the University of Alabama. Having held faculty positions at the U.S. Army War College, Naval War College and Air War College and published over twenty books on national security issues over his career, he has influenced strategic thinking over several generations of military officers. *The Shape of the Future* is a significant update of a work started in 1991 focusing on the political, economic, and military dimensions of the post-Cold War world, utilizing estimates and forecasts.

Secondary Sources

"A Funding Imperative," *The Christian Science Monitor*, November 30, 1998, 10.

Agence France-Presse in Beijing, "Alliances Can Defuse Hegemonism By US," *South China Morning Post*, March 8, 2000.

Allen, Charles T., "Extended Conventional Deterrence: In from the Cold and Out of the Nuclear Fire?" *The Washington Quarterly* 17:3 (Summer 1994): 203–233.

Alberts, David S., John J. Gartska, and Frederick Stein, *Network Centric Warfare: Developing and Leveraging Information Superiority*, 2ᵈ ed. (Washington, D.C.: DOD C⁴ISR Cooperative Research Program, August 1999).

Amnesty International, *Amnesty International 1999 Annual Report: International Organizations* (www.amnesty.org/ailib/aireport/ar99/intorgs.htm).

Anderson, Jennifer, *The Limits of Sino-Russian Strategic Partnership*, International Institute for Strategic Studies, Adelphi Paper 315 (Oxford: Oxford University Press, December 1997).

Anderson, Walter Neal, *Overcoming Uncertainty: U.S.-Chinese Strategic Relations in the 21ˢᵗ Century*, INSS Occasional Paper 29 (U.S. Air Force Academy, CO: Institute for National Security Studies, October 1999).

Arquilla, John, and David Ronfeldt, "Cyberwar is Coming!" *Comparative Strategy* 12:2 (Spring 1993): 141–165.

Archer, Clive, *International Organizations* (London: University of Aberdeen, 1983).

Art, Robert J., "Geopolitics Updated: The Strategy of Selective Engagement," *International Security* 23:3 (Winter 1998/99): 83–85.

Baker, A. D., III, "World Navies in Review," U.S. Naval Institute *Proceedings* 126:3 (March 2000): 30–42.

Baker, Brent, "War and Peace in a Virtual World," U.S. Naval Institute *Proceedings* 123:4 (April 1997): 36–40.

Baker, Howard H., and Ellen L. Frost, "Rescuing the U.S.-Japanese Alliance," *Foreign Affairs* 71:2 (Spring 1992): 97–113.

Baker, James A., "America in Asia—Emerging Architecture for a Pacific Community," *Foreign Affairs* 70:5 (Winter 1991/92): 1–18.

Barnett, Roger W., "Information Operations, Deterrence, and the Use of Force," *Naval War College Review* 51:2 (Spring 1998): 7–19.

Barnett, Thomas P. M., "The Seven Deadly Sins of Network-Centric Warfare," U.S. Naval Institute *Proceedings* 125 (January 1999): 36–39.

Bartholet, Jeffrey, "A Return to Somalia," *Newsweek*, November 1, 1999, 50–51.

Beall, J. H., "Restore the Focus on Technology," U.S. Naval Institute *Proceedings* 126:6 (June 2000): 56–57.

Begert, William J., "Kosovo and Theater Air Mobility," *Aerospace Power Journal* 8:4 (Winter 1999): 11–22.

Bender, Bryan, "USA evaluating defences against nuclear terrorism," *Jane's Defence Weekly* 34:2 (July 12, 2000): 2.

Bergsten, C. Fred, and Marcus Nolan, *Reconcilable Differences?: United States-Japan Economic Conflict* (Washington, D.C.: Institute for International Economics, June 1993).

Bermudez, Joseph S., *A History of Ballistic Missile Development in the DPRK*, Center for Nonproliferation Studies Occasional Paper 2 (Monterey, CA: Monterey Institute of International Studies, November 1999).

Bernstein, Richard, and Ross H. Munro, "China I: The Coming Conflict with America," *Foreign Affairs* 76:2 (March/April 1997): 18–32.

———, *The Coming Conflict with China* (New York: Alfred A. Knopf, 1997).

Bi, Jianxiang, "Managing Taiwan Operations in the Twenty-first Century: Issues and Options," *Naval War College Review* 52 (Autumn 1999): 30–58.

Billigmeier, Scott, and Ed Glabus, "Future War: 'Information Operations Corps' Comes of Age," *Army* 47 (December 1997): 45–51.

Blaker, James R., "The American RMA Force: An Alternative to the QDR," *Strategic Review* 25 (Summer 1997): 29–36.

Blank, Stephen J., *The Dynamics of Russian Weapons Sales to China* (Carlisle, PA: U.S. Army War College, Strategic Studies Institute, March 4, 1997).

————, "Preconditions for a Russian RMA: Can Russia Make the Transition?" *National Security Studies Quarterly* 6:2 (Spring 2000): 1–28.

Bloomfield, Lincoln P., *The Management of Global Disorder: Prospects for Creative Problem Solving* (Lanham, MD: University Press of America, 1987).

Bond, Brian, *British Military Policy Between the Two World Wars* (Oxford: Clarendon Press, 1980).

Bond, Brian, and Williamson Murray, "The British Armed Forces, 1918–39," in Allen R. Millet and Williamson Murray, eds., *Military Effectiveness, Volume II: The Interwar Period* (Boston: Allen and Unwin, 1988): 98–130.

Bonnart, Frederick, "U.S. Starts to Fret Over EU Military Independence . . ." *International Herald Tribune*, May 24, 2000, 1.

Boorujy, James R., "Network-Centric Concepts Can Guarantee Access," U.S. Naval Institute *Proceedings* 126:5 (May 2000): 60–63.

Bowdish, Randall G., and Bruce Woodyard, "A Naval Concepts-Based Vision for Space," U.S. Naval Institute *Proceedings* 125 (January 1999): 50–53.

Bracken, Paul, "Sidewise Technology: A 21st Century Driver," unpublished paper prepared for the Alternative Global Futures 2015 Workshop, (Washington, D.C.: September 26–27, 1999).

Breemer, Jan, "The End of Naval Strategy: Revolutionary Change and the Future of American Naval Power," *Strategic Review* 22 (Spring 1994): 40–53.

Brown, Lester R., et al., *State of the World 2000* (New York: W.W. Norton, 2000).

Brown, Seyom, *The Causes and Prevention of War*, 2d ed. (New York: St. Martin's Press, 1994).

Bruger, Steven J., "Not Ready for the First Space War: What about the Second?" *Naval War College Review* 48 (Winter 1995): 73–83.

Brzezinski, Zbigniew, "Living With China," *The National Interest* 59 (Spring 2000): 5–22.

Builder, Carl H., *The Masks of War: American Military Styles in Strategy and Analysis* (Baltimore: Johns Hopkins University Press, 1989).

Butterworth, Fox, and Joseph Kahn, "Chinese Intellectuals in U.S. Say Spying Case Unfairly Cast Doubts on Their Loyalties, *The New York Times*, May 16, 1999, 1, 32.

Cable, James, *Navies In Violent Peace* (New York: St. Martin's Press, 1989).

Callum, Robert, "Will Our Forces Match the Threat," U.S. Naval Institute *Proceedings* 124 (August 1998): 50–53.

Cancian, Mark F., "Anthrax and the Internet," U.S. Naval Institute *Proceedings* 126 (May 2000): 42–46.

Carothers, Thomas, "Civil Society," *Foreign Policy* 117 (Winter 1999–2000): 18–24.

Cebrowski, Arthur K., and John J. Garstka, "Network-Centric Warfare: Its Origin and Future," U.S. Naval Institute *Proceedings* 124 (January 1998): 28–35.

Center for Counterproliferation Research, *The NBC Threat in 2025* (Washington, D.C.: National Defense University, 1997).

Chanda, Nayan, "Fear of the Dragon," *Far Eastern Review*, April 13, 1995, 24–28.

Chandler, Clay, "Talks Break Off on China Bid to Join WTO," *The Washington Post*, April 1, 2000, A15.

Chandler, Robert W., *Tomorrow's War, Today's Decisions* (McLean, VA: AMCODA Press, 1996).

Chandler, Robert W., with John R. Backschies, *The New Face of War: Weapons of Mass Destruction and the Revitalization of America's Transoceanic Military Strategy* (McLean, VA: AMCODA Press, 1998).

Chang, Felix K., "Conventional War Across the Taiwan Straits," *Orbis* 40:4 (Fall 1996): 577–608.

Chase, Robert S., Emily B. Hill, and Paul Kennedy, "Pivotal States and U.S. Strategy," *Foreign Affairs* 75 (January–February 1996): 33–51.

Chu, Henry, and Richard C. Paddock, "Russia Looks to China as an Ally Amid West's Ire," *Los Angeles Times*, December 8, 1999, 1

Claude, Inis L., *Swords Into Plowshares: The Problems and Progress of International Organization* (New York: Random House, 1971).

Cohen, Eliot A., ed., *Gulf War Air Power Survey: Volume II, Part II* (Washington, D.C.: Government Printing Office, 1993).

———, "The Mystique of U.S. Air Power," *Foreign Affairs* 73 (January/February 1994): 109–124.

———, "A Revolution in Warfare," *Foreign Affairs* 75 (March/April 1996): 37–54.

Cohen, Eliot A., Aaron L. Friedberg, and Stephen Peter Rosen, *The Future Security Environment and American Defense Planning* (John M. Olin Institute for Strategic Studies, November 1999).

Copper, John F., *Taiwan: Nation-State or Province?* 3^d ed. (Boulder, CO: Westview Press, 1999).

Cordesman, Anthony H., and Abraham R. Wagner, *The Lessons of Modern War, Volume Two: The Iran-Iraq War* (Boulder, CO: Westview Press, 1990).

———, *The Lessons of Modern War, Volume IV: The Gulf War* (Boulder, CO: Westview Press, 1996).

Cornish, Edward, et al., *The Study of the Future: An Introduction to the Art and Science of Understanding and Shaping Tomorrow's World* (Washington, D.C.: World Future Society, 1977).

Covault, Craig, "Desert Storm Reinforces Military Space Direction," *Aviation Week and Space Technology*, April 8, 1991, 42.

Covault, Craig, and David A. Fulgham, "Russian Stealth Bomber Design Work Underway," *Aviation Week and Space Technology*, April 10, 2000, 18.

Dahl, Erik J., "We Don't Need an IW Commander," *U.S. Naval Institute Proceedings* 125 (January 1999): 48–49.

Davies, Caroline, "Drinks, drugs, and terror-cocktail that turns boys into killers. Using children in combat has reached a horrifying scale in Africa," *The Daily Telegraph* (London): May 25, 2000, 4.

Dettmer, Jamie, "Requiem for a Heavyweight," *Insight on the News*, February 21, 2000, 22.

Diamond, Larry, "Is the Third Wave Over?" *Journal of Democracy* 7 (July 1996): 20–37.

Didsbury, Howard F., Jr., *Frontier of the 21st Century: Prelude to the New Millenium* (Bethesda, MD: World Future Society, 1999).

DiNardo, R. L., and Daniel J. Hughes, "Some Cautionary Thoughts on Information Warfare," *Airpower Journal* 9 (Winter 1995): 73.

Donnelly, John, "Haiti's Renewal Slow, and Painful Profound Misery Abounds as Foreign Powers Curtail Aid to Country," *The Boston Globe*, December 27, 1999, A1.

Doran, Charles F., "Why Forecasts Fail: The Limits and Potential of Forecasting in International Relations and Economics," *International Studies Review* 1:2 (Summer 1999): 11–42.

Dorgan, Michael, "Few surprised at firing of Los Alamos Scientist; 'Tip of iceberg' seen on Chinese spying," *Arizona Republic*, March 14, 1999, A17.

Downing, John, "A Japanese navy in all but name," *Jane's Navy International* 104:3 (April 1, 1999): 33.

Dudney, Robert S., "Battle of the F–22," *Air Force Magazine* 82:9 (September 1999): 16–17.

Dunlap, Charles J., Jr., "The Origin of the American Military Coup of 2012," *Parameters* 22:4 (Winter 1992–1993): 2–20.

———, "How We Lost the High-Tech War of 2007: A Warning From the Future," *The Weekly Standard*, January 29, 1996, 22–28.

———, "21st Century Land Warfare: Four Dangerous Myths," *Parameters* 27:3 (Autumn 1997): 27–37.

Dunn, Ashley, "The Cutting Edge: Virtual World Leads to Lonely Place, Study Says," *Los Angeles Times*, August 31, 1998, D1.

Ehlers, Vernon J., "Information Warfare and International Security," *The Officer* 75:8 (September 1999): 28–32.

Eikenberry, Karl W., "Does China Threaten Asia-Pacific Regional Stability," *Parameters* 25 (Spring 1995): 82–103.

Eland, Ivan, "Tilting at Windmills: Post-Cold War Threats to U.S. Security," *Policy Analysis* 332 (February 8, 1999); obtained from website www.cato.org.

Eriksson, E. Anders, "Information Warfare: Hype or Reality?" *The Nonproliferation Review* (Spring-Summer 1999): 57–64.

Esposito, John L. "The Islamic Factor," in Phebe Marr, ed., *Egypt at the Crossroads: Domestic Stability and Regional Role* (Washington, D.C.: National Defense University Press, 1999): 47–64.

Estes, Howell M., III, *United States Space Command Long Range Plan* (Peterson Air Force Base, CO: U.S. Space Command, March 1998).

Fahey, Liam, and Robert M. Randall, *Learning From the Future: Competitive Foresight Scenarios* (New York: John Wiley and Sons, 1998).

Falk, Richard A., *A Study of Future Worlds* (New York: Free Press, 1975).

Falk, Richard A., et al., eds., *The United Nations and a Just World Order* (Boulder, CO: Westview Press, 1991).

Fieldhouse, Richard, and Shunji Taoka, *Superpowers at Sea: An Assessment of the Naval Arms Race* (Oxford: Oxford University Press, 1989).

FitzSimonds, James R., and Jan M. van Tol, "Revolutions in Military Affairs," *Joint Force Quarterly* 4 (Spring 1994): 24–31.

Fowles, Jib, ed., *Handbook of Futures Research* (Westport, CT: Greenwood Press, 1978).

Frankel, Charles, "Avoiding Cosmic Catastrophe," *The Futurist* 34:4 (July–August 2000): 23–28.

Friedman, George, and Meredith Lebard, *The Coming War With Japan* (New York: St. Martin's Press, 1991).

Friedman, Norman, *World Naval Weapons Systems 1997–1998* (Annapolis, MD: Naval Institute Press, 1997).

———, "Steaming Into a New World," U.S. Naval Institute *Proceedings* 125:5 (May 1999): 53–59.

———, "The China Puzzle Continues to Baffle the West," U.S. Naval Institute *Proceedings* 126:3 (March 2000): 4–6.

Friedman, Thomas L., *The Lexus and the Olive Tree: Understanding Globalization* (New York: Farrar, Straus and Giroux, 1999).

———, "Was Kosovo World War III?" *The New York Times*, July 2, 1999, A17.

Fulghum, David A., "Air War in Chechnya Reveals Mix of Tactics," *Aviation Week and Space Technology* 152:7 (February 14, 2000): 76–77.

Funabashi, Yoichi, "Japan and the New World Order," *Foreign Affairs* 70:5 (Winter 1991/92): 58–74.

"Future Schlock?" *Foreign Policy* 113 (Winter 1998–99): 82.

Gamboa, John, "The Cost of Revolution," U.S. Naval Institute *Proceedings* 124 (December 1998): 58–61.

Ganguly, Sumut, "South Asia After the Cold War," *The Washington Quarterly* 15 (Autumn 1992): 173–184.

Garrity, Patrick J., "Implications of the Persian Gulf War for Regional Powers," *The Washington Quarterly* 16 (Summer 1993): 153–170.

Gatchel, Theodore L., *At the Water's Edge: Defending Against the Modern Amphibious Assault* (Annapolis, MD: Naval Institute Press, 1996).

Germain, Randall D., ed., *Globalization and its Critics: Perspectives from Political Economy* (New York: St. Martin's Press, 2000).

Gibish, Jane E., comp., *The New World Order: A Second Look* (Carlisle, PA: U.S. Army War College Library, August 1994).

"Globalisation and Tax," *The Economist* 354 (January 29, 2000): 64–68.

"Globalization Fear Runs Deep, Leaders Tell World Forum," *The Toronto Star*, May 24, 1998, B1.

Goldstein, Steve, "Pentagon Planners Gird For Cyber Assault," *The Philadelphia Inquirer*, December 1, 1999, 1.

Gompert, David C., *Right Makes Might: Freedom and Power in the Information Age*, McNair Paper 59 (Washington, D.C.: National Defense University Press, 1998).

Goure, Daniel, "The Resource Gap," *Armed Forces Journal International* 137 (May 2000): 38–42.

Graeves, Rebecca K., "Russia's Biological Weapons Threat," *Orbis* 43 (Summer 1999): 490–491.

Gray, Colin S., *The Geopolitics of the Nuclear Era: Heartland, Rimlands, and the Technological Revolution* (New York: Crane, Russack, 1977).

———, *House of Cards: Why Arms Control Must Fail* (Ithaca, NY: Cornell University Press, 1992).

———, "Combating Terrorism," *Parameters* 23 (Autumn 1993): 17–23.

Gregor, A. James, "Qualified Engagement: U.S. China Policy and Security Concerns," *Naval War College Review* 52:2 (Spring 1999): 74–75.

"Greenpeace's Risky Tactics," *St. Louis Post-Dispatch*, December 7, 1989, A35.

Griffiths, Sian, ed., *Predictions* (Oxford: Oxford University Press, 1999).

Gross, Daniel, "No Plan," U.S. Airways *Attaché* (December 1999): 14–16.

Grundhauser, Larry K., "Sentinels Rising: Commercial High-Resolution Satellite Imagery and Its Implications for U.S. National Security," *Airpower Journal* 12 (Winter 1998): 61–80.

Guehenno, Jean-Marie, "The Impact of Globalisation on Strategy," *Survival* 40 (Winter 1998–99): 5–19.

Hahn, Robert F., II, and Bonnie Jezior, "Urban Warfare and the Urban Warfighter of 2025," *Parameters* 29:2 (Summer 1999): 74–86.

Hallion, Richard P., *Control of the Air: The Enduring Requirement* (Bolling Air Force Base, D.C.: Air Force History and Museums Program, September 8, 1999).

Hammes, T. X., "War Isn't a Rational Business," U.S. Naval Institute *Proceedings* 124:7 (July 1998): 22–25.

Heilbroner, Robert, *Visions of the Future: The Distant Past, Yesterday, Today, Tomorrow* (New York: Oxford University Press, 1995).

Heinl, Robert D., *Dictionary of Military and Naval Quotations* (Annapolis, MD: Naval Institute Press, 1966).

Hirschfeld, Thomas, and W. Seth Carus, "We Need to Understand," U.S. Naval Institute *Proceedings* 123:2 (February 1997): 65–68.

Hoffman, F. G., *Decisive Force: The New American Way of War* (Westport, CT: Praeger, 1996).

———, "Countering Catastrophic Terrorism," *Strategic Review* (Winter 2000): 55–57.

Holbrooke, Richard, "Japan and the United States: Ending the Unequal Partnership," *Foreign Affairs* 70 (Winter 1991/92): 41–57.

"How North Vietnam Won the War," *The Wall Street Journal*, August 3, 1995, A8.

Hoyt, Edwin P., *Mussolini's Empire: The Rise and Fall of the Fascist Vision* (New York: John Wiley and Sons, 1994).

Huisken, Ronald, *The Origin of the Strategic Cruise Missile* (New York: Praeger, 1981).

Huntington, Samuel P., "Democracy's Third Wave," *Journal of Democracy* 2:2 (Spring 1991): 27–29.

———, "The Clash of Civilizations?" *Foreign Affairs* 72:3 (Summer 1993): 22–49.

———, *The Clash of Civilizations and the Remaking of World Order* (New York: Simon and Schuster, 1996)

————, "The West and the World," *Foreign Affairs* 75:6 (November/December 1996): 28–46.

Hyten, John E., *A Sea of Peace or a Theater of War: Dealing with the Inevitable Conflict in Space*, ACDIS Occasional Paper (Champaign, IL, University of Illinois at Urbana-Champaign, April 2000).

Ignatieff, Michael, *Virtual War: Kosovo and Beyond* (New York: Metropolitan Books/Henry Holt and Company, 2000).

Ikle, Fred C., "Comrades in Arms: The Case for a Russian-American Defense Community," *National Interest* 26 (Winter 1991/92): 22–32.

Institute for National Strategic Studies, *The United States and India in the Post-Soviet World* (Washington, D.C.: National Defense University Press, 1993).

Isby, David C., "Russia's once-revered spetsnaz look to rally after Chechnia," *Jane's Intelligence Review* 9 (December 1, 1997): 534–537.

Ishihara, Shintaro, *The Japan That Can Say No* (New York: Simon and Schuster, 1991).

Jenkins, James T., "Use Technology... But Don't Trust It!" U.S. Naval Institute *Proceedings* 124:8 (August 1998): 69–70.

Joergensen, Tim Sloth, "U.S. Navy Operations in Littoral Waters: 2000 and Beyond," *Naval War College Review* 51:2 (Spring 1998): 20–29.

Johnson, Dana J., Scott Pace, and C. Bryan Gabbard, *Space: Emerging Options for National Power* (Santa Monica, CA: RAND, 1998): 31–32.

Johnson, Jay L., "Numbers Do Matter," U.S. Naval Institute *Proceedings* 125 (November 1999): 32.

Johnstone, Chris B., "Redefining the U.S.-Japan Alliance," *Survival* 42 (Spring 2000): 173–181.

Joseph, Robert G., and John F. Reichart, *Deterrence and Defense in a Nuclear, Biological, Chemical Environment*, Occasional Paper of the Center for Counterproliferation Research (Washington, D.C.: National Defense University, 1995).

Joseph, Robert G., and Ronald F. Lehman II, project directors, *U.S. Nuclear Policy in the 21st Century*, Final Report (Washington, D.C.: National Defense University/Lawrence Livermore National Laboratory, 1998).

Kagan, Frederick W., "Star Wars in Real Life: Political Limitations on Space Warfare," *Parameters* 28 (Autumn 1998): 117–118. *Parameters* 29 (Summer 1999): 74–86.

Kagan, Robert, "How China Will Take Taiwan," *The Washington Post*, March 12, 2000, B7.

Kahn, Herman, *Thinking About the Unthinkable In the 1980s* (New York: Simon and Schuster, 1984).

Kaldor, Mary, *New and Old Wars: Organized Violence in a Global Era* (Stanford, CA: Stanford University Press, 1999).

Khalilzad, Zalmay M., and John P. White, eds., *The Changing Role of Information in Warfare* (Santa Monica, CA: RAND, 1999).

Kirk, Don, "New Missile Reported in North Korea," *International Herald Tribune*, February 19–20, 2000, 1.

Klain, David R., "Are We Ready for Tomorrow?" U.S. Naval Institute *Proceedings* 122:4 (April 1996): 55–56.

Klarreich, Kathie, "The legacy of US, UN intervention in Haiti," *The Christian Science Monitor*, March 30, 2000, 7.

Koch, Andrew, "USA rethinks Libya's status," *Jane's Defence Weekly* 34:3 (19 July 2000): 22–23.

Kosnick, Mark E., "The Military Response to Terrorism," *Naval War College Review* 53:2 (Spring 2000): 13–39.

Krasner, Stephen, ed., *International Regimes* (Ithaca, NY: Cornell University Press, 1983).

Krepinevich, Andrew F., Jr., "Calvary to Computer: The Patterns of Military Revolutions," *The National Interest* 37 (Fall 1994): 30–42.

————, *Restructuring for a New Era: Framing the Roles and Missions Debate* (Washington, D.C.: Defense Budget Project, April 1995).

————, "Military Experimentation—Time to Get Serious," www.csba-home.org, March 3, 2000.

Kugler, Richard L., "Nonstandard Contingencies for Defense Planning," in Paul K. Davis, ed., *New Challenges for Defense Planning: Rethinking How Much Is Enough* (Santa Monica, CA: RAND, 1994): 165–196.

Kull, Steven, I. M. Destler, and Clay Ramsey, *The Foreign Policy Gap: How Policymakers Misread the Public* (College Park, MD: Center for International and Security Studies at Maryland University, 1997).

Kurth, James, "American Strategy in the Global Era," *Naval War College Review* 53 (Winter 2000): 7–24.

Laird, Robbin F., and Holger H. Mey, *The Revolution in Military Affairs: Allied Perspectives*, McNair Paper 60 (Washington, D.C.: National Defense University Press, 1999).

Landersman, Stuart D., "Sulfur, Serpents, and Sarin," U.S. Naval Institute *Proceedings* 124.8 (August 1998): 42–43.

Leebaert, Derek, ed., *Soviet Military Thinking* (London: George Allen and Unwin, 1981).

Lewis, William H., and Edward Marks, *Searching for Partners: Regional Organizations and Peace Operations,* McNair Paper 58 (Washington, D.C.: National Defense University Press, 1998).

Libicki, Martin, "Rethinking War: The Mouse's New Roar?" *Foreign Policy* 117 (Winter 1999/2000): 30–43.

Linden, Eugene, *The Future in Plain Sight: Nine Clues to the Coming Instability* (New York: Simon and Schuster, 1998).

Luryi, Surge, Jimmy Xu, and Alex Zaslavsky, *Future Trends in Microelectronics: The Road Ahead* (New York: John Wiley and Sons, 1999).

Luttwak, Edward N., *The Grand Strategy of the Roman Empire: From the First Century A.D. to the Third* (Baltimore: Johns Hopkins University Press, 1976).

———, "Toward Post-Heroic Warfare," *Foreign Affairs* 74:3 (May/June 1995): 109–122.

———, "Give War a Chance," *Foreign Affairs* 78:4 (July/August 1999): 36–44.

MacDonald, D. H. L., "TBMD Could Backfire," U.S. Naval Institute *Proceedings* 124:4 (April 1998): 80–83.

MacKinnon, Darrin W. S., "The Asian Anchor," U.S. Naval Institute *Proceedings* 124:9 (September 1998): 62–66.

Mahnken, Thomas G., "America's Next War," *The Washington Quarterly* 16:3 (Summer 1993): 171–184.

———, "Deny U.S. Access?" U.S. Naval Institute *Proceedings* 124:9 (September 1998): 36–39.

Mann, Charles C., "The End of Moore's Law," *Technology Review*, May/June 2000 (published by M.I.T. at www.techreview.com/articles/may00/mann.htm).

Marghella, Pietro, "December 7, 1999: The Second, Silent Attack on Pearl," U.S. Naval Institute *Proceedings* 125 (May 1999): 60–65.

Martin, Edward L., "The Evolving Missions and Forces of the JMSDF," *Naval War College Review* 68 (Spring 1995): 39–67.

Matthews, Lloyd J., *Challenging the United States Symmetrically and Asymmetrically: Can America Be Defeated?* (Carlisle Barracks, PA: U.S. Army War College, Strategic Studies Institute, July 1998).

Mazarr, Michael J., "Nuclear Weapons After the Cold War," *The Washington Quarterly* 15:3 (Summer 1992): 185–201.

———, "Clinton Foreign Policy, R.I.P.," *The Washington Quarterly* 21:2 (Spring 1998): 11–14.

———, *Global Trends 2005: An Owner's Manual for the Next Decade* (New York: St. Martin's Press, 1999).

McKenzie, Kenneth F., "Beyond Luddites and Magicians: Examining the MTR," *Parameters* 25:2 (Summer 1995): 15–21.

———, *The Revenge of the Melians: Asymmetric Threats and the Next QDR*, McNair Paper 62 (Washington, D.C.: National Defense University Press, 2000).

Mearsheimer, John J., *Conventional Deterrence* (Ithaca, NY: Cornell University Press, 1983).

Megargee, Geoffrey P., *Inside Hitler's High Command* (Lawrence, KS: University Press of Kansas, 2000).

Menon, Rajan, "The Strategic Convergence Between Russia and China," *Survival* 39:2 (Summer 1997): 101–125.

Metz, Steven, *Strategic Horizons: The Military Implications of Alternative Futures* (Carlisle, PA: U.S. Army War College, March 7, 1997).

Miskel, James, "Are We Learning the Right Lessons from Africa's Humanitarian Crises?" *Naval War College Review* 52:3 (Summer 1999): 136–147.

Modis, Theodore, *Predictions: Society's Telltale Signature Reveals the Past and Forecasts the Future* (New York: Simon and Schuster, 1992).

Molander, Roger C., David A. Mussington, and Richard F. Mesic, *Strategic Information Warfare Rising* (Washington, D.C.: RAND, 1998).

Momiyama, Thomas S., "Russia, Inc.—Open for Business," U.S. Naval Institute *Proceedings* 122 (February 1996): 66–69.

Mueller, John, "The Escalating Irrelevancy of Nuclear Weapons," in T.V. Paul, Richard J. Harknett, and James J. Wirtz, *The Absolute Weapon Revisited: Nuclear Arms and the Emerging International Order* (Ann Arbor, MI: University of Michigan Press, 1998): 73–98.

Mufson, Steven, "What's In A Name? U.S. Drops Term 'Rogue State,'" *The Washington Post,* June 20, 2000, 16.

"NMD: The Hard Sell," *Jane's Defence Weekly* 33 (15 March 2000): 19–23.

Nolan, Marcus, "Why North Korea Will Muddle Through," *Foreign Affairs* 76:4 (July/August 1997): 105–118.

North, Robert C., *War, Peace, Survival: Global Politics and Conceptual Synthesis* (Boulder, CO: Westview Press, 1990).

Novichkov, Nickolai, "Four Sovremennys in total for Beijing," *Jane's Defence Weekly* 33 (March 15, 2000): 12.

Nugroho, Anton, "The Dragon Looks South," *U.S. Naval Institute Proceedings* 126:3 (March 2000): 74–76.

Nye, Joseph S., Jr., "What New World Order?" *Foreign Affairs* 71:2 (Spring 1992): 83–96.

———, "Redefining the National Interest," *Foreign Affairs* 78:4 (July/August 1999): 22–35

Nye, Joseph S., Jr., and William A. Owens, "America's Information Edge," *Foreign Affairs* 75:2 (March/April 1996): 20–36.

O'Hanlon, Michael E., "Can High Technology Bring U.S. Troops Home?" *Foreign Policy* 113 (Winter 1998–99): 72–86.

———, *Technological Change and the Future of Warfare* (Washington, D.C.: The Brookings Institution, 2000).

"Operating Abroad," *Air Force Magazine* 81 (December 1998): 28–29.

Orszag-Land, Thomas, "How to Keep Soviet Science Out of the Wrong Hands," *The Christian Science Monitor,* November 8, 1995, 10.

Owens, Mackubin Thomas, "Technology, the RMA, and Future War," *Strategic Review* 26:2 (Spring 1998): 63–70.

———, "In Defense of Classical Geopolitics," *Naval War College Review* 52:4 (Autumn 1999): 59–76.

Owens, William A., with Ed Offley, *Lifting the Fog of War* (New York: Farrar, Straus and Giroux, 2000).

Peeters, Peter, *Can We Avoid a Third World War Around 2010?* (New York: Holmes and Meier Publishers, 1979).

Peters, Katherine McIntire, "Split Decision," *Government Executive*, October 1999, 43–48.

Peters, F. Whitten, "Whit Peters on the Issues," *Air Force Magazine* 82 (October 1999): 47.

Petersen, John L., *The Road to 2015: Profiles of the Future* (Corte Madre, CA: Waite Group Press, 1994).

———, *Out of the Blue: Wild Cards and Other Big Future Surprises* (Washington, D.C.: Arlington Institute, 1997).

———, "Info War: The Next Generation," U.S. Naval Institute *Proceedings* 123 (January 1999).

Pillsbury, Michael, ed., *Chinese Views of Future Warfare*, revised edition (Washington, D.C.: National Defense University Press, 1998).

———, *China Debates the Future Security Environment* (Washington, D.C.: National Defense University Press, 2000).

Pine, Art, "U.S. Targets Heart of Terror," *Los Angeles Times*, August 21, 1998, A1.

Podlesny, Robert E., "MOUT: The Show Stopper," U.S. Naval Institute *Proceedings* 124:2 (February 1998): 51–55.

———, "Infrastructure Networks Are Key Vulnerabilities," U.S. Naval Institute *Proceedings* 125:2 (February 1999): 51–53.

Pohde, William E., "What is Information Warfare?" U.S. Naval Institute *Proceedings* 122:2 (February 1996): 36–38.

Pollack, Jonathan D., and Chung Min Lee, *Preparing for Korean Unification: Scenarios and Implications* (Santa Monica, CA: RAND, 1999).

Porch, Douglas, "The Taiwan Strait Crisis of 1996: Strategic Implications for the United States Navy," *Naval War College Review* 52 (Summer 1999): 15–48.

Postel, Sandra, *Pillar of Sand: Can the Irrigation Miracle Last?* (New York: W.W. Norton, 1999).

Powers, William, "Information Waterbugs," *National Journal* 31:49 (December 4, 1999): 3458–3461.

"Ram Passes OpEval," U.S. Naval Institute *Proceedings* 126:4 (April 2000): 6.

Ranft, Bryan, and Geoffrey Till, *The Sea in Soviet Strategy* (Annapolis, MD: Naval Institute Press, 1983).

Reese, David, *The Prospects for North Korea's Survival*, International Institute for Strategic Studies, Adelphi Paper 323 (Oxford: Oxford University Press, November 1998).

Rempt, Rodney P., "We're in the Enemy's Backyard," U.S. Naval Institute *Proceedings* 127:7 (July 1999): 43–46.

Richter, Andrew, "The American Revolution? The Response of the Advanced Western States to the Revolution in Military Affairs," *National Security Studies Quarterly* 5:4 (Autumn 1999): 1–28.

Richter, Paul, "U.S. Says Raids A Success," *Los Angeles Times*, August 22, 1998, A1.

——, "Sudan Attack Claims Faulty, U.S. Admits," *Los Angeles Times*, September 1, 1998, A1.

Roberts, Brad, "1995 and the End of the Post-Cold War Era," *The Washington Quarterly* 18 (Winter 1995): 5–25.

Roberts, Brad, Robert A. Manning, and Ronald N. Montaperto, "China: The Forgotten Nuclear Power," *Foreign Affairs* 79:4 (July/August 2000): 53–63.

Robertson, Brian, "Security Cooperation in Asia Pacific," U.S. Naval Institute *Proceedings* 122:3 (March 1996): 65–68.

Rodenbeck, Max, "Is Islamism Losing Its Thunder?" *The Washington Quarterly* 21:2 (Spring 1998): 177–194.

Rohrabacher, Dana, "Q: Should Congress be concerned about China and the Panama Canal?" *Insight on the News*, December 27, 1999, 40.

Rona, Thomas P., "Deception and the Formulation of National Intelligence Estimates," in Brian D. Dailey and Patrick J. Parker, *Soviet Strategic Deception* (Lexington, MA: Lexington Books, 1987): 487–508.

Roncolato, Gerard, "Methodical Battle: Didn't Work Then... Won't Work Now," U.S. Naval Institute *Proceedings* 122:2 (February 1996): 32–33.

Rosenau, James N., *Turbulence in World Politics: A Theory of Change and Continuity* (Princeton: Princeton University Press, 1990).

Rosenau, James N., and Ernst-Otto Czempiel, *Governance Without Government: Order and Change in World Politics* (New York: Cambridge University Press, 1992).

Ross, Robert S., "China II: Beijing as a Conservative Power," *Foreign Affairs* 76:2 (March/April 1997): 33–44.

Russett, Bruce, *Grasping the Democratic Peace: Principles for the Post-Cold War World* (Princeton: Princeton University Press, 1993).

"Russia's Chechen War: Second Time Lucky?" *Jane's Defence Weekly* 33 (March 8, 2000): 32–36.

Sagan, Scott D., "The Commitment Trap: Why the United States Should Not Use Nuclear Threats to Deter Biological and Chemical Weapons Attacks," *International Security* 24 (Spring 2000): 85–115.

Sagan, Scott D., and Kenneth N. Waltz *The Spread of Nuclear Weapons: A Debate* (New York: W.W. Norton, 1995).

Segal, Gerald, "What China Threat?" *Foreign Affairs* 78 (September/October 1999): 24–36.

Scalapino, Robert A., "The United States and Asia: Future Prospects," *Foreign Affairs* 70 (Winter 1991/92): 19–40.

Scales, Robert H., Jr., "The Indirect Approach: How U.S. Military Forces Can Avoid the Pitfalls of Future Urban Warfare," *Armed Forces Journal International* 136 (October 1998): 68–74.

———, *Future Warfare* (Carlisle Barracks, PA: U.S. Army War College, 1999).

———, "Russia's Clash in Chechnya: Implications for Future War," *National Security Studies Quarterly* 6:2 (Spring 2000): 49–58.

Schroeder, Paul W., "Rediscovering the New World Order: A Historical Perspective," *The Washington Quarterly* 17:2 (Spring 1994): 25–43.

Scheer, Robert, *With Enough Shovels: Reagan, Bush, and Nuclear War* (New York: Random House, 1982).

Schmalz, Jeffrey, "After Skirmish with Protestors, Navy Tests Missile," *The New York Times*, December 5, 1989, A1.

Schmitt, Gary, and Thomas Donnelly, "Our Interests Lie With Theirs," *The Washington Post*, April 23, 2000, B4.

Schnurrpusch, Gary W., "Asian Crisis Spurs TBMD," *U.S. Naval Institute Proceedings* 125:9 (September 1999): 46–49.

Schoettle, Peter, "Key Geostrategic Trends: A Cloudy Crystal Ball," *Naval War College Review* 48 (Winter 1995): 63–72.

Schwartz, Peter A., *The Art of the Long View* (New York: Currency Doubleday, 1996).

Shambaugh, David, "China's Military Views the World: Ambivalent Security," *International Security* 24:3 (Winter 1999/2000): 52–79.

———, "Sino-American Strategic Relations: From Partners to Competitors," *Survival* 42 (Spring 2000): 97–115.

Sheldon, Raymond S., "No Democracy Can Feel Secure," U.S. Naval Institute *Proceedings* 124:8 (August 1998): 39–44.

"Ship rams Greenpeace; sub unleashes Trident 2," *The San Diego Union Tribune*, December 5, 1989, A-10.

Sidhu, Waheguru Pal Singh, *Enhancing Indo-U.S. Strategic Cooperation*, International Institute for Strategic Studies, Adelphi Paper 313 (Oxford: Oxford University Press, September 1997).

Siegrist, David W., and Janice M. Graham, *Countering Biological Terrorism in the U.S.: An Understanding of Issues and Status* (Dobbs Ferry, NY: Oceana Publications, 1999).

Singh, Sanjay, "Indian Ocean Navies—Learn from War," U.S. Naval Institute *Proceedings* 118:3 (March 1992): 51–54

"Sins of the Secular Missionaries," *The Economist* 354 (January 29, 2000): 25–27.

Smith, W. Y., "U.S. National Security After the Cold War," *The Washington Quarterly* 15:4 (Autumn 1992): 23–34.

Sokolski, Henry D., ed., *Prevailing in a Well-Armed World: Devising Competitive Strategies Against Weapons Proliferation* (Carlisle, PA: U.S. Army War College, March 2000).

Solarz, Stephen J., and Michael E. O'Hanlon, "Humanitarian Intervention: When is Force Justified?" *The Washington Quarterly* 20 (Autumn 1997): 3–14.

Spacey, William L., II, *Does the United States Need Space-Based Weapons?*, Cadre Paper 4 (Maxwell Air Force Base, AL: Air University Press, September 1999).

Sprinzak, Ehud, "The Great Superterrorism Scare," *Foreign Policy* 112 (Fall 1998): 110–119.

Staar, Richard F., *The New Military in Russia: Ten Myths that Shape the Image* (Annapolis, MD: Naval Institute Press, 1996).

Starobin, Paul, "What Went Wrong," *National Journal* 49 (December 1999): 3451–53.

Stauffer, Don, "Electronic Warfare: Battles Without Bloodshed," *The Futurist* 34 (January–February 2000): 23–26.

Stevens, Pete, "The Silence of the Labs," U.S. Naval Institute *Proceedings* 126 (June 2000): 96.

Stokes, Mark A., *China's Strategic Modernization: Implications for the United States* (Carlisle, PA: U.S. Army War College, Strategic Studies Institute, 1999).

stratfor.com, "Global Intelligence Update—January 6, 2000" (website, posted January 5, 2000).

———, "Herding Pariahs: Russia's Dangerous Game," Stratfor.com Weekly Global Intelligence Update, February 8, 2000.

———, "The Geopolitics of Fidel," Stratfor.com Weekly Global Intelligence Update, April 10, 2000.

———, "I Love You and the Problem of Cyberforce," May 15, 2000, 3.

———, "Global Intelligence Update—5 June 2000; Retrieving the Irretrievable: The Clinton Foreign Policy Legacy," June 4, 2000.

———, "Russian Military Quarrel Winds Down," Stratfor.com Weekly Global Intelligence Update, August 2, 2000.

Sullivan, John D., "Democracy and Global Economic Growth," *The Washington Quarterly* 15:2 (Spring 1992): 175–186.

Sullivan, Kevin, "North Korea Says It Is Running Out of Food," *The Washington Post*, March 3, 1998, 11.

Summers, Harry G., Jr., *The New World Strategy: A Military Policy for America's Future* (New York: Simon and Schuster, 1995).

Sun Tzu, *The Art of War*, trans. by Samuel B. Griffith (London: Oxford University Press, 1963).

Talbot, David, and Ed Hayward, "Students say focus is studies, not spying," *The Boston Herald*, May 26, 1999, 030.

Tangredi, Sam J., "Naval Strategy and Arms Control," *The Washington Quarterly* 14:3 (Summer 1991): 201–209.

————, "The Fall and Rise of Naval Forward Presence," U.S. Naval Institute *Proceedings* 126:5 (May 2000): 28–32.

Tanter, Raymond, *Rogue Regimes: Terrorism and Proliferation* (New York: St. Martin's Press, 1998).

"The Access Issue," *Air Force Magazine* 81 (October 1998): 42–46.

Thomas, Timothy L., "The Battle for Grozny: Deadly Classroom for Urban Combat," *Parameters* 29:2 (Summer 1999): 87–102.

Tilford, Earl H., Jr., *The Revolution in Military Affairs: Prospects and Cautions* (Carlisle, PA: U.S. Army War College, Strategic Studies Institute, June 23, 1995).

Tipak, John A., "Can the Fighter Force Hold Its Edge?" *Air Force Magazine* 83 (January 2000): 25–31.

Train, John, "Foreign Intelligence Penetration," *Strategic Review* 27:4 (Fall 1999): 78–79.

Trottier, Dave, "The Emerging 21st Century Force Structure Paradigm" (unpublished paper, National War College, 2000).

Tsouras, Peter G., *Warrior's Words* (London: Cassell, 1992).

Tucker, David, "Fighting Barbarians," *Parameters* 28:2 (Summer 1998): 69–79.

United States Advisory Panel to Assess Domestic Response Capabilities for Terrorism Involving Weapons of Mass Destruction, *First Annual Report: Assessing the Threat* (Washington, D.C.: RAND, December 15, 1999).

United States Air Force, *Information Operations*, Air Force Doctrine Document 2–5 (August 5, 1998).

United States Commission on National Security/21st Century [Philip L. Ritcheson, primary author], "Study Addendum" to *New World Coming* (published on website only; not released with report text): September 15, 1999.

United States, Congressional Research Service, CRS Report to Congress 97–75 ENR by Zachary S. Davis, *Weapons of Mass Destruction: New Terrorist Threat?* (Washington, D.C.: Congressional Research Service, January 8, 1997).

United States, General Accounting Office, *Information Superhighway: An Overview of Technology Challenges*, Report to Congress GAO/AIMD–95–23, January 23, 1995.

United States, General Accounting Office, *Nuclear Nonproliferation: Concerns With DOE's Efforts to Reduce the Risks Posed by Russia's Unemployed Weapons Scientists* (Washington, D.C.: Report to the Chairman, Committee on Foreign Relations, U.S. Senate, February 1999).

United States, House of Representatives, 105th Cong., 2d Sess., *Report of the Select Committee on U.S. National Security and Military/Commercial Concerns With the People's Republic of China*, Report 105–851 (Washington, D.C.: Government Printing Office, 1999).

United States, House of Representatives, 106th Cong., 1st Sess., *National Defense Authorization Act for Fiscal Year 2000* (Conference Report to Accompany S. 1059): August 6, 1999.

United States, Joint Chiefs of Staff, *Joint Vision 2010* (Washington, D.C.: Department of Defense, 1996).

United States, Joint Chiefs of Staff, *National Military Strategy of the United States—Shape, Respond, Prepare Now: A Military Strategy for a New Century* (Washington, D.C.: Department of Defense, 1997).

United States, Joint Chiefs of Staff, *Joint Doctrine for Command and Control Warfare*, Joint Pub. 3-13.1 (Washington, D.C.: Department of Defense, February 7, 1996).

United States, Office of Naval Intelligence, *Challenges to Naval Expeditionary Warfare* (Washington, D.C.: Office of Naval Intelligence, 1997).

United States, Office of the Secretary of Defense, Defense Science Board, *1997 DSB Summer Study: DOD Responses to Transnational Threats*, Volume 1–Final Report (December 9, 1997).

United States, Office of the Under Secretary of Defense for Acquisition and Technology, *Defense Science Board 1997 Summer Study Task Force on DOD Responses to Transnational Threats* (Washington, D.C.: Department of Defense, October 1997).

van Creveld, Martin, *The Rise and Decline of the State* (Cambridge: Cambridge University Press, 1999).

Van Riper, Paul K., and Robert H. Scales, Jr., "Preparing for War in the 21st Century," *Strategic Review* 25 (Summer 1997): 14–20.

Van Riper, Paul K., and F. G. Hoffman, "Pursuing the Real Revolution in Military Affairs: Exploiting Knowledge-Based Warfare," *National Security Studies Quarterly* 4 (Summer 1998): 1–19.

Vandergriff, Donald E., "truth@readiness.mil," U.S. Naval Institute *Proceedings* 125 (June 1999): 56–60.

Varney, James, "Democracy Falters and Haiti Flirts With Chaos: A Nation in Tatters," *New Orleans Times-Picayune*, March 12, 2000, A01.

Vego, Milan N., *Naval Strategy and Operations in Narrow Seas* (Portland, OR: Frank Cass Publishers, 1999).

Veit, Petert, ed., *Africa's Valuable Assets: A Reader in Natural Resource Management* (Washington, D.C.: World Resources Institute, 1998).

Vogt, Larry G., "China's Strategic Seapower," *The Submarine Review*, July 1997, 47–56.

Wack, Pierre, "The Gentle Art of Reperceiving" (article in two parts) *Harvard Business Review* 85 (September–October 1985): 73–89; 85 (November–December 1985): 139–150.

Wallace, William, and Jan Zielonka, "Misunderstanding Europe," *Foreign Affairs* 77:6 (November–December 1998): 65–79.

Wallerstein, Immanuel, *The Capitalist World Economy* (Cambridge: Cambridge University Press, 1979).

Walt, Stephen M., "Why Alliances Endure or Collapse," Survival 39 (Spring 1997): 163–165.

Waltz, Kenneth N., *The Spread of Nuclear Weapons: More May Be Better*, International Institute for Strategic Studies, Adelphi Paper 171 (London: International Institute for Strategic Studies, 1981).

Weaver, Greg, and D. J. Glaes, *Inviting Disaster: How Weapons of Mass Destruction Undermine U.S. Strategy for Projecting Military Power* (McLean, VA: AMCODA Press, no date).

Weinberger, Caspar, with Peter Schweitzer, *The Next War* (Washington, D.C.: Regnery Publishing, 1996).

Wilson, Andrew, "Russian Military Haunted by Past Glories," *International Defense Review* 29 (May 1, 1996): 25.

Wirtz, James J., "QDR 2001: The Navy and the Revolution in Military Affairs," *National Security Studies Quarterly* 5 (Autumn 1999): 52–53.

Woodward, Susan L., "Failed States: Warlordism and 'Tribal Warfare,'" *Naval War College Review* 52 (Spring 1999): 55–68.

Wright, Robin, "Democracy: Challenges and Innovations in the 1990s," *The Washington Quarterly* 20 (Summer 1997): 23–36.

Ya'ari, Yedidia, "The Littoral Arena: A Word of Caution," *Naval War College Review* 48:2 (Spring 1995): 7–21.

Zimmermann, Tim, "All propaganda, all the time," *U.S. News and World Report*, November 11, 1996, 48–49.

Zinni, Anthony C., "A Commander Reflects," U.S. Naval Institute *Proceedings* 126 (July 2000): 34–36.

Endnotes

[1] The last volumes of the Sibylline Books were destroyed in the great fire during the reign of the emperor Nero. This was considered the beginning of Rome's collapse caused by a series of unforeseen dangers. Once the books had been sold, Amalthaea was never seen again.

[2] The U.S. Commission on National Security/21st Century, "Study Addendum" to *New World Coming: American Security in the 21st Century* (published at *http://www.nssg.gov/Reports/reports.html* only; not released with report text), September 15, 1999, 10–11. Not all of these studies are designed to address the overall character of the future security environment; many address a more narrow set of topics, or provide an indirect assessment.

[3] Some studies published in 1996 might not have achieved wide circulation by the May 1997 completion of the Quadrennial Defense Review 1997; hence the inclusion of sources which appeared in that year. Two 1995 studies were included because they represent organizations that did not sponsor a later study on the future security environment.

[4] Chapter one includes a listing of common subjects as well as details on methodology. A summary of the 36 primary sources is found in appendix A.

[5] An approximately 85 percent agreement among sources was considered a majority.

[6] The consensus points are discussed in detail in chapter five and the points of divergence are discussed in chapter six.

[7] The dissenting positions are also discussed in detail in chapter five. A bibliography of the more than three hundred secondary sources constitutes appendix B. In general, publications from the 1996–2000 period were used to identify dissenting views; older sources were used as background.

[8] These wild cards are described in chapter seven.

[9] Quoted in Peter G. Tsouras, *Warrior's Words* (London: Cassell, 1992), 322.

[10] An emerging fad in business literature can be termed "jamming instead of planning." In a December 1999 article, Daniel Gross argues that "in today's chaotic economic environment, the best business plan might be to have no plan at all." His logic is that plans, particularly long-range plans, are quickly overtaken by events, and that the entrepreneur must operate more like a jazz musician in a "jam" session than a driver following a detailed road map. Gross unconvincingly links the futility of planning argument to chaos theory, but his primary inspiration is John Kao's *Jamming: The Art and Discipline of Business Creativity* (New York: Harperbusiness, 1997). Though citing the statistic that only 14 percent of small businesses have annual business plans in writing, Gross appears to eventually contradict himself by admitting that even jam sessions need to be scheduled. See Daniel Gross, "No Plan," U.S. Airways *Attaché* (December 1999): 14–16. According to one source, Richard Holbrooke, special envoy to the Balkans who negotiated the Dayton Accords of 1995, also likens diplomacy to jazz rather than chess—its traditional metaphor. Michael Ignatieff, *Virtual War: Kosovo and Beyond* (New York: Metropolitan Books/Henry Holt and Company, 2000), 17, 35.

[11] From the DOD perspective, QDR 1997 followed in the mode of an earlier series of Secretary of Defense-directed reviews, conducted at approximately four-year intervals, including the Bush administration's Base Force/New National Security Strategy of 1989–1990 and the Clinton administration Bottom-Up Review of 1993. The distinction is the Congressional mandate for the QDR series.

[12] Officially the National Security Study is chartered by the Secretary of Defense, rather than Congressional mandate. In reality, it was the brainchild of then-Speaker of the House Newt Gingrich and its funding was originally a part of legislation. De facto, it is a Congressionally-mandated study.

[13] "We lack a clear threat to provide an identifiable template against which we can shape our forces." From James R. Blaker, "The American RMA Force: An Alternative to the QDR," *Strategic Review* 25:3 (Summer 1997): 29–30. For discussion of the "optimistic thesis" predicting the "end of all forms of major military conflict," see Richard L. Kugler, "Nonstandard Contingencies for Defense Planning," in Paul K. Davis, ed., *New Challenges for Defense Planning: Rethinking How Much Is Enough* (Santa Monica, CA: RAND, 1994), especially 168–170.

[14] "During the current strategic lull, the absence of a clear competitor removes one of the major motivations and compasses for change and innovation." Blaker, 29.

[15] Among early discussions of the difficulties in identifying threats in the post-Cold War era is W.Y. Smith, "U.S. National Security After the Cold War," *The Washington Quarterly* 15 (Autumn 1992): 23–34.

[16] This idea that the post-Cold War world was brief is still under debate. For an opposing argument see Paul W. Schroeder, "Rediscovering the New World Order: A Historical Perspective," *The Washington Quarterly* 17 (Spring 1994): 25–43. An argument that the period of strategic euphoria was an illusion can be found in Joseph S. Nye, "What New World Order?" *Foreign Affairs* 71 (Spring 1992): 83–96.

[17] A discussion that uses nuclear and weapons of mass destruction proliferation as a benchmark for a post-post-Cold War world is Brad Roberts, "1995 and the End of the Post-Cold War Era," *The Washington Quarterly* 18 (Winter 1995): 5–25.

[18] National Intelligence Council, *Global Trends 2010* (Washington, D.C.: National Intelligence Council, November 1997).

[19] U.S. Commission on National Security/21st Century, "Study Addendum" to *New World Coming*, 10–11.

[20] A number of studies do pick and choose supporting documentation from their predecessors. But none appear to begin with an across-the-board survey of previous assessments. Philip Ritcheson's effort for the National Security Study Group supporting the U.S. Commission on National Security/21st Century does not appear to have had a significant impact on their published report. The World Future Society's publication *Future Survey* provides "a monthly abstract of books, articles, and reports concerning forecasts, trends, and ideas about the future." This is the most comprehensive effort to collect alternative views, but it does not attempt to compare and contrast them. *Future Survey* also tends to highlight normative and prescriptive publications that focus on peace building rather than defense analysis.

[21] These categories were initially derived from the topics addressed in the future security environment section of the QDR 1997 report. However, the results of the surveys and analyses required a narrowing of these categories. For clarity, the findings identified in chapter five are recategorized as threats, military technology, and opposing strategies.

[22] Appendix B is a listing of these secondary, consulted sources.

[23] All the material presented in this study comes exclusively from unclassified information. Although several of the primary sources have an overall classification level above unclassified, the information derived from such sources came solely from sections within the document that are unclassified. As a further guarantee that classified material is not inadvertently presented, there are no footnotes citing any source with a higher overall classification level. Therefore, there are no direct citations in this study for the following sources: *Transformed World, 2015,* "The Projected Security Environment" from *Defense Planning Guidance 1999,* and *Joint Strategy Review 1998.*

[24] As is always the case with such selections, judgments were required as to how closely particular material conformed to the criteria; not all sources conform to the same degree.

[25] An additional, particularly useful study is the report of the Harvard University-sponsored 1999 Wianno Summer Study. Although conducted by an independent working group, the findings of the Wianno study were integrated into and form the basis for the 1999 OSD Office of Net Assessment Summer Studies. Because of that, the Wianno study was consulted, but not surveyed as a primary source. Its published version is: Eliot A. Cohen, Aaron L. Friedberg, and Stephen Peter Rosen, *The Future Security Environment and American Defense Planning* (Cambridge, MA: John M. Olin Institute for Strategic Studies, November 1999).

[26] It should be noted that IFPA conducts contract research for the U.S. Government.

[27] Zalmay Khalilzad and Ian O. Lesser, eds., *Sources of Conflict in the 21st Century: Regional Futures and U.S. Strategy* (Santa Monica, CA: RAND, 1998), 34.

[28] U.S. House of Representatives, 106th Cong., 1st Sess., *National Defense Authorization Act for Fiscal Year 2000* (Conference Report to Accompany S. 1059), August 6, 1999, 782.

[29] Ibid., 781.

[30] Peter A. Schwartz, *The Art of the Long View* (New York: Currency Doubleday, 1996), 29.

[31] Cold War era discussions of the capabilities versus intentions controversy can be found in Derek Leebaert, ed., *Soviet Military Thinking* (London: George Allen and Unwin, 1981), 12–13, and Thomas Rona, "Deception and the Formulation of National Intelligence Estimates," in Brian D. Dailey and Patrick J. Parker, *Soviet Strategic Deception* (Lexington, MA: Lexington Books, 1987), 487–508.

[32] "Study Addendum" to *New World Coming*, 2. The addendum does not state that Delphi variants are most frequently used; this conclusion is based on the author's survey.

[33] Liam Fahey and Robert M. Randall, *Learning From the Future: Competitive Foresight Scenarios* (New York: John Wiley and Sons, 1998), 6.

[34] Ibid.

[35] Harry G. Summers, Jr., *The New World Strategy: A Military Policy for America's Future* (New York: Simon and Schuster, 1995), 61.

[36] An echo of Summers' views in the sound bites from other critics can be found in "Future Schlock?" *Foreign Policy* 113 (Winter 1998–99): 82.

[37] In his introduction to a new edition of Kahn's classic work, Brent Scowcroft points out that it was Kahn's deliberate efforts to broaden his scope beyond "the technical aspects of the nuclear threat and potential" that made his scenario work unique. Kahn himself originally referred to scenario work as "Gedanken (thought) experiments." Herman Kahn, *Thinking About the Unthinkable in the 1980s* (New York: Simon and Schuster, 1984), 11, 55, 58.

[38] Schwartz, xiv.

[39] Ibid., 8.

[40] Ibid., 9.

[41] Ibid., 227–239.

[42] Although the effort, *Project 2025*, may have been designed in part to prepare the Air Force for future comprehensive defense reviews, the timing of QDR 1997 was such that it is difficult to determine if the project had any impact on the QDR. It is also difficult to link Air Force resource requirements planning to project 2025, primarily because of the impact of such subsequent real world events as NATO intervention in Bosnia and Kosovo. Because of that, and the significant effort involved, *Project 2025* is included among the current (i.e., post-QDR 1997) futures studies.

[43] Joseph A. Engelbrecht, Jr., et al., *Alternative Futures for 2025: Security Planning to Avoid Surprise* (Maxwell Air Force Base, AL: Air University Press, September 1996), 14.

[44] Arguably, many aspects of human behavior are well known and can be reasonably predicted in a particular context or set of circumstances. This is, in fact, the very rationale behind the use of wargames (or other decisionmaking games) as preparatory tools and training in decisionmaking. However, the nature of human behavior is hotly debated throughout the realms of psychology, philosophy, and religion and most estimates shy away from *overtly* incorporating a particular philosophy of human decision-making. This is discussed in greater detail in chapter three.

[45] A harsher criticism by Ed Smith, Boeing Corporation: "Intelligence—the military kind—doesn't work [in predicting out to 2020]. [It is] only good for 5–10 years out. [It relies on] evidence based projections, [but, there] may be no evidence [and the] projections are probably wrong." From "What . . . *From the Sea* Didn't Say" (Boeing Corporation briefing, presented June 2000).

[46] While acknowledging the use of forecasting for commodity speculation, Charles F. Doran argues that the traders ultimately expect forecasting to fail. See Doran, "Why Forecasts Fail: The Limits and Potential of Forecasting in International Relations and Economics," *International Studies Review* 1 (Summer 1999): 11–42.

[47] Pierre Wack, "Scenarios: Uncharted Waters Ahead" (article in two parts) *Harvard Business Review* 63 (September–October 1985): 73–89, and 63 (November–December 1985): 139–150.

[48] Schwartz, 9.

[49] Ibid., 75.

[50] National Defense Panel, *Transforming Defense: National Security in the 21st Century*, December 1997, 8–11; U.S. Commission on National Security/21st Century, *New World Coming: Supporting*

Research and Analysis, 133–139. However, the scenarios appear to have little direct connection to the recommendations of the National Defense Panel for transformation, nor to the "Major Themes and Implications" identified by the Commission members.

[51] Richard Danzig, *The Big Three: Our Greatest Security Risks and How to Address Them* (Washington, D.C.: National Defense University Press, 1999), 6.

[52] Quoted in Robert D. Heinl, *Dictionary of Military and Naval Quotations* (Annapolis, MD: Naval Institute Press, 1966), 239.

[53] Brian Bond and Williamson Murray, "The British Armed Forces, 1918–39," in Allen R. Millet and Williamson Murray, eds., *Military Effectiveness, Volume II: The Interwar Period* (Boston: Allen and Unwin, 1988), 101.

[54] Brian Bond, *British Military Policy Between the Two World Wars* (Oxford: Clarendon Press, 1980), 96.

[55] Ibid., 96–97.

[56] Ibid., 97.

[57] See discussion in David C. Gompert, *Right Makes Might: Freedom and Power in the Information Age*, McNair Paper 59 (Washington, D.C.: National Defense University Press, 1998), 15–39.

[58] Behavior discussed in William Powers, "Information Waterbugs," *National Journal* 31 (December 4, 1999): 3458–3461.

[59] The impossibility of value-free research in the social sciences, and the necessity to be value-explicit, are reflected in the foreign policy analysis writings of James N. Rosenau. See Rosenau, *Turbulence in World Politics: A Theory of Change and Continuity* (Princeton: Princeton University Press, 1990), 33–34.

[60] Discussed in W. Warren Wagar, "Utopias, Futures and H.G. Well's Open Conspiracy," in Howard F. Didsbury, Jr., ed., *Frontier of the 21st Century: Prelude to the New Millenium* (Bethesda, MD: World Future Society, 1999), 141–147.

[61] Abridged version published in Howard F. Didsbury, Jr., ed., *Frontier of the 21st Century: Prelude to the New Millenium* (Bethesda, MD: World Future Society, 1999), 148–154.

[62] Public organizations that promote futures research, such as the World Future Society, generally have two faces. On the one hand, they encourage discussion of rigorous, scholarly futures analysis from various sources. On the other hand, they also provide a forum for a wide variety of normative prescriptions for the future dressed in scholarly language. Often the normative prescriptions are themselves the aspirations of noted scholars, or are the underlying motives for a whole field of academic inquiry, such as peace research. It must be noted that the World Future Society has continued to move in the direction of value explicitness, particularly in its professional journal, *Futures Research Quarterly*.

[63] For discussion, see Carl H. Builder, *The Masks of War: American Military Styles in Strategy and Analysis* (Baltimore: Johns Hopkins University Press, 1989).

[64] The Commission on America's National Interests admonishes that "interests are not just whatever the current government says they are." Graham T. Allison and Robert Blackwill, lead authors, *America's National Interests* (The Commission on America's National Interests, July 2000, available at http://www.nixoncenter.org/publications/monographs/nationalinterests.pdf), 16.

[65] Address given at the Naval War College-sponsored "Alternative Futures in War and Conflict" Conference, Pell Center for International Relations, Salve Regina University, Newport, RI, November 30, 1999.

[66] I have been unable to identify any current study that is explicitly based on a particular view of human nature or exclusively based on historical analysis.

[67] See for example Robert Scheer, *With Enough Shovels: Reagan, Bush, and Nuclear War* (New York: Random House, 1982).

[68] An excellent discussion of economic thinking in this period can be found in Paul Starobin, "What Went Wrong," *National Journal* 49 (December 1999): 3451–53.

[69] Ibid., 3451–3452.

[70] The reigning classic on this subject is John J. Mearsheimer, *Conventional Deterrence* (Ithaca, NY: Cornell University Press, 1983). An excellent survey of the literature is Charles T. Allen, "Extended Conventional Deterrence: In from the Cold and Out of the Nuclear Fire?" *The Washington Quarterly* 17 (Summer 1994): 203–233.

[71] A detailed analysis is Kenneth F. McKenzie, *The Revenge of the Melians: Asymmetric Threats and the Next QDR*, McNair Paper 62 (Washington, D.C.: National Defense University Press, 2000).

[72] Department of Defense, *Report of the Quadrennial Defense Review*, May 1997, v. Hereafter refered to as *QDR 1997*.

[73] U.S. Commission on National Security/21st Century, "Study Addendum ," 16.

[74] *QDR 1997*, 5.

[75] Ibid., 11.

[76] An excellent categorization and description of such operations from a traditional, primarily naval, point of view can be found in James Cable, *Navies in Violent Peace* (New York: St. Martin's Press, 1989).

[77] *QDR 1997*, 11.

[78] Ibid., iv.

[79] National Defense Panel, *Transforming Defense*, 6.

[80] Khalilzad and Lesser, 121–122.

[81] On January 5, 2000, Italy announced that it intended to recognize North Korea. Italy is the first of the G-7 states to do so, and the move appears to indicate some success of the North Korea regime to break out of its pariah state status. See stratfor.com, "Global Intelligence Update—January 6, 2000" (website, posted Jan 5, 2000).

[82] The RAND study discusses the argument that the United States should take the lead in preventing the complete collapse of North Korea (the so-called "soft landing school") because the "negative and destabilizing aftershocks" are not in the interests of the United States, Japan, or South Korea. However, the study concludes that a North Korean collapse is inevitable, given that "the root causes of collapse are entrenched within the North Korean system." Actions taken by other states could postpone, but not prevent such a collapse. (p. 123)

[83] See discussion in Jacquelyn K. Davis and Michael J. Sweeney, *Strategic Paradigms 2025: U.S. Security Planning for a New Era* (Dulles, VA: Brassey's, 1999), 106–107.

[84] National Defense Panel, *Transforming Defense*, 23.

[85] Ibid.

[86] There may be, in fact, political reasons for not publicly discussing American defense policy in terms other than the threat of rogue states. However, this approach has a stifling effect on open public debate on the future security environment.

[87] The term "prominent dissenters" is meant to describe those analytical, political, or scholarly sources who are likely to have an effect on U.S. defense policy. Generally, these are authorities who are used by the Department of Defense for analysis or have a track record of influencing the thinking of government decisionmakers. Other scholarly dissenters without such a track record have not been included, even if prominent within their fields of study.

[88] Recent scholarship appears somewhat ambivalent about the role of ideology in modern conflict. Marxists and others have often argued that economic factors are the prime drivers of conflict. Since Marxism itself became a dogmatic ideology, there is no small irony in this argument. More recently, others have questioned whether conflict studies have been too focused on ideology or "grand causes" as motives for conflict. An illustrative statement by David Tucker is that "with the end of the Cold War, commentators began to notice that men fought for reasons other than ideology." David Tucker, "Fighting Barbarians," *Parameters* 28 (Summer 1998): 71.

[89] A particularly elegant statement of this argument can be found in Starobin, 3452.

[90] A brief discussion on the role of the United States as "an ideological power" from a military perspective is contained in Norman Friedman, "Steaming Into a New World," U.S. Naval Institute *Proceedings* 125 (May 1999): 53–59.

[91] A recent discussion of Fidel Castro's unique ability to blend Soviet-style communism with his own style of anti-American politics and cult of the personality is www.stratfor.com , "The Geopolitics of Fidel," Stratfor.com Weekly Global Intelligence Update, 10 April 2000.

[92] Brian R. Sullivan states directly: "Chinese Communism is dead as an ideology, and the Party survives only as a tool of the national government." From Sullivan, "A World of Great Powers," in Patrick M. Cronin, ed., *2015: Power and Progress* (Washington, D.C.: National Defense University Press, 1996), 34.

[93] John Train, "Foreign Intelligence Penetration," *Strategic Review* 27 (Fall 1999): 78.

[94] *National Military Strategy of the United States—Shape, Respond, Prepare Now: A Military Strategy for a New Century* (1997), 9.

[95] A succinct statement of this argument can be found in Donald M. Snow, *The Shape of the Future: World Politics in a New Century*, 3d ed. (Armonk, NY: M.E. Sharpe, 1999), 128–130.

[96] Davis and Sweeney, 14–15.

[97] A discussion of democratic claims and illiberal democracy appears in *Strategic Assessment 1999: Priorities for a Turbulent World* (Washington, D.C.: National Defense University Press, 1999), 195–199.

[98] "Evolutionary" is a key word in this assessment. A number of previously enthusiastic authorities on the post-Cold War expansionism of democratic values now suggest that exponential growth in democracies may be over. See, for example, Larry Diamond, "Is the Third Wave Over?" *Journal of Democracy* 7 (July 1996): 20–37.

[99] Perhaps one of the most powerful arguments that such discouragement and disillusionment not only are already occurring, but should be expected as natural human reactions with international security implications, is Ralph Peters, "Our Old New Enemies," in Lloyd J. Matthews, *Challenging the United States Symmetrically and Asymmetrically: Can America Be Defeated?* (Carlisle Barracks, PA: U.S. Army War College, Strategic Studies Institute, July 1998), 215–238. Peters states: "Our future enemies will be of two kinds—those who have seen their hopes disappointed, and those who have no hope. Do not worry about a successful China. Worry about a failing China." (p. 223). See also Robin Wright, "Democracy: Challenges and Innovations in the 1990s," *The Washington Quarterly* 20 (Summer 1997): 23–36.

[100] The White House, *A National Security Strategy for a New Century*, October 1998, iv.

[101] The December 1999 version of *A National Security Strategy for a New Century*, does not use the same language and is not explicit concerning potential disillusionment. However, such a possibility is implied in discussions on "Promoting Prosperity" and "Promoting Democracy" in Section III, "Integrated Regional Approaches," 32–34, 37–39, 40–41, 44, 46–47.

[102] Samuel P. Huntington, *The Clash of Civilizations and the Remaking of World Order* (New York: Simon and Schuster, 1996); Samuel P. Huntington, "The Clash of Civilizations?" *Foreign Affairs* 72 (Summer 1993): 22–49.

[103] See discussion on separation of authority in Islam in Samuel P. Huntington, "Democracy's Third Wave," *Journal of Democracy* 2 (Spring 1991): 27–29.

[104] Huntington, *The Clash of Civilizations and the Remaking of World Order*, 109–110.

[105] Ibid., 111.

[106] Ibid., 116.

[107] U.S. Commission on National Security/21st Century, *New World Coming: Supporting Research and Analysis*, 88. *A National Security Strategy for a New Century*, December 1999 version, seeks to distance itself from any implication that Islamic views on separation of religious and secular power are a potential for conflict. See p. 45.

[108] John L. Esposito, "The Islamic Factor," in Phebe Marr, ed., *Egypt at the Crossroads: Domestic Stability and Regional Role* (Washington, D.C.: National Defense University Press, 1999), 61–62.

[109] See Max Rodenbeck, "Is Islamism Losing Its Thunder?" *The Washington Quarterly* 21 (Spring 1998): 177–194.

[110] The thesis of democratic peace is given official standing in *A National Security Strategy for a New Century*, 2. Scholarly support is given by Bruce Russett, *Grasping the Democratic Peace: Principles for the Post-Cold War World* (Princeton: Princeton University Press, 1993), 119. Detractors among current futures assessments include Sullivan, 3–4.

[111] Globalism is thought by some to be the replacement to nationalism, which itself has often been decried as the source of war. This trend is rapidly becoming common wisdom. As described by Paul Bracken: "The unquestioned assumption in the West is that globalization is the force of the future, while nationalism stands for the world of the past." Paul Bracken, *Fire in the East: The Rise of Asian Military Power and the Second Nuclear Age* (New York: HarperCollins, 1999), xxiv.

[112] Thomas Friedman, "Was Kosovo World War III?" *The New York Times*, July 2, 1999, A17. Friedman does admit that Belgrade, Serbia, along with all the NATO countries, had McDonald's franchises during the NATO air strikes of 1999.

[113] This perception was particularly prevalent following the collapse of communism and the Chinese freedom movement that led to the Tiananmen Square standoff. However, recent arguments maintain that "democracy lost the information war," and that authoritarian control of the media (including the Internet) is now shaping perspectives. See, for example, Tim Zimmermann, "All propaganda, all the time," *U.S. News and World Report*, November 11, 1996, 48.

[114] Derived from discussion in Stephen M. Walt, "Why Alliances Endure or Collapse," *Survival* 39 (Spring 1997): 163–165.

[115] An example is the Italian Fascist dictator Benito Mussolini's view of Hitler and his motives for joining the invasion of France. Mussolini's commitment to the Axis Pact initially appeared ambiguous because he did not want Germany's power to eclipse Italy's glory. See, for example, Edwin Hoyt, *Mussolini's Empire: The Rise and Fall of the Fascist Vision* (New York: John Wiley and Sons, 1994), 163–194. Scholarly interest in Mussolini appeared to have a revival in the mid-1990s. Hitler himself seemed to have concerns that "... the British Empire would collapse, to the net benefit of Japan, America, and others, rather than Germany." He preferred a negotiated peace with Britain in 1940 rather than allowing others to benefit. Geoffrey Megargee, *Inside Hitler's High Command* (Lawrence, KS: University Press of Kansas, 2000), 89.

[116] Sullivan, 3.

[117] Ibid.

[118] Steven M. Walt, "Coalitions," in Patrick M. Cronin, ed., *2015: Power and Progress* (Washington, D.C.: National Defense University Press, 1996), 92.

[119] See discussion in www.stratfor.com, "Global Intelligence Update—5 June 2000; Retrieving the Irretrievable: The Clinton Foreign Policy Legacy," June 4, 2000.

[120] Snow, 39.

[121] Ibid., 39–40.

[122] However, there are discussions of how an independent European military structure could balance American power. See, for example, Jean-Marie Guehenno, "The Impact of Globalisation on Strategy," *Survival* 40 (Winter 1998–99): 16–18; Frederick Bonnart, "U.S. Starts to Fret Over EU Military Independence . . ." *International Herald Tribune,* May 24, 2000, 1.

[123] Russia as "honorary member" is Snow's interpretation of WTO activities. As of May 2000, Chinese membership was not concluded. See Clay Chandler, "Talks Break Off on China Bid to Join WTO," *The The Washington Post,* April 1, 2000, A15.

[124] However, in contrast to Snow, Samuel Huntington argues that economic ties do not create a common culture and that "the image of an emerging universally Western world is misguided, arrogant, false, and dangerous." Huntington, "The West and the World," *Foreign Affairs* 75 (November/December 1996): 28–46.

[125] Even sources concerned with the possible expansion of Chinese military power argue that "given the favorable conditions presented by the international economic order, it is still very much in China's self-interest to work within a system from which it has profited so greatly." Karl W. Eikenberry, "Does China Threaten Asia-Pacific Regional Stability," *Parameters* 25 (Spring 1995): 96. See also Felix K. Chang, "Conventional War Across the Taiwan Straits," *Orbis* 40 (Fall 1996): 606.

[126] Davis and Sweeney, 226.

[127] Ibid.

[128] Others suggest that a massive military strike without warning—spearheaded by ballistic missile attack—would be the more likely method for China to employ against Taiwan. See, for example, Robert Kagan, "How China Will Take Taiwan," *The Washington Post,* March 12, 2000, B7; and Gary Schmitt and Thomas Donnelly, "Our Interests Lie With Theirs," *The Washington Post,* April 23, 2000, B4.

[129] Ibid., 238.

[130] Henry Chu and Richard C. Paddock, "Russia Looks to China as an Ally Amid West's Ire," *Los Angeles Times,* December 8, 1999, 1. Rajan Menon describes Russian-Chinese rapprochement as a "strategic convergence" directed toward the U.S. rather than "trust or goodwill." Menon, "The Strategic Convergence Between Russia and China, *Survival* 39 (Summer 1997): 101–125. For the impact of Russian-Chinese arm sales on "a strategic cooperative partnership," see Stephen J. Blank, *The Dynamics of Russian Weapons Sales to China* (Carlisle, PA: U.S. Army War College, Strategic Studies Institute, March 4, 1997).

[131] www.stratfor.com, "Herding Pariahs: Russia's Dangerous Game," Stratfor.com Weekly Global Intelligence Update, February 8, 2000.

[132] Agence France-Presse in Beijing, "Alliances Can Defuse Hegemonism by US," *South China Morning Post,* March 8, 2000.

[133] However, their willingness to support security cooperation with the United States is discussed in Brian Robertson, Royal Australian Navy, "Security Cooperation in Asia Pacific," U.S. Naval Institute *Proceedings* 122 (March 1996): 65–68.

[134] For a study of recent Sino-Russian relations that argues an effective alliance is unlikely, see Jennifer Anderson, *The Limits of Sino-Russian Strategic Partnership*, International Institute for Strategic Studies, Adelphi Paper 315 (Oxford: Oxford University Press, December 1997). Her conclusion is

that: "Russia and China's strategic partnership is unwieldy and imprecise . . . weighed down by contradictory commitments, hyperbolic rhetoric . . . [and] inherently and deliberately vague." (p. 79) Additional Russian-Chinese contentions are discussed in Norman Friedman, "The China Puzzle Continues to Baffle the West," U.S. Naval Institute *Proceedings* 126 (March 2000): 4–6.

[135] *QDR 1997*, 5.

[136] Ibid.

[137] National Defense Panel, *Transforming Defense*, 77.

[138] Ibid., 5.

[139] See, for example, the debates in: Richard Bernstein and Ross H. Munro, "China I: The Coming Conflict with America," and Robert S. Ross, "China II: Beijing as a Conservative Power," *Foreign Affairs* 76 (March/April 1997): 18–44, and Gerald Segal, "What China Threat?" 78 *Foreign Affairs* (September/October 1999): 24–36. A balanced "neither partner nor adversary" assessment is David Shambaugh, "Sino-American Strategic Relations: From Partners to Competitors," *Survival* 42 (Spring 2000): 97–115.

[140] *Joint Vision 2010*, the current joint military vision of future capabilities, states "power projection, enabled by overseas presence, will likely remain the fundamental strategic concept of our future force." Chairman, Joint Chiefs of Staff, *Joint Vision 2010* (Washington, D.C.: Department of Defense, 1996), 3.

[141] *Strategic Assessment 1999*, 91–99; Davis and Sweeney, 60–64.

[142] *Strategic Assessment 1999*, 129–130.

[143] Despite the name and presumed constitutional restrictions, the JMSDF "is in fact a navy in all but name and the most powerful one in Asia-Pacific after the U.S. Navy." John Downing, "A Japanese navy in all but name," *Jane's Navy International* 104 (April 1, 1999): 33. See also Edward L. Martin, "The Evolving Missions and Forces of the JMSDF," *Naval War College Review* 68 (Spring 1995): 39–67.

[144] *QDR 1997*, 12.

[145] Ibid., 33.

[146] Ibid., 12.

[147] As a foreign commentator on the lessons of the Gulf War noted: "The 'super-power' of the U.S. stemmed not simply from its size or its superior resources, but from its ability to harness its power and concentrate it effectively. . . . Above all it came from an ability to mount an integrated effort across a broad spectrum of capabilities and to marshal the resources—social and political—as well as economic and military in an integrated manner." Quoted in Patrick J. Garrity, "Implications of the Persian Gulf War for Regional Powers," *The Washington Quarterly* 16 (Summer 1993): 154.

[148] Khalilzad and Lesser use the term "global peer competitor," defined as "an adversarial power that would attempt to challenge the United States and its interests worldwide." Zalmay Khalilzad and Ian O. Lesser, eds., *Sources of Conflict in the 21st Century: Regional Futures and U.S. Strategy* (Santa Monica, CA: RAND, 1998), 19.

[149] The total number of nuclear warheads permitted by the START 1 treaty for the U.S. and Russia is 6,000 on each side. START 2, which is planned for implementation in 2007 calls for a total of 3,500 for each nation. Source: *Jane's Intelligence Review* 10 (November 1, 1998): 10.

[150] The National Defense Panel argues that although China's current nuclear arsenal may be small, "China has the capability to be a more significant nuclear power by 2010–2020." National Defense Panel, 50. Shambaugh provides an estimate of 17 to 20 ICBMs capable of reaching the U.S. Shambaugh, "Sino-American Strategic Relations," 112. Others argue that the U.S. Government should be more concerned about China's nuclear modernization programs, but concede that at present "China's nuclear missile force is closer in size to a so-called rogue state's than it is to Russia." Brad Roberts, Robert A. Manning, and Ronald N. Montaperto, "China: The Forgotten Nuclear Power," *Foreign Affairs* 79 (July/August 2000): 58. A brief discussion of the Chinese ballistic missile submarine program is Larry G. Vogt, "China's Strategic Seapower," *The Submarine Review*, July 1997, 47–56.

[151] Robert J. Art, "Geopolitics Updated: The Strategy of Selective Engagement," *International Security* 23 (Winter 1998/99): 83–85.

[152] As the Commission on America's National Interests asserts: "The United States is unique in its ability to conduct large-scale military operations at great distances from its own territory. This ability to fight and win wars in the 'backyards' of potential adversaries is essential to preventing the emergence of a hostile hegemon and to ensuring the survival of American allies." Allison and Blackwill, 52.

[153] Although Khalilzad and Lesser argue that it is doubtful a competitor with such "suprare-gional" capabilities will develop before 2025, they hedge their assessment by stating that "the rise of a 'global competitor' is uncertain." Their argument, however, is very similar to that above. Khalilzad and Lesser, 19–20.

[154] Davis and Sweeney suggest that China would not be able to integrate RMA-type technologies until 2030. See Davis and Sweeney, 92.

[155] Under Secretary of Defense (Policy), 1999 Summer Study Final Report, *Asia 2025* (assembled briefing slides and text), Newport, RI, July 25–August 4, 1999, 102–114.

[156] A discussion of factors that limit Chinese power projection capabilities can be found in Davis and Sweeney, 86–92.

[157] Ibid., 127–141.

[158] There are, however, sources that argue that "prudent force planning must take such a worse case scenario into account." See, for example: William T. Johnsen, *Force Planning Considerations for Army XXI* (Carlisle, PA: U.S. Army War College, Strategic Studies Institute, February 18, 1998).

[159] The leading examples being the politician and filmmaker Shintaro Ishihara and Sony Corporation Chairman Akio Morita. See Shintaro Ishihara, *The Japan That Can Say No* (New York: Simon and Schuster, 1991).

[160] George Friedman and Meredith Lebard, *The Coming War With Japan* (New York: St. Martin's Press, 1991).

[161] See Secretary of State James A. Baker, "America in Asia—Emerging Architecture for a Pacific Community," *Foreign Affairs* 70 (Winter 1991/92): 1–18; Robert A. Scalapino, "The United States and Asia: Future Prospects," *Foreign Affairs* 70 (Winter 1991/92): 19–40; Yoichi Funabashi, "Japan and the New World Order," *Foreign Affairs* 70 (Winter 1991/92): 58–74; Howard H. Baker and Ellen L. Frost, "Rescuing the U.S.-Japanese Alliance," *Foreign Affairs* 71 (Spring 1992): 97–113. Even articles largely critical of Japan, such as Richard Holbrooke, "Japan and the United States: Ending the Unequal Partnership," *Foreign Affairs* 70 (Winter 1991/92): 41–57, insist that the U.S.-Japanese security alliance is unassailable.

[162] A recent essay on the linkage between economic and military competition with China is Dana Rohrabacher, "Q: Should Congress be concerned about China and the Panama Canal?" *Insight on the News*, December 27, 1999, 40. A discussion on American fears of a competition with the European Union can be found in William Wallace and Jan Zielonka, "Misunderstanding Europe," *Foreign Affairs* 77 (November–December 1998): 65–79.

[163] See C. Fred Bergsten and Marcus Nolan, *Reconcilable Differences? United States-Japan Economic Conflict* (Washington, D.C.: Institute for International Economics, June 1993). A review of recent sources on U.S.-Japanese security arrangements is Chris B. Johnstone, "Redefining the U.S.-Japan Alliance," *Survival* 42 (Spring 2000): 173–181.

[164] See Thomas L. Friedman, *The Lexus and the Olive Tree: Understanding Globalization* (New York: Farrar, Straus and Giroux, 1999); Davis and Sweeney, 14–15.

[165] *New World Coming*, 141.

[166] Allen Hammond, *Which World? Scenarios for the 21st Century* (Washington, D.C.: Island Press, 1998), 110–112. For extended water scarcity assessment, see also Sandra Postel, *Pillar of Sand: Can the Irrigation Miracle Last?* (New York: W.W. Norton, 1999).

[167] This view also has its roots in the perception of the worldwide advance of democracy in the 1980s. A representative argument that economic liberalization precedes and helps create the conditions for political change to democratization (and more peaceful relations) is John D. Sullivan, "Democracy and Global Economic Growth," *The Washington Quarterly* 15 (Spring 1992): 175–186.

[168] www.stratfor.com, "Decade Forecast—Decade Through 2005," December 24, 1994 (currently available on website), 1.

[169] Ibid.

[170] Ibid.

[171] Ibid., 3.

[172] *QDR 1997*, 3.

[173] Current MTW planning focuses on Iraq rather than Iran. However, the two contingencies are often linked when addressing American foreign policy objectives in the Gulf region. "This approach is consistent with the dual containment policy of the United States, which treats Iran and Iraq as twin pariahs. Although both reject being classified as a pair, American policy groups them together." From Raymond Tanter, *Rogue Regimes: Terrorism and Proliferation* (New York: St. Martin's Press, 1998), xiii.

[174] An opposing view is that of Thomas Hirschfeld and W. Seth Carus who argue that "with any luck, the adversaries of the two major regional conflicts . . . will disappear by the early days of the next century." They base their conclusions on the fact that "rogue status" is transitory, with such authoritarian states prone to frequent regime changes. "In reality, the history of the states presently labeled 'rogue' suggests that relatively few will pursue hostile policies over an extended period." Hirschfeld and Carus, "We Need to Understand," U.S. Naval Institute *Proceedings* 123 (February 1997): 66.

[175] Although *Global Trends 2010* issued by the National Intelligence Council argues that internal contradictions in both states would prevent such dominance in the near term. See 8–10.

[176] *New World Coming*, 47.

[177] If the START 2 treaty is implemented in 2007, the Russian arsenal of nuclear warheads will be reduced to 3,500, which would still massively dwarf the arsenals of China, Britain, and France.

[178] National Intelligence Council, *Global Trends 2010*, 8. Richard F. Staar estimates that Russia has retained approximately 70 percent of the former Soviet Union's military-industrial complex. See Richard F. Staar, *The New Military in Russia: Ten Myths that Shape the Image* (Annapolis, MD: Naval Institute Press, 1996), 76–79.

[179] The consensus of the literature on military operations in Chechnya is that Russian forces performed poorly and would not have been successful were if not for absolute air supremacy. On the most recent fighting in Chechnya, see: "Russia's Chechen War: Second Time Lucky?" *Jane's Defence Weekly* 33 (March 8, 2000): 32–36; Jamie Dettmer, "Requiem for a Heavyweight," *Insight on the News*, February 21, 2000, 22, and David A. Fulghum, "Air War in Chechnya Reveals Mix of Tactics," *Aviation Week and Space Technology* 152 (February 14, 2000): 76. On previous operations, see Andrew Wilson, "Russian Military Haunted by Past Glories," *International Defense Review* 29 (May 1, 1996): 25. An assessment of overall lessons learned is Robert H. Scales, Jr., "Russia's Clash in Chechnya: Implications for Future War," *National Security Studies Quarterly* 6 (Spring 2000): 49–58.

[180] Special forces and elite units, such as *spetsnaz*, were considered the most reliable troops in the Soviet armed forces. Although the readiness of Russian *spetsnaz* is nowhere near Cold War standards, and they did not fight as well as expected in Chechnya, they are one of the few forces of the Russian military apparently not slated for further cuts. It is easier to increase the readiness of these units than the Russian army as a whole. See David C. Isby, "Russia's once-revered *spetsnaz* look to rally after Chechnia," *Jane's Intelligence Review* 9 (December 1, 1997): 534–537. In fact, it was announced in July 2000 that Russia would increase elite airborne troops by 5,000 by the end of 2001. See www.stratfor.com, "Russian Military Quarrel Winds Down," Stratfor.com Weekly Global Intelligence Update—August 2, 2000.

[181] Some sources view this dominance as fleeting. See, for example, forecasts contained in Howell M. Estes III, *United States Space Command Long Range Plan* (Peterson Air Force Base, CO: U.S. Space Command, March 1998).

[182] A brief discussion of the ASEAN community's efforts to prevent Chinese military confrontation in the South China Sea is contained in A. James Gregor, "Qualified Engagement: U.S. China Policy and Security Concerns," *Naval War College Review* 52 (Spring 1999): 74–75. An eloquent view on Chinese military expansion into South East Asia from an Asian perspective is Anton Nugroho, "The Dragon Looks South," U.S. Naval Institute *Proceedings* 126 (March 2000): 74–76.

[183] China also appears to view NATO expansion and the extension of the Partnership for Peace program to Central Asian states as "separate pincers in a grand strategy of containment against China." Shambaugh, "Sino-American Strategic Relations," 104.

[184] See notes in Engelbrecht et al., 91–92.

[185] *New World Coming*, 77; see explanation in footnote 53 (p. 29), which demonstrates that by conventional measurements this forecast is unrealistic.

[186] Reports indicate that China increased defense spending by over 200 percent between 1988 (near end of Cold War) and 1995. Nayan Chanda, "Fear of the Dragon," *Far Eastern Review*, April 13, 1995, 24. See also the assessment of new technologies under study by China in Mark A. Stokes, *China's Strategic Modernization: Implications for the United States* (Carlisle, PA: U.S. Army War College, Strategic Studies Institute, 1999).

[187] For example, see the translations of Chinese military writings contained in Michael Pillsbury, ed., *Chinese Views of Future Warfare*, revised edition (Washington, D.C.: National Defense University Press, 1998), especially 249–420.

[188] Roberts, Manning, and Montaperto argue that: "It is time Washington turned its eyes to the East and came to grips with the fact that over the next decade it will likely be China, not Russia or any rogue, where nuclear weapons policy will concern America most." Roberts et al., 53.

[189] Paul Bracken discusses this perception of China's willingness to use force as "the will to bomb," which is why, he argues, Britain—with an impressive nuclear arsenal—has never been taken seriously as a nuclear power, yet China—with a small arsenal—has always evoked fear. See Bracken, *Fire in the East*, 108–109.

[190] Khalilzad and Lesser argue that this threat to Beijing's legitimacy, combined with a Taiwanese declaration of independence, is such that "a Chinese resort to force would likely occur regardless of the state of the military balance at the time or the adverse consequences such actions would pose for Chinese reform policies and Beijing's relations with other powers." Khalilzad and Lesser, 85.

[191] This is a perspective of the Kuomintang (KMT) as the historical ideological opponent of Chinese marxism rather than the current state of the KMT as a political party. See John F. Copper, *Taiwan: Nation-State or Province?* 3d ed. (Boulder, CO: Westview Press, 1999), 42–48; Zbigniew Brzezinski, "Living With China," *The National Interest* 59 (Spring 2000): 12–13; and Chang, 577.

[192] Khalilzad and Lesser, 84–85. Part of the irony is that it is less likely that the KMT—presumably the ideological opponent of the mainland—is less likely to declare Taiwanese independence than other Taiwanese political parties that have no claim whatsoever to the loyalty of mainlanders.

[193] See discussion in Jianxiang Bi, "Managing Taiwan Operations in the Twenty-first Century: Issues and Options," *Naval War College Review* 52 (Autumn 1999): 30–58.

[194] A particularly thorough discussion of this possibility is Douglas Porch , "The Taiwan Strait Crisis of 1996: Strategic Implications for the United States Navy," *Naval War College Review* 52 (Summer 1999): 15–48. A good summary of the dilemma between America's support of democracy and human rights and the desire to develop a strategic relationship with China is Walter Neal Anderson, *Overcoming Uncertainty: U.S.-Chinese Strategic Relations in the 21st Century*, INSS Occasional Paper 29 (U.S. Air Force Academy, CO: Institute for National Security Studies, October 1999). See also *Asia 2025*, 67–72; *Strategic Assessment 1999*, 127–128. On the other hand, informal interviews with leaders of the U.S. business community indicate that there is some sentiment that the U.S. Government will ultimately abandon its support of Taiwanese self-determination in exchange for a dominant position in the Chinese import market.

[195] An excellent source for Chinese military writings on the potential for future conflict is Michael Pillsbury, *China Debates the Future Security Environment* (Washington, D.C.: National Defense University Press, 2000). See also the discussion of the anti-U.S. focus of the PLA in David Shambaugh, "China's Military Views the World: Ambivalent Security," *International Security* 24 (Winter 1999/2000): 52–79.

[196] Such a scenario, entitled "The New South Asian Order," is developed in *Asia 2025*, 83–100.

[197] A useful brief history of the change in relations between the U.S., Pakistan and India is Sumut Ganguly, "South Asia After the Cold War," *The Washington Quarterly* 15 (Autumn 1992): 173–184.

[198] These incentives are discussed in Waheguru Pal Singh Sidhu, *Enhancing Indo-U.S. Strategic Cooperation*, International Institute for Strategic Studies, Adelphi Paper 313 (Oxford: Oxford University Press, September1997), 37–78; *Strategic Assessment 1999*, 151; Institute for National Strategic Studies, *The United States and India in the Post-Soviet World* (Washington, D.C.: National Defense University Press, 1993); and Darrin W. S. MacKinnon, "The Asian Anchor," U.S. Naval Institute *Proceedings* 124 (September 1998): 62–66.

[199] *Asia 2025*, 73–76.

[200] Sources referring to these states as "pivotal states" advise that the United States should design its foreign policy primarily to maintain such positive relations. See Robert S. Chase, Emily B. Hill, and Paul Kennedy, "Pivotal States and U.S. Strategy," *Foreign Affairs* 75 (January–February 1996): 33–51.

[201] While no formal definition of rogue state may exist, the general description "... correlates closely to those states that support aggression and terrorism. A rogue state is an outlaw country capable of instigating conflict with the United States and its allies." *Strategic Assessment 1999*, 3. In his study, *Rogue Regimes*, Raymond Tanter identifies the "primary criteria" for rogue status as "large conventional forces, [support for] international terrorism, and [desire to possess] weapons of mass destruction. . . . secondary criteria is appearance on the State Department's *Patterns of Global Terrorism*, a list released annually by the Office of the Coordinator for Counterterrorism." Tanter, 261, note 1.

[202] Specifically conflict with North Korea and Iraq. There is no official list of rogue states. However, there are usually five that are included in intelligence assessments: North Korea, Iraq, Iran, Syria, and Libya. Common characteristics are the support of terrorism and a history of hostility toward the United States by the current regimes. For diplomatic purposes, and to "encourage reentry into the community of nations," one or the other of these states, most recently Syria, is removed from the rogue list. At the moment, sources suggest that Libya has reduced its support for terrorism and may be a candidate for reentry. North Korea and Iraq under Saddam Hussein appear to be implacable. Tanter includes Cuba under the category of rogue regimes because it appears to support international terrorism. Sudan, which is also considered a rogue because of its support for terrorism, generally is not included in the list because it is thought to be a client state of another rogue—Iran—and does not possess large conventional forces. (Tanter, 261, note 1.) On June 19, 2000, Secretary of State Madeleine K. Albright announced that the Clinton administration would no longer use the term rogue states, but that "henceforth nasty, untrustworthy, missile-equipped countries would be known as 'states of concern.'" This would appear to be a reaction to a recent meeting of the South and North Korean heads of state. See Steven Mufson, "What's In A Name? U.S. Drops Term 'Rogue State,'" *The Washington Post*, June 20, 2000, 16. However, the term rogue state is ubiquitous within the analytical literature and, therefore, has been retained in this study.

[203] *Strategic Assessment 1999*, 219–228.

[204] The National Intelligence Council paints the rogue states as opponents to globalization and insisting on retaining regional ambitions and the "trappings of power" in opposition to a more cooperative world community. This contrasts with a more common view that rogue states oppose the status quo and are trying to promote violent change in the international system. National Intelligence Council, *Global Trends 2010*, 2. A brief survey of potential rogue states based on open source literature can be found in Kori N. Schake, "Beyond Russia and China: A Survey of Threats to U.S. Security From Lesser States," in Lloyd J. Matthews, *Challenging the United States Symmetrically and Asymmetrically: Can America Be Defeated?* (Carlisle Barracks, PA: U.S. Army War College, Strategic Studies Institute, 1998), 303–326.

[205] Sullivan, 3–6.

[206] A discussion of factors contributing to North Korean resilience can be found in Jonathan D. Pollack and Chung Min Lee, *Preparing for Korean Unification: Scenarios and Implications* (Santa Monica, CA: RAND, 1999), 27–34.

[207] There is a wealth of published recommendations in this regard. Prominent among them is Ashton B. Carter and William J. Perry, *Preventive Defense: A New National Security Strategy for America* (Washington, D.C.: The Brookings Institution, March 1999), which discusses the immediate need for engagement of both Russia and China.

[208] A particularly witty treatment of this argument is Hank Gaffney, "Oh, to be weak" (unpublished paper circulated in 1998; available from author at Center for Naval Analyses).

[209] An excellent bibliography of sources on the new world order debate is Jane E. Gibish, comp., *The New World Order: A Second Look* (Carlisle, PA: U.S. Army War College Library, August 1994).

[210] The terms "core" and "periphery" were frequently used in studies on complex interdependence in the 1970s and 1980s to describe the developed nations/West and the less-developed nations/Third World. Although the terms are tinged with neo-marxist philosophy, they can be traced to earlier studies of geopolitics. On the neo-marxist use see Immanuel Wallerstein, *The Capitalist World Economy* (Cambridge: Cambridge University Press, 1979). One of the best brief discussions of geopolitical writing remains Colin S. Gray, *The Geopolitics of the Nuclear Era: Heartland, Rimlands, and the Technological Revolution* (New York: Crane, Russack, 1977). A recent update is Mackubin Thomas Owens, "In Defense of Classical Geopolitics," *Naval War College Review* 52 (Autumn 1999): 59–76.

[211] *New World Coming*, 142.

[212] *QDR 1997*, 3.

[213] Ibid.

[214] Steven Kull, I. M. Destler, and Clay Ramsey, *The Foreign Policy Gap: How Policymakers Misread the Public* (College Park, MD: Center for International and Security Studies at Maryland University, 1997), 91–92.

[215] On postintervention developments in Haiti, see Kathie Klarreich, "The legacy of US, UN intervention in Haiti," *The Christian Science Monitor*, March 30, 2000, 7; James Varney, "Democracy Fal-

ters and Haiti Flirts With Chaos: A Nation in Tatters," *New Orleans Times-Picayune*, March 12, 2000, A01; and John Donnelly, "Haiti's Renewal Slow, and Painful Profound Misery Abounds as Foreign Powers Curtail Aid to Country," *The Boston Globe*, December 27, 1999, A1.

[216] A critical assessment of the Clinton administration's shift from promotion of democracy to a "pragmatic status quo as the benchmark for safeguarding U.S. interests" is Michael J. Mazarr, "Clinton Foreign Policy, R.I.P.," *The Washington Quarterly* 21 (Spring 1998): 11–14. David Tucker argues that "after Somalia the Clinton administration's policy of 'aggressive multilateralism' disappeared." Tucker, 71.

[217] One argument for intervention to prevent massive but not normal levels of war-related deaths can be found in Stephen J. Solarz and Michael E. O'Hanlon, "Humanitarian Intervention: When is Force Justified?" *The Washington Quarterly* 20 (Autumn 1997): 3–14.

[218] David Tucker makes this case pointedly: "Contrary to what proponents of the coming anarchy imply . . . it is not the case that instability and conflict anywhere requires us to respond militarily. In the current strategic setting there are very few places where we would be justified in deploying forces or to police civil unrest." Tucker, 73.

[219] *New World Coming*, 142.

[220] National Intelligence Council, *Global Trends 2010*, 2–3.

[221] A dissenting viewpoint that argues that the cumulative effect of failed states is a significant international security threat is Susan L. Woodward, " Failed States: Warlordism and 'Tribal Warfare,'" *Naval War College Review* 52 (Spring 1999): 55–68.

[222] Based on evaluation of the Somalia and Bosnia experiences, Donald Snow identifies four limitations that the American people have implicitly placed on humanitarian intervention: (1) "there is little public support for more than small efforts," (2) "involvement must be relatively bloodless if support is to be sustained," (3) "when atrocity becomes widely evident through publicity, there will be a strong tendency to want to 'do something,' but that reaction will be highly ephemeral," and (4) "ultimately, public support for this kind of action will almost certainly depend on whether any lasting good comes from involvement." Snow, 170–172.

[223] On food shortages, see Kevin Sullivan, "North Korea Says It Is Running Out of Food," *The Washington Post*, March 3, 1998, 11. A more detailed discussion argues that "North Korea's economic crisis is so severe that the economy cannot be sustained without outside help." See David Reese, *The Prospects for North Korea's Survival*, International Institute for Strategic Studies, Adelphi Paper 323 (Oxford: Oxford University Press, November 1998).

[224] A brief economic analysis of North Korean staying power is Marcus Nolan, "Why North Korea Will Muddle Through," *Foreign Affairs* 76 (July/August 1997): 105–118.

[225] An open-source assessment on the history of North Korean ballistic missile development efforts is Joseph S. Bermudez, *A History of Ballistic Missile Development in the DPRK*, Center for Nonproliferation Studies, Occasional Paper No. 2 (Monterey, CA: Monterey Institute of International Studies, November 1999).

[226] The vital interest most often noted is "the whereabouts and control of North Korean weapons of mass destruction." See Davis and Sweeney, 105–106. Of additional concern are the reports that North Korea has already developed a ballistic missile capable of hitting the continental United States. See Don Kirk, "New Missile Reported in North Korea," *International Herald Tribune*, February 19–20, 2000.

[227] See, for example, the discussions in *New World Coming*, 80–82, and Davis and Sweeney, 107–110.

[228] The National Defense Panel hedges slightly by envisioning "a reconciled, if not unified Korea" in the timeframe. National Defense Panel, 6.

[229] Khalilzad and Lesser, 24.

[230] *QDR 1997*, 5.

[231] As David Tucker notes: "Every briefing on the future now contains an obligatory slide on 'failed states.'" Tucker, 71.

[232] *New World Coming*, 96–99. Several NGOs claim that pessimistic forecasts for Africa discourage investment, therefore perpetuating instability. The implication is that they should be balanced by more optimistic assessments. See, for example, Peter Veit, ed., *Africa's Valuable Assets: A Reader in Natural Resource Management* (Washington, D.C.: World Resources Institute, 1998).

[233] *New World Coming*, 99.

[234] See discussion in James Miskel, "Are We Learning the Right Lessons from Africa's Humanitarian Crises?" *Naval War College Review* 52 (Summer 1999): 136–147.

[235] As noted earlier, these are profuse. Many are listed in the World Future Society's *Future Survey*, sometimes without a clear separation between subjective and objective literature.

[236] National Defense Panel, *Transforming Defense*, 16–17.

[237] As an example, it is perceived that in expelling Kosovar refugees, "Milosevic had perfected a new weapon of war: the use of refugee flows to destabilize neighboring countries, to immobilize the logistics of NATO forces by handing them a humanitarian catastrophe, then keeping them off-balance by turning on and off the flow of refugees at the border and finally—following the adage that a guerilla swims in the local population like a fish in the sea—by draining the sea, exposing the guerillas, the Kosovo Liberation Army, who were left behind so they could be finished off." Ignatieff, 41.

[238] The White House, *A National Security Strategy for a New Century*, December 1999, 14.

[239] Examples include: Clive Archer, *International Organizations* (London: University of Aberdeen, 1983); Richard Falk, *A Study of Future Worlds* (New York: Free Press, 1975); Stephen Krasner, ed., *International Regimes* (Ithaca, NY: Cornell University Press, 1983); and Robert C. North, *War, Peace, Survival: Global Politics and Conceptual Synthesis* (Boulder, CO: Westview Press, 1990). All four have been used as texts for graduate courses in international relations.

[240] Examples include Inis L. Claude, *Swords Into Plowshares: The Problems and Progress of International Organization* (New York: Random House, 1971); Richard A. Falk et al., eds., *The United Nations and a Just World Order* (Boulder, CO: Westview Press, 1991); and James N. Rosenau and Ernst-Otto Czempiel, *Governance Without Government: Order and Change in World Politics* (New York: Cambridge University Press, 1992). A collection of essays that includes virtually every such proposal and titles itself "Readings for Leaders" is Lincoln Bloomfield, *The Management of Global Disorder: Prospects for Creative Problem Solving* (Lanham, MD: University Press of America, 1987).

[241] On OAU and peacekeeping, see William H. Lewis and Edward Marks, *Searching for Partners: Regional Organizations and Peace Operations*, McNair Paper 58 (Washington, D.C.: National Defense University Press, June 1998), 96–99, 108–110.

[242] For such a critique of IGOs from an NGO, *see Amnesty International 1999 Annual Report: International Organizations* at www.amnesty.org/ailib/aireport/ar99/intorgs.htm.

[243] An opposing view is that of Martin van Creveld, whose historical and theoretical perspectives have had some influence on current military thinking. Van Creveld argues that because the development of the nation-state was primarily the result of organizing for war, the "waning" of interstate conflict (a development presumably caused by the existence of nuclear weapons) necessarily brings about the weakening of the state. Additionally, reduction of the postwar guarantees of social welfare, growing internal disorders, and the destruction of faith in government will eventually cause the concept of state to dissipate. However, van Creveld is unable to clearly identify what will replace the state in maintaining civil order; the implication is that order and security functions will be carried out by a blend of for-profit multinational companies, nongovernmental organizations, and regional agreements. See van Creveld, *The Rise and Decline of the State* (Cambridge: Cambridge University Press, 1999), 336–421.

[244] David Tucker argues that "migration and conflict, even civil war, historically have helped build states as often as they have destroyed them." Tucker, 72.

[245] Ibid.

[246] From a military perspective, nonstate and transnational threats are but one end of a spectrum of conflict that has been largely consistent throughout history. As the Defense Science Board stated in 1997: "Transnational threats *do not* represent a new mission for DOD, but a different and difficult challenge to the traditional mission." Office of the Secretary of Defense, Defense Science Board, *1997 DSB Summer Study: DOD Responses to Transnational Threats*, Volume 1—Final Report (December 9, 1997), vii. Thomas Hirschfeld and W. Seth Carus maintain: "Claims about the growing numbers of internal conflicts and more ethnic strife are . . . hard to sustain. Internal wars and ethnic conflicts are not increasing in number or intensity; they just have become more visible now that our anxieties about the danger of global war have receded." Hirschfeld and Carus, 66.

[247] A brief discussion on self-imposed risks, particularly as concerns computer network attack, is contained in Martin Libicki, "Rethinking War: The Mouse's New Roar?" *Foreign Policy* 117 (Winter 1999/2000): 35–36.

[248] This is not meant to label NGOs as nonstate "threats" or imply a direct linkage to the threats identified by the National Defense Panel. Rather, it is an intellectual convenience to identify international actors (whether "threats" or "solutions") as either states or nonstates.

[249] "Sins of the secular missionaries," *The Economist* 354 (January 29, 2000): 25–27.

[250] It is also argued that within nations, the power of emerging NGOs is "outweighed by more traditional parts of civil society" such as religious organizations and labor unions. See Thomas Carothers, "Civil Society," *Foreign Policy* 117 (Winter 1999–2000), 18–24. (Quote is from p. 20.)

[251] "Ship rams Greenpeace; sub unleashes Trident 2," *The San Diego Union-Tribune*, December 5, 1989, A-10; Jeffrey Schmalz, "After Skirmish with Protestors, Navy Tests Missile," *The New York Times*, December 5, 1989, A1. On public reaction: "Greenpeace's Risky Tactics," *St. Louis Post-Dispatch*, December 7, 1989, A35.

[252] *New World Coming*, 141.

[253] Ibid.

[254] The potential for an anti-technology backlash is linked to fear of globalization. See "Globalization Fear Runs Deep, Leaders Tell World Forum," *The Toronto Star*, May 24, 1998, B1.

[255] A discussion of potential effects on democracy can be found in Edward Wenk, "Socio-Pychological Aspects of Information in a Democracy," in Didsbury, 129–140. See also Ashley Dunn, "The Cutting Edge: Virtual World Leads to Lonely Place, Study Says," *Los Angeles Times*, August 31, 1998, D1.

[256] An extensive discussion on this point and the effects of globalization on taxation in general can be found in "Globalisation and Tax," *The Economist* 354 (January 29, 2000): 64–68.

[257] Ibid., 142.

[258] However, there are technologies that might be useful in countering chemical and biological terrorism. See Randy D. Curry and Thomas Clevenger, "New Approaches to Countering Biological Terrorism with Electrotechnologies: an Overview," in David W. Siegrist and Janice M. Graham, *Countering Biological Terrorism in the U.S.: An Understanding of Issues and Status* (Dobbs Ferry, NY: Oceana Publications, 1999), 161–174. Most of the technologies are useful as elements of consequence management, but others may prove useful in detection of weapons prior to use.

[259] There is a difference between assessing the future security environment as the result of actions and reactions, and viewing it as a worse case scenario. The Department of Defense has formally recognized the importance of preparing for nonstate and transnational threats, as well as the need to devote increased resources to defending against them and providing for consequence management. An influential statement of this view is Office of the Under Secretary of Defense for Acquisition and Technology, *Defense Science Board 1997 Summer Study Task Force on DOD Responses to Transnational Threats* (Washington, D.C.: October 1997). An underlying assumption of the "evolving nature" view assumes actions are carried out to respond to such threats.

[260] An argument that "superterrorism" is unlikely and that measures taken to prevent it may be counter-productive is made in Ehud Sprinzak, "The Great Superterrorism Scare," *Foreign Policy* 112 (Fall 1998): 110–119.

[261] A short, balanced assessment of this possibility is the Congressional Research Service Report to Congress 97–75 ENR by Zachary S. Davis, *Weapons of Mass Destruction: New Terrorist Threat?* (Washington, D.C.: Congressional Research Service, January 8, 1997). A more recent and lengthier official source is: Advisory Panel to Assess Domestic Response Capabilities For Terrorism Involving Weapons of Mass Destruction, *First Annual Report: Assessing the Threat* (Washington, D.C.: RAND, December 15, 1999). A list of current sources on the topic of catastrophic terrorism can be found in *New World Coming*, footnote 95, p. 48.

[262] McKenzie, 29, 32, 35–36.

[263] Some argue that terrorist information warfare or cyber-terrorism is much harder to do than is popularly claimed. See Libicki, 35–36, 38.

[264] A number of sources identify information operations or information warfare as "weapons of mass destruction." The logic of this argument is that death and destruction on a large scale can occur by attacks on the computer networks controlling public utilities and transportation. However, these sources are unable to convincingly demonstrate that such attacks would result in casualties in the numbers expected from a successful nuclear or biological attack. From that perspective, the WMD label for computer network attack (CNA) is largely used for attracting attention or identifying its potential seriousness. In *New World Coming*, the more realistic term "weapons of mass disruption" is used (p. 52). On the lower end of the spectrum, information operations using new media, such as the

Internet, can have effects on the morale of combatants without actually causing any physical casualties. This would put it in the category of nonlethal weapon, a category that can include propaganda throughout history.

[265] During the mid-1980s, the SS–N–22 was considered the most potent Soviet anti-ship weapon because its Mach 2.0–2.5 speed made it very difficult for U.S. close-in weapons systems to shoot down. It was reportedly sold to Iran in the late 1980s, but that report was apparently incorrect. It was, however, sold to China in the mid-1990s. An authoritative source states that the U.S. considered buying the entirety of the Russian inventory (841 missiles) in 1994 to prevent it from being sold to potential opponents, but a price was not agreed upon. See Norman Friedman, *World Naval Weapons Systems 1997–1998* (Annapolis, MD: Naval Institute Press, 1997), 243–244. In April 2000, it was reported that the U.S. point defense system Rolling Airframe Missile (RAM) had successfully engaged a simulated SS–N–22 conducting a high speed weave. See "RAM Passes OpEval," *U.S. Naval Institute Proceedings* 126 (April 2000): 6.

[266] As detailed in House of Representatives, 105th Cong. 2nd Sess., *Report of the Select Committee on U.S. National Security and Military/Commercial Concerns With the People's Republic of China*, Report 105–851 (Washington, D.C.: Government Printing Office, 1999); otherwise known as the "Cox Report." See especially, Vol. 1 19–52, 80–82, 116–118, and Vol. II, 2–5, 47–48, 68–75, 161–171.

[267] See Thomas Orszag-Land, "How to Keep Soviet Science Out of the Wrong Hands," *The Christian Science Monitor*, November 8, 1995, 10; "A Funding Imperative," *The Christian Science Monitor*, November 30, 1998, 10; Rebecca K. Graeves, "Russia's Biological Weapons Threat," *Orbis* 43 (Summer 1999): 490–491; U.S. General Accounting Office, *Nuclear Nonproliferation: Concerns with DOE's Efforts to Reduce the Risks Posed by Russia's Unemployed Weapons Scientists* (Washington, D.C.: Report to the Chairman, Committee on Foreign Relations, U.S. Senate, February 1999.)

[268] *New World Coming*, 51. See discussion in Center for Counterproliferation Research, *The NBC Threat in 2025* (Washington, D.C.: National Defense University, 1997).

[269] Paul Bracken, "Sidewise Technology: A 21st Century Driver," unpublished paper prepared for the Alternative Global Futures 2015 Workshop, Washington, D.C.: September 26–27, 1999.

[270] Eliot A. Cohen, "The Mystique of U.S. Air Power," *Foreign Affairs* 73 (January/February 1994): 112.

[271] *New World Coming*, 51. See also *Strategic Assessment 1999*, 293–294.

[272] Frederick Thompson et al., *Vision-21 Source Book, Volume 1: The Process* (Alexandria, VA: Center for Naval Analyses, November 26, 1996), 62.

[273] Libicki, 31–32.

[274] See discussion in Andrew Richter, "The American Revolution? The Response of the Advanced Western States to the Revolution in Military Affairs," *National Security Studies Quarterly* 5 (Autumn 1999): 1–28.

[275] See discussion on "the Burundi Exercise" of the 1996 Commission on the Roles and Capabilities of U.S. Intelligence in Robert D. Steele, "Information Peacekeeping: The Purest Form of War," in Matthews, *Challenging the United States*, 169–170 (note 18).

[276] See discussion on the commercialization of remote sensing in Dana J. Johnson, Scott Pace, and C. Bryan Gabbard, *Space: Emerging Options for National Power* (Santa Monica, CA: RAND, 1998), 31–32.

[277] Ibid., 32.

[278] Thompson, 62.

[279] *New World Coming*, 54.

[280] Ibid. On this point, *New World Coming* cites Roger C. Molander, David A. Mussington, and Richard F. Mesic, *Strategic Information Warfare Rising* (Washington, D.C.: RAND, 1998) as its source.

[281] This is supported by the language carefully chosen for the *U.S. Space Command Long Range Plan*, which states: "*Prior to hostilities or during peace operations* [emphasis added], an adversary will have sophisticated regional situational awareness." Estes, 2.

[282] (2) is suggested by insights from the "Zaibatsu" alternative future developed by the Air University's *2025* study. Engelbrecht et al., 49–53, 150, 169. See also Larry K. Grundhauser, "Sentinels Rising: Commercial High-Resolution Satellite Imagery and Its Implications for U.S. National Security," *Airpower Journal* 12 (Winter 1998): 74–76. A source that cites wargaming experience as indicative that a commercial cut-off cannot be presumed is Frederick W. Kagan, "Star Wars in Real Life: Political Limitations on Space Warfare," *Parameters* 28 (Autumn 1998): 117–118.

[283] For definitions and discussion of RMAs by proponents, see Eliot A. Cohen, "A Revolution in Warfare," *Foreign Affairs* 75 (March/April 1996); James R. FitzSimonds and Jan M. van Tol, "Revolutions in Military Affairs," *Joint Force Quarterly* 4 (Spring 1994): 24–31; and Andrew F. Krepinevich, "Calvary to Computer: The Patterns of Military Revolutions," *The National Interest* 37 (Fall 1994): 30–42. A more skeptical discussion that is supportive of transformation is Michael E. O'Hanlon, "Can High Technology Bring U.S. Troops Home?" *Foreign Policy* 113 (Winter 1998–99): 72–86; and further developed in O'Hanlon, *Technological Change and the Future of Warfare* (Washington, D.C.: The Brookings Institution, 2000).

[284] A particularly direct criticism of the concept of an ongoing RMA can be found in Steele, who charges that, "The Revolution in Military Affairs is a joke. It is nothing more than lip service, substituting astronomically expensive systems with no sensor-to-shooter guidance . . . for outrageously expensive systems with no sensor-to-shooter guidance . . ." (p. 144).

[285] One of the most enthusiastic advocates of pursuing the RMA, William A. Owens, describes the result as proving a "system of systems" in which information can be drawn from a wide array of sources so that knowledge of a targeted area could be near absolute. Recently, he has argued that the RMA would require creating a state-of-the-art military force from scratch, but that it would cost 35 percent less than current military capabilities. See William A. Owens with Ed Offley, *Lifting the Fog of War* (New York: Farrar, Straus and Giroux, 2000), especially chapter 6, "Winning the Revolution."

[286] Technical discussions on the potential for moving "from microelectronics to nanoelectronics" can be found in Surge Luryi, Jimmy Xu, and Alex Zaslavsky, *Future Trends in Microelectronics: The Road Ahead* (New York: John Wiley and Sons, 1999).

[287] But in the case of biological weapons, technological "advances" are seen as pushing us closer to a bloody killing field filled with dying and panic-stricken civilians. Richard Danzig refers to this as "traumatic attack." See Danzig, 34–39.

[288] The overall theme of Earl H. Tilford, Jr., *The Revolution in Military Affairs: Prospects and Cautions* (Carlisle, PA: U.S. Army War College, Strategic Studies Institute, June 23, 1995). See also Kenneth F. McKenzie, "Beyond Luddites and Magicians: Examining the MTR," *Parameters* 25 (Summer 1995): 15–21.

[289] *New World Coming*, 143.

[290] As Andrew Richter explains: "Only one country—the United States—currently has capabilities in all [RMA] areas, thereby indicating its centrality in any discussion of the RMA." Richter, 3.

[291] FitzSimonds and van Tol, 29.

[292] Ronald Huisken, *The Origin of the Strategic Cruise Missile* (New York: Praeger, 1981), 20–21, 28.

[293] "The Soviet Navy was at its most innovative when it developed various classes of submarines capable of firing cruise missiles." From Bryan Ranft and Geoffrey Till, *The Sea in Soviet Strategy* (Annapolis, MD: Naval Institute Press, 1983), 111.

[294] *New World Coming* suggests that "the relative U.S. technological edge may actually grow over the next quarter century." (pp. 122–123)

[295] In the words of *New World Coming*: "American commercial successes should also keep the United States the leader in command and intelligence systems development, systems integration, and information management." (p. 56).

[296] See Robbin F. Laird and Holger H. Mey, *The Revolution in Military Affairs: Allied Perspectives*, McNair Paper 60 (Washington D.C.: National Defense University Press, April 1999), 97–104.

[297] Engelbrecht et al., 171–172.

[298] From this perspective, all war planning and technology development are efforts at adaptation. As Robert H. Scales, Jr., writes: "The evolving sequence from dominance through challenge and adaptive response has been the hallmark of the Western way of war." Scales, *Future Warfare* (Carlisle Barracks, PA: U.S. Army War College, 1999), 36.

[299] *New World Coming*, 120.

[300] Michael Dorgan, "Few surprised at firing of Los Alamos Scientist; 'Tip of iceberg' seen on Chinese spying," *The Arizona Republic*, March 14, 1999, A17; Fox Butterworth and Joseph Kahn, "Chinese Intellectuals in U.S. Say Spying Case Unfairly Cast Doubts on Their Loyalties," *The New York Times*, May 16, 1999, 1:32 David Talbot and Ed Hayward, "Students say focus is studies, not spying," *Boston Herald*, May 26, 1999, 030.

[301] For example: Andrew F. Krepinevich, Jr., "Military Experimentation—Time to Get Serious," *www.csbahome.org* , March 3, 2000.

[302] Concerning a lack of funding for the RMA, see John Gamboa, "The Cost of Revolution," U.S. Naval Institute *Proceedings* 124 (December 1998): 58–61. For commentary on a loss of focus on development of military technology, see J. H. Beall, "Restore the Focus on Technology," U.S. Naval Institute *Proceedings* 126 (June 2000): 56–57, and Pete Stevens, "The Silence of the Labs," U.S. Naval Institute *Proceedings* 126 (June 2000): 96.

[303] The potential for such a leapfrog has been the "dreadnought factor." In 1906, the Royal Navy commissioned the first big gun, steam-turbine battleship, HMS *Dreadnought*, which was widely perceived as making all other warships, and thus the naval fleets of all other nations, instantly obsolete. Although other weapons systems were developed to defeat the dreadnought (submarines, carrier-based aviation), the leapfrogging of existing naval technology allowed the Royal Navy to maintain a military advantage that was thought to have been slipping away to Germany, Japan, and the United States. (This later came to pass due to organizational choices concerning naval air power, rather than loss of the technological lead.) See discussion in Andrew F. Krepinevich, Jr., *Restructuring for a New Era: Framing the Roles and Missions Debate* (Washington, D.C.: Defense Budget Project, April 1995), 44–47. Elsewhere Krepinevich points out that in many cases, as in the *Dreadnought* case, the initial advantage of a technical revolution is ephemeral, and "there do not seem to be any prolonged 'monopolies' exercised by a single competitor in periods of military revolution . . . [However,] it may be that although the period of competitive advantage appears to be fairly short there may be a potentially great advantage from being first, as the French discovered to their dismay and the Germans to their elation in the spring of 1940." Krepinevich, "Calvary to Computers: The Pattern of Military Revolutions," 37.

[304] See Chris Hables Grey, "Our Future as Post-Modern Cyborgs," in Didsbury, 20–40, and Robert B. Mellert, "The Future of God," in Didsbury, 76–82.

[305] See discussion in Schwartz, 73–78.

[306] However, the dominant authority in future scenario building, Peter Schwartz, claims that novels, "even science fiction novels," have not been useful in his scenario research because "the ideas are not surprising enough." Schwartz, 80.

[307] Andrew Richter articulates this view in reference to the RMA: "At present, the vast majority of countries in the developing world appear totally unprepared to adapt to the RMA, and thus any study that focused on them would, by definition, be brief." See Richter, 1.

[308] Additionally, there are future studies devoted specifically to potential wildcards, such as John L. Petersen, *Out of the Blue: Wild Cards and Other Big Future Surprises* (Washington, D.C.: Arlington Institute, 1997).

[309] Khalilzad and Lesser, 36. The chapter in which this appears was written by Zalmay Khalilzad and David Shlapak, with Ann Flanagan.

[310] Ibid.

[311] Ibid. A similar proposal is by David R. Klain, "Are We Ready for Tomorrow?" U.S. Naval Institute *Proceedings* 122 (April 1996): 55–56.

[312] In contrast, Davis and Sweeney mention technological surprise but do not include it among their "three wildcards worth considering." (pp. 219–221).

[313] Although sources maintaining that the United States is not taking the biological warfare threat seriously use the Pearl Harbor rhetoric to describe a potential biological attack on the continental United States. See, for example, Pietro Marghella, "December 7, 1999: The Second, Silent Attack on Pearl," U.S. Naval Institute *Proceedings* 125 (May 1999): 60–65.

[314] The lethality of massive cruise missile attacks against surface ships is a current concern. However, such a potential attack would be conceptually similar in intensity to that experienced in the Okinawa campaign of April 1945 when over 355 *kamikazes* struck at the U.S. fleet. It is estimated that Japan could have generated as many as 7,500 *kamikaze* sorties to defend the home islands from the anticipated amphibious invasion (McKenzie, 8). But these attacks, even on that level, could do little to enable Japan to regain the control of the seas it held in 1941–1942.

[315] "Indeed, it is true to say that, with a single exception [the U.S.], most states no longer maintain ocean-going navies at all." Van Creveld, 346.

[316] The concept of a distinctively transoceanic navy—one that can operate across oceans to project combat power onto land—originated with Samuel P. Huntington, "National Policy and the Transoceanic Navy," U.S. Naval Institute *Proceedings* 80 (May 1954): 483–493. Under a rigorous application of Huntington's definition, the Navy is the world's sole transoceanic maritime force.

[317] It should be noted that some sources would object to "the use of major platforms as the prime units of account for comparing particular military capabilities with those of another country" because of resulting analytic "distortions." Hirschfeld and Carus, 67–68. However, the two tables in this chapter are intended to illustrate relative force size rather than directly compare capabilities.

[318] Danzig, 22–24.

[319] There are indications of an increased emphasis on such aircraft programs under Russian President Vladimir Putin's leadership. See Craig Covault and David A. Fulgham, "Russian Stealth Bomber Design Work Underway," *Aviation Week and Space Technology*, April 10, 2000, 18.

[320] James J. Wirtz, "QDR 2001: The Navy and the Revolution in Military Affairs," *National Security Studies Quarterly* 5 (Autumn 1999): 52–53.

[321] Ibid., 50–51.

[322] Jan S. Breemer refers to this circumstance as "the end of naval strategy," implying that U.S. forces can focus on directly influencing effects on land. Jim Wirtz refers to it as "the golden age of United States seapower." See Breemer, "The End of Naval Strategy: Revolutionary Change and the Future of American Naval Power," *Strategic Review* 22 (Spring 1994): 40–53; Wirtz, 43–60.

[323] See discussion in A. D. Baker III, "World Navies in Review," U.S. Naval Institute *Proceedings* 126 (March 2000): 30–42.

[324] Illustrative of this argument is John A. Tipak, "Can the Fighter Force Hold Its Edge?" *Air Force Magazine* 83 (January 2000): 25–31.

[325] Ibid. See also Robert S. Dudney, "Battle of the F–22," *Air Force Magazine* 82 (September 1999): 16–17; and Richard Hallion, *Control of the Air: The Enduring Requirement* (Bolling Air Force Base, D.C.: Air Force History and Museums Program, September 8, 1999).

[326] At first glance this seems to contradict the concept of network-centric warfare, which claims to shift the focus away from platforms to network. Network-centric operations promise to increase the value of individual units by providing effective information linkages and a common operational picture, that, in turn, allow for the optimization of weapons and effects. Presumably that would allow for achieving a greater operational effect from fewer platforms. However, as recently argued by the Navy leadership, "numbers do count," since, ultimately, the weapons are launched from platforms. If network-centric operations increase the value of a small, widely dispersed but highly networked force, then logically it would increase even more the dominance of a larger, widely dispersed but highly networked force. The concept of overwhelming force—a principle that the U.S. armed forces and the American public seems most comfortable with—requires dominance in numbers as well as capabilities. On network-centric warfare, see Arthur K. Cebrowski and John J. Garstka, "Network-Centric Warfare: Its Origin and Future," U.S. Naval Institute *Proceedings* 124 (January 1998): 28–35, and David S. Alberts, John J. Gartska, and Frederick Stein, *Network-Centric Warfare: Developing and Leveraging Information Superiority*, 2ᵈ ed. (Washington, D.C.: DOD C⁴ISR Cooperative Research Program, August 1999). On "numbers count," see Jay L. Johnson, "Numbers Do Matter," U.S. Naval Institute *Proceedings* 125 (November 1999): 32. On the doctrine of overwhelming force, see F. G. Hoffman, *Decisive Force: The New American Way of War* (Westport, CT: Praeger, 1996).

[327] See discussion in Thomas S. Momiyama, "Russia, Inc.—Open for Business," U.S. Naval Institute *Proceedings* 122 (February 1996): 66–69. However, Stephen Blank—among other sources—maintains that the Russian military complex is in a period of "comprehensive demodernization" and will prove unable to develop future RMA-type systems. See Blank, "Preconditions for a Russian RMA: Can Russia Make the Transition?" *National Security Studies Quarterly* 6 (Spring 2000): 1–28.

[328] As of March 2000, the 44,570-ton VSTOL-aircraft carrier *Admiral Gorshkov* had not been transferred to the Indian Navy, although a protocol to buy the ship was signed on November 8, 1999. Reports indicate that India wants the carrier modified to operate conventional fixed-wing aircraft and will purchase several dozen MIG–29K aircraft as a possible complement. See A. D. Baker, "World Navies in Review," U.S. Naval Institute *Proceedings* 126 (March 2000): 31–32. On the *Sovremenny*-class destroyer sale, see Nikolai Novichkov, "Four Sovremennys in total for Beijing," *Jane's Defence Weekly* 33 (March 15, 2000).

[329] The debate on whether such an arms race dynamic exists is heated and extensive. Whether or not it is a reality, naval construction has historically been identified as a cause or propellant of arms races. See, as a historically recent example, Richard Fieldhouse and Shunji Taoka, *Superpowers at Sea: An Assessment of the Naval Arms Race* (Oxford: Oxford University Press, 1989). For an opposing view, see Colin S. Gray, *House of Cards: Why Arms Control Must Fail* (Ithaca, NY: Cornell University Press, 1992), 37–47.

³³⁰ Along these lines, van Creveld maintains that the warmaking abilities of the modern state will continue to weaken, ensuring large-scale clashes of naval or air forces will not occur. In a sense, his overall argument implies that all states will become failing states. See van Creveld, 337–354, 419.

³³¹ The most recent work by the Office of Net Assessment emphasizing that "increasingly, other countries strategies will be oriented around keeping the U.S. out of their region" is the Office of the Under Secretary of Defense (Policy), 1999 Summer Study Final Report, *Maintaining U.S. Military Superiority* (assembled briefing slides and text), Newport, RI: July 25–August 4, 1999. (The quotation is found on page 19.)

³³² The naval roots of the antiaccess or area-denial concepts can be traced from such sources as Sanjay Singh, "Indian Ocean Navies—Learn from War," U.S. Naval Institute *Proceedings* 118 (March 1992): 51–54, and Yedidia Ya'ari, "The Littoral Arena: A Word of Caution," *Naval War College Review* 48 (Spring 1995): 7–21. The Office of Net Assessment construct originated in a series of briefings by Pat Curry, in the mid-1990s.

³³³ See Tim Sloth Joergensen, "U.S. Navy Operations in Littoral Waters: 2000 and Beyond," *Naval War College Review* 51 (Spring 1998): 20–29.

³³⁴ Detailed in, *Challenges to Naval Expeditionary Warfare* (Washington, D.C.: Office of Naval Intelligence, 1997).

³³⁵ These weapons can be considered asymmetric because the Navy is largely configured for open-ocean operations. From an historical perspective, use of such weapons or their antecedents would be considered a normal aspect of naval warfare in narrow seas. An excellent study of the historical and environmental factors influencing near-shore naval operations is Milan N. Vego, *Naval Strategy and Operations in Narrow Seas* (Portland, OR: Frank Cass Publishers, 1999).

³³⁶ With the development of theater ballistic missile defense systems, cruise missiles could replace ballistic missiles as the prime area-denial threat. See Rodney Rempt, "We're in the Enemy's Backyard," U.S. Naval Institute *Proceedings* 127 (July 1999): 43–46.

³³⁷ A skeptical view of the ballistic missile threat to CONUS can be found in "NMD: The Hard Sell," *Jane's Defence Weekly* 33 (March 15, 2000): 19–23.

³³⁸ See discussion in McKenzie, 4–6.

³³⁹ The most detailed discussion is Theodore L. Gatchel, *At the Water's Edge: Defending Against the Modern Amphibious Assault* (Annapolis, MD: Naval Institute Press, 1996).

³⁴⁰ See discussion in Thomas G. Mahnken, "America's Next War," *The Washington Quarterly* 16 (Summer 1993): 171–184.

³⁴¹ See discussion in McKenzie, 22–23. Sources that link antiaccess strategies with WMD include Robert W. Chandler, *Tomorrow's War, Today's Decisions* (McLean, VA: AMCODA Press, 1996) and Greg Weaver and D. J. Glaes, *Inviting Disaster: How Weapons of Mass Destruction Undermine U.S. Strategy for Projecting Military Power* (McLean, VA: AMCODA Press, no date).

³⁴² Quoted in Robert G. Joseph and John F. Reichart, *Deterrence and Defense in a Nuclear, Biological, and Chemical Environment*, Occasional Paper of the Center for Counterproliferation Research (Washington, D.C.: National Defense University, 1995), 4.

³⁴³ The battle of Thermopylae is well known in military literature as one of the great episodes of self-sacrificing heroism in battle. Thus, it makes a useful example in pointing out the timeless nature of antiaccess strategies.

³⁴⁴ A typology of antiaccess strategies that could be used against power projection forces can be found in McKenzie, 47.

³⁴⁵ An example of the willingness of rogue states to use such means is the Iraq-Iran war of 1980–1988 in which ballistic missiles and chemical weapons were used. See discussion of potential "alternative operational concepts" of rogue states in McKenzie, 39–40.

³⁴⁶ Sources suggesting that emerging military technology can neutralize antiaccess strategies include: James R. Boorujy, "Network-Centric Concepts Can Guarantee Access," U.S. Naval Institute *Proceedings* 126 (May 2000): 60–63; Gary W. Schnurrpusch, "Asian Crisis Spurs TBMD," U.S. Naval Institute *Proceedings* 125 (September 1999): 46–49. Other sources argue that long-range aviation in "extended range operations"—particularly stealth bombers—can effectively defeat antiaccess strategies.

³⁴⁷ See discussion in Sam J. Tangredi, "The Fall and Rise of Naval Forward Presence," U.S. Naval Institute *Proceedings* 126 (May 2000): 28–32.

³⁴⁸ John Jumper: "Access is an issue until you begin to involve the vital interests of the nation that you want and need as a host. Then access is rarely an issue . . ." James R. Callard: "The issue of

access is a red herring . . . Is access a problem when our vital interests are threatened? The short answer is no. . . . When our vital interests are threatened, we will have access. The American people will demand it. . . . The American people will not allow us to protect an ally that refuses to allow us access." Quoted in "The Access Issue," *Air Force Magazine* 81 (October 1998): 42–46. See also "Operating Abroad," *Air Force Magazine* 81 (December 1998): 28–29.

[349] The willingness to use such weapons to prevent the defeat of NATO or in response to nuclear use by the Soviets was considered to have considerable deterrent value. At what point permission to use these weapons would be given was kept ambiguous to forestall Soviet calculations. Yet, this remained essentially a last resort strategy. Whether NATO leaders would actually bring themselves to use nuclear weapons is now a moot point. There is, however, considerable literature that suggests that the absolute distinction between nuclear and conventional weapons was not a view held by Soviet military planners. See, for example, Fritz W. Ermath, "Contrasts in American and Soviet Strategic Thought," in Derek Leebaert, ed., *Soviet Military Thinking* (Boston: George Allen and Unwin, 1981), 50–69.

[350] For an assessment of the military effectiveness of chemical warfare in the Iraq-Iran conflict, see Anthony H. Cordesman and Abraham R. Wagner, *The Lessons of Modern War, Volume Two: The Iran-Iraq War* (Boulder, CO: Westview Press, 1990), 495–529, 598–600.

[351] See Art Pine, "U.S. Targets Heart of Terror," *Los Angeles Times*, August 21, 1998, A1; Paul Richter, "U.S. Says Raids A Success," *Los Angeles Times*, August 22, 1998, A1; Paul Richter, "Sudan Attack Claims Faulty, U.S. Admits," *Los Angeles Times*, September 1, 1998, A1.

[352] Robert W. Chandler with John R. Backschies, *The New Face of War: Weapons of Mass Destruction and the Revitalization of America's Transoceanic Military Strategy* (McLean, VA: AMCODA Press, 1998), 199–223; Anthony H. Cordesman and Abraham R. Wagner, *The Lessons of Modern War, Volume IV: The Gulf War* (Boulder, CO: Westview Press, 1996), 879–915.

[353] See, for example, discussion in Gerard Roncolato, "Methodical Battle: Didn't Work Then . . . Won't Work Now," U.S. Naval Institute *Proceedings* 122 (February 1996): 32–33.

[354] Dunlap argues: "Given the West's still-sizable nuclear arsenal and its *relatively* robust capability to deal with other-than-nuclear WMD warfare, are WMD really asymmetrical to the West? So long as the West maintains its current capabilities, it seems rather unlikely that an adversary could *decisively* employ WMD against it." Dunlap, "Preliminary Observations: Asymmetrical Warfare and the Western Mindset," in Matthews, *Challenging the United States*, 5.

[355] Robert Kupperman and David Siegrist, "Strategic Firepower in the Hands of Many?" in David W. Siegrist and Janice M. Graham, *Countering Biological Terrorism in the U.S.: An Understanding of Issues and Status* (Dobbs Ferry, NY: Oceana Publications, 1999), 49.

[356] Danzig, 32–34.

[357] Davis and Sweeney urge greater emphasis and more "candid evaluations of the impact of WMD on U.S. operations . . ." Davis and Sweeney, 325.

[358] On the effectiveness of the "Scud hunt," see Eliot A. Cohen, ed., *Gulf War Air Power Survey: Volume II, Part II* (Washington, D.C.: Government Printing Office, 1993), 330–339, which implies that allied attacks reduced both the Iraqi launch rate and the Scud operating areas, even if fewer launchers were destroyed than originally estimated. See also Anthony H. Cordesman and Abraham R. Wagner, *The Lessons of Modern War, Volume IV: The Gulf War*, 860–867.

[359] Based on historical survey, Stuart D. Landersman maintains that "Chemical warfare is employed when there is no chance of reciprocal use." Landersman, "Sulfur, Serpents, and Sarin," U.S. Naval Institute *Proceedings* 124 (August 1998): 42–43.

[360] He did, however, routinely use poisonous gas in the concentration camps to destroy Jews, other targeted peoples, and potential domestic opponents of the Nazi regime or its control over conquered territories. Likewise, Saddam Hussein elected not to use chemical weapons against coalition forces even though he demonstrated that he possessed the capability. But, he has used it against his own people to suppress revolts. See Anthony H. Cordesman and Abraham R. Wagner, *The Lessons of Modern War, Volume IV: The Gulf War*, 886–887. For a discussion of the effects of Saddam's use of chemical weapons against the Kurdish village of Halabjah in 1998, see Chandler with Backschies, 215, 403–405.

[361] National Defense Panel 1977, *Transforming Defense*, 25.

[362] See discussion in McKenzie, 1–2.

[363] *New World Coming*, 141.

[364] Ibid.

[365] Hirschfeld and Carus maintain that: "Repeated claims that the post-Cold War world has become more dangerous for the United States are hard to justify. It is absurd to compare the remaining dangers to threats we faced during the Cold War." Hirschfeld and Carus, 65.

[366] "Although the dangers of proliferation and backlash states are real, the demise of the Soviet Union and the reduction of its strategic nuclear threat mean that the U.S. has never, in recent memory, been safer." Peter Schoettle, "Key Geostrategic Trends: A Cloudy Crystal Ball," *Naval War College Review* 48 (Winter 1995): 70.

[367] Khalilzad and Lesser argue: "Moscow's behavior will be conditioned by the same cold war calculus of deterrence that kept the peace during the years of East-West confrontation. The emerging and more immediate threat is not one of societal destruction, but of smaller, damaging attacks, some of which could originate from states or groups less susceptible to the 'logical' cost-benefit accounting of 'rational' deterrence theory." Khalilzad and Lesser, 18–19.

[368] McKenzie, 3–4, 10–12; *New World Coming,* 49–50

[369] Arguably, it was naval power, not the oceans and distance, that provided the sanctuary. In the case of Britain, the Atlantic proved a convenient maneuver space for the Royal Navy throughout the War of 1812, as it frequently did for pirates in earlier years. In the initial period of naval weakness, the United States rushed to build a series of coastal fortifications to prevent otherwise unopposed attacks from the sea. It was not until Americans had confidence in their own naval power that they began to see the blessings that ocean borders provided.

[370] National Defense Panel, *Transforming Defense,* 25; Representative arguments include Chandler with Backschies, 177–194;. Raymond S. Sheldon, "No Democracy Can Feel Secure," U.S. Naval Institute *Proceedings* 124 (August 1998): 39–44.

[371] National Defense Panel, *Transforming Defense,* 26–27.

[372] See discussion in F. G. Hoffman, "Countering Catastrophic Terrorism," *Strategic Review* (Winter 2000): 55–57.

[373] Gray argues that the American people would likely demand a "healthily disproportionate action" in response. See Colin S. Gray, "Combating Terrorism," *Parameters* 23 (Autumn 1993): 22.

[374] This interpretation of information warfare as having two facets—(1) the use of advanced information systems for military operation, a category which also includes corresponding attempts to deny information to or destroy such advanced systems, and (2) the control or manipulation of publicly available information of military significance via media or other methods—is derived from common elements found in most references on information warfare and information operations. However, sources include a wide variety of activities within the term. As R. L. DiNardo and Daniel J. Hughes argue: "Unfortunately, *information warfare* has become so expansive a term that it now threatens to become a tautology by encompassing nearly everything beyond the most primitive forms of combat. Some include traditional intelligence as information warfare, while others include the capabilities inherent in certain weapons systems. . . . This logic could be extended to acts of politics, advances in weaponry, and uses of propaganda." DiNardo and Hughes, "Some Cautionary Thoughts on Information Warfare," *Airpower Journal* 9 (Winter 1995): 73.

[375] A discussion of the vulnerability of these systems can be found in Steve Goldstein, "Pentagon Planners Gird For Cyber Assault," *The Philadelphia Inquirer,* December 1, 1999, 1; and Robert E. Podlesny, "Infrastructure Networks Are Key Vulnerabilities," U.S. Naval Institute *Proceedings* 125 (February 1999): 51–53.

[376] Almost every discussion of information warfare cites "Moore's Law"—which postulates (thus far correctly) that computing power will roughly double every year—as evidence of the exponential increase of future information processing capabilities. This leads to the claim that there is "a new world coming" in which information warfare will be the dominant style of war. However, rarely cited is Moore's *Second* Law, which postulates that the cost of microchip production is increasing faster than revenues. In other words, there is a limit to commercially affordable computer technology. This may imply that information warfare will not be as ubiquitous as anticipated—most states and nonstate actors will not be able to afford top-of-the line systems. See Charles C. Mann, "The End of Moore's Law," *Technology Review,* May/June 2000 (published by M.I.T. at www.techreview.com/articles/may00/mann.htm).

[377] Three particular areas of vulnerability include: maintaining security and privacy, achieving interoperability, and network reliability. See U.S. General Accounting Office, *Information Superhighway: An Overview of Technology Challenges,* Report to Congress GAO/AIMD–95–23, January 23, 1995.

[378] Vernon J. Ehlers, "Information Warfare and International Security," *The Officer* 75 (September 1999): 28–32.

[379] "Second-generation information warfare will probably look a lot like advertising." John L. Petersen, "Info War: The Next Generation," U.S. Naval Institute *Proceedings* 123 (January 1999): 62.

[380] Engelbrecht et al., 169–171.

[381] The linkage between command and control (C²) warfare and psychological operations as elements of information warfare is detailed in Joint Pub. 3-13.1, *Joint Doctrine for Command and Control Warfare*, (Washington, D.C.: Department of Defense, February 7, 1996).

[382] A discussion of the effect of the Internet on the debate over the Department of Defense anthrax vaccination policy is Mark F. Cancian, "Anthrax and the Internet," U.S. Naval Institute *Proceedings* 126 (May 2000): 42–46. Cancian suggests that distrust of government fuels the misinformation and conspiracy theories that can be found on the Web.

[383] A North Vietnamese commander is quoted as saying: "The conscience of America was part of its war-making capability, and we were turning that power in our favor. America lost because of its democracy; through dissent and protest it lost the ability to mobilize a will to win." From "How North Vietnam Won the War," *The Wall Street Journal*, August 3, 1995, A8. For a discussion of future effects, see Brent Baker, "War and Peace in a Virtual World," U.S. Naval Institute *Proceedings* 123 (April 1997): 36–40; and Ignatieff, 191–196.

[384] Robert Callum, "Will Our Forces Match the Threat," U.S. Naval Institute *Proceedings* 124 (August 1998): 51–52. A contrary view is that of E. Anders Eriksson who argues that "the cyber WMD problem is likely to be transitional in the sense that as information technology matures, defense will outweigh offense." From Eriksson, "Information Warfare: Hype or Reality?" *The Nonproliferation Review* (Spring–Summer 1999): 58.

[385] www.stratfor.com, "I Love You and the Problem of Cyberforce," May 15, 2000, 3.

[386] The contrast between resources given to information processing and efforts at information security is discussed in William E. Pohde, "What is Information Warfare?" U.S. Naval Institute *Proceedings* 122 (February 1996): 36–38.

[387] Roger Barnett argues that the United States is "the country with the greatest capability to conduct information operations" and therefore has considerable ability to deter attack through punishment or denial. This deterrence capacity would be effective even against masked attacks. See Roger W. Barnett, "Information Operations, Deterrence, and the Use of Force," *Naval War College Review* 51 (Spring 1998): 7–19.

[388] Davis and Sweeney, 14–15.

[389] An argument that e-mail provided an alternative and more accurate means for military personnel to identify shortfalls in military readiness to Congress is made by Donald E. Vandergriff, "truth@readiness.mil," U.S. Naval Institute *Proceedings* 125 (June 1999): 56–60.

[390] "Information superiority" is the term used in the 1997 *National Military Strategy* and in *Joint Vision 2010* to indicate "the capability to collect, process, and disseminate an uninterrupted flow of precise and reliable information, while exploiting or denying an adversary's ability to do the same." (*National Military Strategy*, 18) "Knowledge superiority" is the term used in a U.S. Navy briefing to describe the objective of developing network-centric warfare capabilities.

[391] As Air Force Doctrine Document 2-5, *Information Operations* (August 5, 1998) states: "Information has long been an integral component of human competition—those with a superior ability to gather, understand, control and use information have had a substantial advantage on the battlefield. History is replete with examples of how information has influenced political and military struggles—from the earliest battles of recorded history to current military operations in Bosnia." (p. i)

[392] See discussion in Joseph S. Nye, Jr., and William A. Owens, "America's Information Edge," *Foreign Affairs* 75 (March–April 1996): 20–36.

[393] A primary implication of John Arquilla and David Ronfeldt, "Cyberwar is Coming!" *Comparative Strategy* 12 (Spring 1993): 141–165.

[394] This is an anecdote that was included in classified intelligence briefings in 1999. I have yet to be able to ascertain its accuracy, although it seems plausible.

[395] A representative discussion is James T. Jenkins, "Use Technology... But Don't Trust It!" U.S. Naval Institute *Proceedings* 124 (August 1998): 69–70.

[396] See argument in Erik J. Dahl, "We Don't Need an IW Commander," U.S. Naval Institute *Proceedings* 125 (January 1999): 48–49.

[397] Thomas P. M. Barnett, "The Seven Deadly Sins of Network-Centric Warfare," U.S. Naval Institute *Proceedings* 125 (January 1999): 36–39; Vandergriff, 56–57.

[398] A representative argument is T. X. Hammes, "War Isn't a Rational Business," U.S. Naval Institute *Proceedings* 124 (July 1998): 22–25.

[399] Charles Dunlap argues that potential opponents can combine selected high-tech operations with low-tech redundancies common to less technologically-sophisticated cultures. See Charles J. Dunlap, "How We Lost the High-Tech War of 2007: A Warning From the Future," *The Weekly Standard*, January 29, 1996, 22–28. See also Paul K. Van Riper and Robert H. Scales, Jr., "Preparing for War in the 21st Century," *Strategic Review* 25 (Summer 1997): 14–20.

[400] See discussion in Katherine McIntire Peters, "Split Decision," *Government Executive*, October 1999, 43–48.

[401] Paul K. Van Riper and F. G. Hoffman, "Pursuing the Real Revolution in Military Affairs: Exploiting Knowledge-Based Warfare," *National Security Studies Quarterly* 4 (Summer 1998): 1–19; Mackubin Thomas Owens, "Technology, the RMA, and Future War," *Strategic Review* 26 (Spring 1998): 63–70; Charles J. Dunlap, Jr., "21st Century Land Warfare: Four Dangerous Myths," *Parameters* 27 (Autumn 1997): 27–37.

[402] Primary proponents of this view are William A. Owens and James R. Blaker. Perhaps the ultimate expression of this aspiration is a fictional essay by Scott Billigmeier and Ed Glabus, "Future War: 'Information Operations Corps' Comes of Age," *Army* 47 (December 1997): 45–51.

[403] National Defense Panel, *Transforming Defense*, 23.

[404] "To the German military leaders, allies were a nuisance that, at best, one could expect to do one's bidding without any concern for their own interests." Megargee, x.

[405] However, the German armed forces command staff posited an American Germany-first strategy for worst-case planning. See Megargee, 170–171.

[406] Ibid., 137–138.

[407] See discussion in Daniel Goure, "The Resource Gap," *Armed Forces Journal International* 137 (May 2000): 38–42.

[408] Allison and Blackwill, 52.

[409] Secretary of the Air Force F. Whitten Peters: "I think everyone has agreed that what we did in Kosovo was equivalent to a single Major Theater War." "Whit Peters on the Issues," *Air Force Magazine* 82 (October 1999): 47. William J. Begert, uses this argument to assert: "To the surprise of many, air power played the deciding role in a major theater war." Begert, "Kosovo and Theater Air Mobility," *Aerospace Power Journal* 8 (Winter 1999): 11.

[410] The phenomenon of a "world of warriors" is also referred to as "the new warrior class." See Ralph Peters, *Fighting for the Future: Will America Triumph?* (Mechanicsburg, PA: Stackpole Books, 1999), 32–47. See commentary on child warriors in Caroline Davies, "Drinks, drugs, and terror-cocktail that turns boys into killers. Using children in combat has reached a horrifying scale in Africa," *The Daily Telegraph* (London), May 25, 2000, 4.

[411] "In our lifetimes, this morally savage, unruly killer, not the trained, disciplined soldier, will be the type of enemy most frequently encountered by Euro-American militaries." Peters, *Fighting for the Future*, 48.

[412] See the rhetoric of Don Stauffer, "Electronic Warfare: Battles Without Bloodshed," *The Futurist* 34 (January–February 2000), 23–26.

[413] Billigmeier and Glabus, 50.

[414] *New World Coming*, 143.

[415] Cairns, 29.

[416] Ignatieff, 210–212.

[417] As Ralph Peters argues: "The U.S. Army will fight warriors far more often than it fights soldiers in the future." Peters, *Fighting for the Future*, 44.

[418] Peters calls for an increase in humint—human means of intelligence collection—in order to build databases on active "warrior leaders." "If electronic collection means can't acquire it, we pretend we don't need it—until we find ourselves in downtown Mogadishu with everybody shooting at us." Peters, *Fighting for the Future*, 45–46.

[419] This is the conventional wisdom for states concerned about holding down collateral damage. As seen in the wars in Chechnya, another approach is to mass firepower from ground and air so as to devastate a killing zone in which the opposing guerrillas presumably operate.

[420] An opposing view from a technologist: "Telling the good guys from the bad guys requires old fashioned, hard detective work. Technology is not likely to solve this problem anytime soon." Robert E. Podlesny, "MOUT: The Show Stopper," U.S. Naval Institute *Proceedings* 124 (February 1998): 51.

[421] This is an illustrative, if somewhat extreme interpretation of the arguments made in Joseph S. Nye, Jr., "Redefining the National Interest," *Foreign Affairs* 78 (July/August 1999): 22–35 and Edward N. Luttwak, "Give War a Chance," *Foreign Affairs* 78 (July/August 1999): 36–44. Anthony C. Zinni attributes the following quote to "an earlier Chairman of the Joint Chiefs of Staff: '... real men don't do OOTW' [operations other than war]." Zinni, "A Commander Reflects," U.S. Naval Institute *Proceedings* 126 (July 2000): 34.

[422] Term developed in Edward N. Luttwak, "Toward Post-Heroic Warfare," *Foreign Affairs* 74 (May/June 1995): 109–122.

[423] Luttwak sees patience as a defining virtue of post-heroic warfare. The objective should be long-term cumulative effects, rather than a swift, decisive effect, which he considers illusory. Luttwak, "Toward Post-Heroic Warfare," 117–121.

[424] See discussion in Zinni, 34–36.

[425] For example, see discussion of Marine Corps capabilities in Thompson, 77–81.

[426] Other sources include Robert F. Hahn II and Bonnie Jezior, "Urban Warfare and the Urban Warfighter of 2025," *Parameters* 29 (Summer 1999): 74–86.

[427] Charles C. Krulak, "The Three Block War: Fighting in Urban Areas," speech presented at National Press Club, Washington, D.C., October 10, 1997; published in *Vital Speeches of the Day*, December 15, 1997, 139–141. Podlesny postulates MOUT (military operations in urban terrain) as a major obstacle to achieving *Joint Vision 2010* objectives. Podlesny, "MOUT: The Show Stopper," 50–54.

[428] Hahn and Jezior concentrate on the emerging military technologies that can prepare ground forces for urban warfare. Although arguing for "transformation of the current infantry soldier into a truly lethal urban warrior," they appear to view technology and training as more important than changes in U.S. military organization (which is the target of the transformation school writ large). Hahn and Jezior, 75. See also Timothy L. Thomas, "The Battle for Grozny: Deadly Classroom for Urban Combat," *Parameters* 29 (Summer 1999): 87–102.

[429] Thompson, 10.

[430] The term "chaos in the littorals" is adopted from a joint U.S. Naval Institute-Armed Forces Communications and Electronics Association conference of that title held in San Diego, California, on February 10–11, 2000.

[431] Danzig, 42–49.

[432] Ibid., 40–42.

[433] A representative argument is Robert H. Scales, Jr., "The Indirect Approach: How U.S. Military Forces Can Avoid the Pitfalls of Future Urban Warfare," *Armed Forces Journal International* 136 (October 1998): 68–74.

[434] Current ambivalence in the official DOD position is illustrated by strong support for NMD, on the one hand, and comments made by Secretary of Defense William Cohen in July 2000: "I think the act of terrorism taking place on the United States is more likely than intercontinental missile [attack]." See Bryan Bender, "USA evaluating defences against nuclear terrorism," *Jane's Defence Weekly* 34 (July 12, 2000): 2.

[435] Craig Covault, "Desert Storm Reinforces Military Space Direction," *Aviation Week and Space Technology*, April 8, 1991, 42. See also: Steven J. Bruger, "Not Ready for the First Space War: What about the Second?" *Naval War College Review* 48 (Winter 1995): 73–83.

[436] William L. Spacey II, *Does the United States Need Space-Based Weapons?* Cadre Paper 4 (Maxwell Air Force Base, AL: Air University Press, September 1999), 1–7, 109. Also see discussion in Randall G. Bowdish and Bruce Woodyard, "A Naval Concepts-Based Vision for Space," U.S. Naval Institute *Proceedings* 125 (January 1999): 50–53.

[437] An excellent summary of the debates can be found in John E. Hyten, *A Sea of Peace or a Theater of War: Dealing with the Inevitable Conflict in Space*, ACDIS Occasional Paper (Champaign, IL, University of Illinois at Urbana-Champaign, April 2000). As is obvious from the title, Hyten's study favors the space-conflict-is-inevitable side.

[438] *New World Coming*, 143.

[439] Estes, 10.

[440] Hyten, 33–34.

[441] Ibid., 2.

[442] Ibid.

[443] According to the former Commander-in-Chief of the U.S. Space Command, General Joseph W. Ashy: "It's politically sensitive, but it's going to happen. Some people don't want to hear this, and it sure isn't in vogue . . . but—absolutely—we're going to fight in space. We're going to fight from space and we're going to fight into space." Quoted in Spacey, 1.

[444] Spacey, 107.

[445] Ibid.

[446] For detailed discussion, see McKenzie, 38–43.

[447] Or other political constraints. See Kagan, "Star Wars in Real Life," 112–118.

[448] For a more extensive discussion, see Spacey, 95–103.

[449] Recommendations on a U.S. approach to such negotiations can be found in Hyten, 70.

[450] The full quote as often cited is: "Treaties are like roses and pretty girls, they last while they last." Quoted in (among other sources): Summers, 65.

[451] Sheila E. Widnall, Secretary of the Air Force, "The Space and Air Force of the Next Century," address to the National Security Forum, Maxwell Air Force Base, AL, May 29, 1997 (www.af.mil/news/speech/current/The_Space_and_Air_Force_of.html); quoted in Spacey, 4.

[452] Quoted in Spacey, 4.

[453] For a study that seeks to identify the implications for defense policy of Rome's politico-military experience, see Edward N. Luttwak, *The Grand Strategy of the Roman Empire: From the First Century A.D. to the Third* (Baltimore: Johns Hopkins University Press, 1976). These are the implications applied in Luttwak, "Toward Post-Heroic Warfare."

[454] In terms of the current status of the United States, see Davis and Sweeney, 286–288.

[455] Seyom Brown has repeatedly argued that "gross imbalances in military power" combined with "inherently destabilizing deployments" are the culprits that cause such competition. See Brown, *The Causes and Prevention of War*, 2ᵈ ed. (New York: St. Martin's Press, 1994), 94–98.

[456] A similar approach (concerning Russia) was suggested earlier by Fred C. Ikle. See Ikle, "Comrades in Arms: The Case for a Russian-American Defense Community," *National Interest* 26 (Winter 1991/92): 22–32.

[457] This is the basis behind the planning methodology known as "competitive strategies." See Henry D. Sokolski, ed., *Prevailing in a Well-Armed World: Devising Competitive Strategies Against Weapons Proliferation* (Carlisle, PA: U.S. Army War College, March 2000), 10–11. See also Khalilzad and Lesser, 19–20.

[458] One proposed approach is to allow other powers to have their own geographic spheres of influence as suggested in James Kurth, "American Strategy in the Global Era," *Naval War College Review* 53 (Winter 2000): 7–24.

[459] Cronin, 136–137.

[460] Bracken, *Fire in the East*, 63–70.

[461] Cohen, Friedberg, and Rosen, 6; Bracken, *Fire in the East*, 45–50.

[462] Bracken, *Fire in the East*, 31–36.

[463] A view implied by the conclusions of *2015: Power and Progress*: ". . . while American military presence overseas would retain its value, the form and context of the presence must be adapted to the shifting parameters of conventional warfare." Cronin, 145.

[464] Davis and Sweeney, 324–325.

[465] Thomas G. Mahnken argues: "the forces most useful for projecting a tangible U.S. presence within a region, such as aircraft carriers and air wings, will be highly vulnerable . . . . What is at stake is nothing short of our ability to protect our interests around the globe. Failure to address this threat in the near term will only multiply the problems we face in the future." Mahnken, 39.

[466] Office of Naval Intelligence, 26–31.

[467] A discussion on the force structure implications for the Army can be found in Davis and Sweeney, 306–313.

[468] See discussion in Sam J. Tangredi, "Naval Strategy and Arms Control," *The Washington Quarterly* 14 (Summer 1991): 201–209.

[469] See, for example, John Mueller, "The Escalating Irrelevance of Nuclear Weapons," in T. V. Paul, Richard J. Harknett, and James J. Wirtz, *The Absolute Weapon Revisited: Nuclear Arms and the Emerging International Order* (Ann Arbor, MI: University of Michigan Press, 1998), 73–98.

[470] Joseph and Lehman, 1.13–1.16.

[471] See an early post-Cold War discussion in Michael J. Mazarr, "Nuclear Weapons After the Cold War," *The Washington Quarterly* 15 (Summer 1992): 185–201.

[472] One source argues that the threat of nuclear retaliation is more effective than denial (active defenses) and that building theater ballistic missile defenses would actually *reduce* the deterrent effect of the perception of an overwhelming nuclear response. See D.H.L. MacDonald, "TBMD Could Backfire," U.S. Naval Institute *Proceedings* 124 (April 1998): 80–83.

[473] A source that argues that nuclear weapons *should not* be used to deter other forms of WMD is Scott D. Sagan, "The Commitment Trap: Why the United States Should Not Use Nuclear Threats to Deter Biological and Chemical Weapons Attacks," *International Security* 24 (Spring 2000): 85–115.

[474] An ongoing debate stimulated by Kenneth N. Waltz, *The Spread of Nuclear Weapons: More May be Better,* International Institute for Strategic Studies Adelphi Paper 171 (London: International Institute for Strategic Studies, 1981), and more recently renewed in Scott D. Sagan and Kenneth N. Waltz *The Spread of Nuclear Weapons: A Debate* (New York: W.W. Norton, 1995).

[475] "Traditional methods of deterrence have inherent limitations and tend to be ineffective in countering proliferation of WMD today." Siegrist and Graham, 7, 18. An opposing view is implied by the discussion in Robert G. Joseph and Ronald F. Lehman II, project directors, *U.S. Nuclear Policy in the 21ˢᵗ Century, Final Report* (Washington, D.C.: National Defense University/Lawrence Livermore National Laboratory, 1998), 1.13, 2.40–2.41.

[476] "For example, deterrence may prove difficult against religiously-motivated terrorists who believe they are carrying out the will of their Supreme Being. The components of deterrence need to be reexamined, then *refocused*, with other more pertinent options added." Siegrist and Graham, 18.

[477] As Gray maintains: "If their strategy can be beaten, terrorists can be defeated." See Colin S. Gray, "Combating Terrorism," 20.

[478] Ibid., 22.

[479] See Mark E. Kosnik, "The Military Response to Terrorism," *Naval War College Review* 53 (Spring 2000): 13–39.

[480] In July 2000, the U.S. Government considered the eventual lifting of sanctions on Libya because of its current lack of support for international terrorism and its apparent suspension of chemical weapons production. See Andrew Koch, "USA rethinks Libya's status," *Jane's Defence Weekly* 34 (July 19, 2000): 22–23.

[481] Quoted in Jonathon Green, *Morrow's International Dictionary of Contemporary Quotations* (New York: William Morrow and Company, 1982), 24.

[482] The term "permitted defense planning" reflects the limits that the political structure imposes on its defense establishment. For example, in a democracy with a long-standing tradition of military subordination to civilian authority—and in which the military is sworn to uphold the constitution—planning for the conduct of a coup d'etat would be treasonous. Likewise, planning for military conflict under conditions in which civilian authority has lost control of the military would not be considered permissible.

[483] Davis and Sweeney maintain that "basing studies of the future security environment on such unexpected and unanticipated events ill serves the defense planner or the foreign policy professional, since it is almost impossible to prepare for such eventualities. . . . Putting aside for a moment whether or not these [wild cards] are even valid arguments, the broader point remains that such possibilities are useless to long range planning" (Davis and Sweeney, 218). I disagree with their conclusions and see great value in developing hedging strategies against selected wild cards. Apparently, so do Davis and Sweeney, who later suggest that there are at least "three wild cards worth considering." See discussion in Davis and Sweeney, 219–221.

[484] The one exception was the Korean War, which was officially a United Nations action, even if primarily conducted by U.S. forces. The Soviet Union was boycotting the Security Council at the time the Articles were evoked.

[485] Summarized in Michael Marien, ed., *World Futures and the United Nations* (Bethesda, MD: World Future Society, 1995), 4, 52–53.

[486] The obvious exception is the U.S. Coast Guard. Although one of the Armed Services, the Coast Guard operates in peacetime under the authority of the Department of Commerce. Maritime law enforcement is one of its primary missions. Other services have provided support to the Coast Guard and other law enforcement agencies for counterdrug operations. However, considerable effort has been made to ensure that the powers of domestic search and arrest are made exclusively by the supported agencies.

[487] A lively debate about the effects of such a fundamental break was generated by Charles J. Dunlap, Jr., "The Origin of the American Military Coup of 2012," *Parameters* 22 (Winter 1992–1993): 2–20.

[488] Snow, 200.

[489] Stratfor.com refers to this as "global economic de-synchronization." See www.stratfor.com, "Decade Forecast 2000–2010," December 20, 1999 (remains currently available on website).

[490] Davis and Sweeney, 221.

[491] Lester R. Brown et al., *State of the World 2000* (New York: W.W. Norton, 2000), 22–24, 37–38.

[492] "*2015* suggests that the United States and other great powers may command the means to mitigate such tragedies, but they rarely need the intervention of combat forces to deal with such crises." Cronin, 150.

[493] See Ivan Eland, "Tilting at Windmills: Post-Cold War Threats to U.S. Security," *Policy Analysis* 332 (February 8, 1999), obtained from website www.cato.org.

[494] This shock can be attributed in part to a "yawning 'gap of intolerance' between advanced western civilizations and the [rest of] world" where intolerant cultures abound. See argument in Dave Trottier, "The Emerging 21st Century Force Structure Paradigm" (unpublished paper, National War College, 2000), 6.

[495] Quoted in Rudolph Flesch, *The New Book of Unusual Quotations* (New York: Harper and Row, 1966), 130–131.

[496] Davis and Sweeney, 2.

[497] Charles Frankel, "Avoiding Cosmic Catastrophe," *The Futurist* 34 (July–August 2000): 23–28.

[498] Arguably, stockpiling strategic materials could be considered a hedge against an economic downturn or unanticipated rise in prices.

[499] Sun Tzu, *The Art of War,* trans. by Samuel B. Griffith (London: Oxford University Press, 1963), 86–87.

[500] See discussion on conditions in Somalia in Jeffrey Bartholet, "A Return to Somalia," *Newsweek*, November 1, 1999, 50–51.

[501] McKenzie, 39–42.

[502] Pillsbury, *China Debates the Future Security Environment*, xxiii.

[503] National Intelligence Council, *National Intelligence Council 1999* (pamphlet).

[504] Ritcheson's survey describes it as "minimal" or "truncated" scenario building methodology. "Instead of providing multiple strategic environments, qualitative descriptions of various trends are proffered." Ritcheson, 15–16.